D0763709

NARRATIVE OF A JOURNEY ACROSS THE ROCKY
MOUNTAINS TO THE COLUMBIA RIVER

Narrative of a Journey

across the Rocky Mountains to the Columbia River

John Kirk Townsend

Introduction by Donald Jackson

University of Nebraska Press
Lincoln and London

For permission to use the map of the Route of Nathaniel Wyeth's Party from Independence to Fort Hall in Year 1834, the University of Nebraska Press is indebted to the Oregon Historical Society. The map by Aubrey L. Haines, ed., is Plate I from Osborne Russell's Journal of a Trapper, published by the Oregon Historical Society, 1955.

Introduction Copyright © 1978 by the University of Nebraska Press

First Bison Book printing: 1978

Most recent printing indicated by first digit below:

2   3   4   5   6   7   8   9   10

Library of Congress Cataloging in Publication Data

Townsend, John Kirk, 1809–1851.
  Narrative of a journey across the Rocky Mountains to the Columbia River.

Originally published in 1839.
  Reprint of the abridged version published in 2. 21, 1905 of Early Western travels, edited by R. G. Thwaites.
  Includes bibliographical references.
  1. Overland journeys to the Pacific. 2. The West—Description and travel—To 1848. 3. Oregon—Description and travel. 4. Hawaii—Description and travel—To 1950. 5. Natural history—Oregon. 6. Natural history—The West. 7. Townsend, John Kirk, 1809–1851. I. Title.
F592.T73   1978   917.9   78–17422
ISBN 0–8032–4402–9
ISBN 0–8032–9401–8 pbk.

This edition is reproduced from the 1970 edition published by Ye Galleon Press, Fairfield, Washington.

Manufactured in the United States of America

INTRODUCTION
Donald Jackson

THE YOUNG TRAVELER was standing on a spot which the American people would someday consider hallowed ground. About four and a half miles southwest of what is now Astoria, Oregon, he had reached a place grown high with wild currant bushes and other brambles and he had found the remains of a small fort without a roof. It was Fort Clatsop, where Lewis and Clark had spent the winter of 1805–1806. Now, thirty years later, the young man was here as a tourist, enjoying a day's diversion from the assignment that had brought him across the continent as a scientific collector and observer. Thus had parts of the West become, in a generation, a busy land swarming with men of vast ideas.

John Kirk Townsend (1809–51), a Philadelphia Quaker, already a physician and skilled ornithologist though still in his twenties, had come west with the Wyeth trading expedition. His traveling companion was Thomas Nuttall (1786–1859), an English botanist almost twice his age who already had made notable exploring trips in the trans-Missouri country. Nuttall traveled under the auspices of his employer, Harvard College, where he was curator of the botanical gardens. Townsend's sponsorship was much less formal. He had learned of the expedition from Nuttall, with whom he had been corresponding on scientific matters, and who had encouraged him to go along. The American Philosophical Society and the Academy of Natural Sciences of Philadelphia each had subscribed $125.00 to help outfit him for his trip, and he was to bring back natural history specimens for their collections—retaining duplicates for his own use.

The spring of 1834, when the expedition had left St. Louis, had been a bustling one in the West. On the Arkansas River, Bent's Fort was being completed. A spring caravan under trader Josiah Gregg was making its way to Santa Fe. Far up the Missouri, Prince Maximilian of Wied-Neuwied, with his artist companion Karl Bodmer, was returning from a collecting and exploring expedition, while headed upstream was the steamer *Assiniboine*, bound for Fort Union at the mouth of the Yellowstone. By midsummer, the 1st U.S. Dragoons would be heading out for the Comanche and Kiowa country in what is now southwest Oklahoma, accompanied by the great painter of Indians George Catlin.

It was also a time when the fur trade was in turmoil. Rival combines were at one another's throats, new schemers combating the inevitable fact that the flourishing era of the fur trade was about to end. The annual Green River rendezvous of trappers and traders was losing its vigor. In Europe, men were beginning to prefer top hats made of silk instead of brushed beaver. The day of the permanent settler, however, was just beginning. As Reuben Gold Thwaites remarked in his original preface to this work, "It was bona-fide settlers, not fur-traders or trappers, that captured Oregon for the United States."

Among the first to escort a company of such settlers was Capt. Nathaniel Jarvis Wyeth, of Cambridge, Massachusetts. Inspired by another New Englander, Hall J. Kelley, who was obsessed with the notion that Oregon must become American territory, Wyeth organized his first party of westering companions in the winter of 1831–32. They proceeded overland in the spring of that year while a supply vessel set out to round Cape Horn and meet the party at the mouth of the Columbia. Although this expedition was far from successful (the vessel and cargo were lost), Wyeth and his men were received amicably by the British at the Hudson's Bay

Company post called Fort Vancouver, and Wyeth was inspired to try again. He returned home overland to organize his second expedition, the one to which Townsend was to attach himself.

In Boston, Wyeth organized the Columbia River Fishing and Trading Company, recruited an overland party, and engaged the *May Dacre* to sail for Oregon by way of the cape. The parallel approach by land and sea had been conceived by John Jacob Astor, who had established Astoria on the Oregon coast in 1811, and it seemed the only logical procedure for a large-scale operation. This time it was to fail again for Wyeth.

The new expedition was the first of 1834 to take the trail, leaving Independence, Missouri, with 70 men and 250 horses in late April; other fur company expeditions followed close behind. Besides Townsend and Nuttall, there were several other notable men in the group. Osborne Russell, of Maine, had been a seaman and fur trader, and his experiences with Wyeth would become part of his published diary, *Journal of a Trapper*. Jason Lee was a Methodist missionary whom Bernard De Voto has characterized as a tall, slow, awkward man, "hearty, adaptable, courageous, and ingenious." He had asked to be sent west and thought he was going to establish a mission among the Flatheads of Montana; later he would decide to go on to the Columbia with Wyeth and settle on the Willamette River. Lee was accompanied by his nephew Daniel and three other dedicated young men.

The landmarks of travel to Oregon were soon to become familiar to thousands. Court House Rock, Chimney Rock, Scott's Bluff, Independence Rock, South Pass, and a new post called Laramie. By the Fourth of July, the expedition had reached Ham's Fork of the Green River, scene of the annual rendezvous.

It was here, where the traders annually transacted much of their business, that Wyeth began to see his enterprise dissolve once more. He had brought with him three thousand dollars' worth of goods for the Rocky Mountain Fur Company, a business venture conducted by such well-known mountain men as Milton and William Sublette and Thomas Fitzpatrick. With this start, Wyeth—still optimistic despite his earlier mishaps—hoped to become a freighter for other fur trading companies. To his surprise and anger, the Sublettes and Fitzpatrick refused to honor their contract and accept Wyeth's shipment. There was more than just chicanery and shrewd dealing involved; the Rocky Mountain Fur Company was folding completely. A rearrangement of partnerships left the American Fur Company as the newly organized leader of the industry.

Wyeth then decided to "roll a stone into their garden," as he later said, by taking the goods on to the Snake River, building a trading post, and leaving a few men there to engage in the fur trade. The post he built in present Idaho was named Fort Hall in honor of his oldest partner. It was soon to become another renowned landmark on the Oregon Trail, but was of little help in salvaging Wyeth's investment.

Traveling on to the Columbia, and welcomed by his old friend Dr. John McLoughlin, the factor at Fort Vancouver, Wyeth met with further business reverses, including the failure of his fishing interests. His ship had been delayed three months after being struck by lightning, arriving too late for the fishing season. Modern students of the West consider Wyeth an honorable and competent businessman who failed because only unlimited resources could have countered his bad luck and the dogged opposition of his competitors.

The drama of transactions in furs, of mergers and shifting loyalties, was of less interest to Townsend the naturalist than the excitement of a new landscape and new life-forms. He had read James Fenimore Cooper, and liked his own new image as a westering woodsman. He felt the poignancy of the moment when he left one final reminder of civilization, a church bell ringing at Fulton, Missouri. "The peal gave rise to many reflections," he wrote. "I felt that I was leaving the scenes of my childhood. . . . I was entering a land of strangers, and would be compelled hereafter to mingle with those who might look upon me with indifference, or treat me with neglect."

But upon leaving Independence he was full of anticipation. When he rode away from the column to view it in perspective, the cavalcade of armed men and prancing horses "was altogether so exciting that I could scarcely contain myself. Every man in the company," he wrote, "seemed to feel a portion of the same kind of enthusiasm; uproarious bursts of merriment, and gay and lively songs, were constantly echoing along the line."

Of his companion, the botanist Nuttall, Townsend often seemed disrespectful although the older man had much to teach him. He spoke of Nuttall's "dreaming of weeds" and often seemed unconcerned with the importance of the plant collecting. He was an ornithologist, a bird man, and delighted with the taking of each specimen hitherto unknown to his fellow scholars back home.

His birds were collected with a gun, of course, and he was not averse to killing for legitimate purposes. But remorse overcame him when he needlessly shot a beautiful pronghorn at a time when the camp was not in need of meat: "As I stood over her, and saw her cast her large, soft, black eyes upon me with an expression of the most touching sadness, while the great tears rolled over her face, I felt myself the meanest and most abhorrent thing in creation."

Townsend worked in a period when every bend in the river or turn of the trail might reveal a new creature or plant. He was the first trained zoologist to cross the continent. On a day when he had seen an especially large variety of new birds, he reflected upon the exciting scientific discoveries that awaited his fellow scientists:

> None but a naturalist can appreciate a naturalist's feelings— his delight amounting to ecstacy—when a specimen such as he has never before seen, meets his eye, and the sorrow and grief which he feels when he is compelled to tear himself from a spot abounding with all that he has anxiously and unremittingly sought for. . . . What valuable and highly interesting accessions to science might not be made by a party, composed exclusively of naturalists, on a journey through this rich and unexplored region! The botanist, the geologist, the mamalogist, the ornithologist, and tho entomologist, would find a rich and almost inexhaustible field for the prosecution of their inquiries.

Being young and far from home, Townsend did not confine his thoughts to science. At the Ham's Fork rendezvous he observed that some of the Nez Percé girls were "rather handsome," although they were dressed "in truly savage taste." Like most western travelers of the period, he had several encounters with the great and powerful grizzly bear. Fascinated also by the buffalo, he borrowed a double-barreled rifle to see if it would kill a specimen with bullets weighing twenty to the pound, and found he could not penetrate the animal's skull with such a weapon.

The pleasant welcome given the Wyeth party by British members of the Hudson's Bay Company, at both Walla Walla and Fort Vancouver, persuaded Townsend to remain in the area. Although he spent several months in Hawaii during the winter of 1834–35, most of his time in the West was employed as a physician at Fort Vancouver. When he was relieved of that assignment by the arrival of a British surgeon in March 1836, he continued to roam the country in search of specimens.

He was most successful in obtaining new specimens of birds, and he worried that he was not obtaining materials—especially geological specimens—wanted by the

America Philosophical Society. Writing to Samuel George Morton, corresponding secretary of the Academy of Natural Sciences, he said he felt some embarrassment on that score. He had failed to collect rocks and minerals on the expedition overland, he said, because they were heavy to transport and hard to find quickly while trying to keep up with a column of mounted men.

Nuttall decided to return home by way of Cape Horn, carrying some of Townsend's specimens as well as his own. He had gone as far as San Diego when he unwittingly became part of a famous travel narrative. Richard Henry Dana, on a voyage that would result in *Two Years before the Mast*, saw him on the beach—a white-haired old man picking up shells—and recognized him as the gifted lecturer and scholar from Harvard. Townsend's attitude toward Nuttall's return is curious, as shown in a letter he wrote to Samuel George Morton: "I did not expect the old gentleman would have deserted me—but let that pass."

Actually, Nuttall's early return may have helped to ensure Townsend's reputation. A list of his bird specimens so excited John J. Audubon, who was then in the final stages of producing his monumental work on birds, that he hurried from New York to Philadelphia to see the preserved skins. His wish to include drawings of these new birds in his publication was thwarted at first by dissension among the officers of the Academy of Natural Sciences. But Audubon persevered, and was able to purchase duplicate skins not only from this preliminary collection but also from the second set which Townsend himself brought home. Birds and also mammals collected by Townsend were to appear in Audubon's books.

Townsend's return home was a long ordeal, aggravated by illness. He spent a year in making his way to the East Coast, a voyage that included stopovers in Hawaii and Chile. And, once home, he was reminded that scientists do not spend all their hours in pursuit of knowledge and the enjoyment of lofty thoughts; they often squabble among themselves.

He appears to have presented all of his bird and animal specimens to the academy. His other sponsor, the American Philosophical Society, felt it had been slighted. In April 1838, a special committee met to consider Townsend's obligations to the society. The report said, "All they have obtained from him is a small collection of shells, a few ordinary specimens of rocks, and some Indian vocabularies." They called the materials "trifling" and said he refused to give the society any birds or animals although he had agreed to do so. One of the men who signed the report was Titian Ramsay Peale, an artist who had himself explored parts of the Plains and Rockies and knew what the society had a right to expect from the returning scientist.

One of Townsend's valuable contributions to the society's holdings was a set of Indian vocabularies, obtained in the Northwest "by dictation from natives and halfbreeds, and Hudson's Bay Company traders." The two-volume manuscript took its place beside others collected for the society by such members as Thomas Jefferson, Benjamin Smith Barton, and Peter S. DuPonceau.

Townsend's new bird discoveries were first described in the *Journal* of the academy, volumes 7 (1837) and 8 (1839). They were then pictured in the last volumes (1844) of Audubon's *Birds of America*. His mammals were described and illustrated by Audubon and John Bachman in their later work, *Quadrupeds of North America* (1845–49). He decided to produce his own work on birds but was able to issue only one part, *Ornithology of the United States of North America* (1840).

The remaining years of Townsend's life were relatively undistinguished. He studied dentistry but never practiced, and died in Washington in 1851 while planning a trip around the Cape of Good Hope. His contribution to knowledge was secure, however, in the works of Audubon and in the collections of the academy in Philadelphia. Today the Townsend Collection at the academy still contains more than seventy specimens, collected mainly in the Rockies and the Pacific Northwest. They include the lark bunting, which Townsend first collected near Ash Hollow in present Nebraska and is now the state bird of Colorado, and such now familiar species as the chestnut-collared longspur and chestnut-backed chickadee, the dark-eyed junco, and the hairy woodpecker.

One of his admirers was Bernard De Voto, who said of his work in the West: "For the first time an effort [was] made to add exact observation and classification to the empirical knowledge of the Far West that had been heaped up by the mountain men and almost wholly confined to them."

This book is a reprint of Townsend's journal as it appeared in volume 8 of Reuben Gold Thwaites, ed., *Early Western Travels* (Cleveland: Arthur H. Clark, 1905), 30 vols. Thwaites reprinted the text of the original edition (Philadelphia, 1839), but omitted a scientific appendix and some journal material not related to North America. In editing his version he gave the page numbers of the 1839 edition in brackets in the text. Thwaites also made many footnote references to other volumes in the series which, of course, are not applicable here.

Several members of the expedition besides Townsend left accounts of the journey. Wyeth's own story is in "Correspondence and Journals of Captain Nathaniel J. Wyeth, 1831–6," *Sources of the History of Oregon*, vol. 1, pts. 3–6 (Eugene, Ore., 1899). See also Rev. Jason, "Diary of Rev. Jason Lee," *Oregon Historical Quarterly* 17 (1916): 116–46, 240–66, 397–430. For more on the missionary contingent, see Daniel Lee and J. H. Frost, *Ten*

Years in Oregon (New York, 1844). Osborne Russell's account is *Journal of a Trapper*, first published in 1955 and now Bison Book 316 (Lincoln: University of Nebraska Press, 1965). See also Dale L. Morgan and Eleanor T. Harris, eds., *The Rocky Mountain Journals of William Marshall Anderson* (San Marino, Calif.: Huntington Library, 1967). Thomas Nuttall published no narrative of his journal. Thwaites's first footnote refers to his journal of earlier travels into the Arkansas River country.

Letters and documents about Townsend's dealings with the two learned societies are in the holdings of the American Philosophical Society. See especially his agreement with the society of March 12, 1834; a committee report expressing dissatisfaction with his work, April 30, 1834; and Townsend's letters to Samuel George Morton of September 20, 1835, and March 13, 1836. Morton was corresponding secretary of the Academy of Natural Sciences of Philadelphia.

Biographies of both Townsend and Nuttall appear in the *Dictionary of American Biography*. Scientific journals, such as *Madroño* 2 (1934): 143–44, and *Bartonia* 18 (1936): 1–51, have dealt with the zoological and botanical aspects of their travels.

For John J. Audubon's frustrating attempts to study the Townsend collection, see Francis H. Herrick, *Audubon the Naturalist*, 2 vols. (New York: Appleton-Century, 1917), especially pp. 147, 153–54, 170–73.

An engaging account of the second Wyeth expedition is to be found in Bernard De Voto, *Across the Wide Missouri* (Boston: Houghton Mifflin, 1947). See especially chapter 8.

For a recent popular article on the scientific aspects of the expedition, see John I. Merritt III, "Naturalists across the Rockies," *American West* 24 (March–April 1977): 4–9, 62–63.

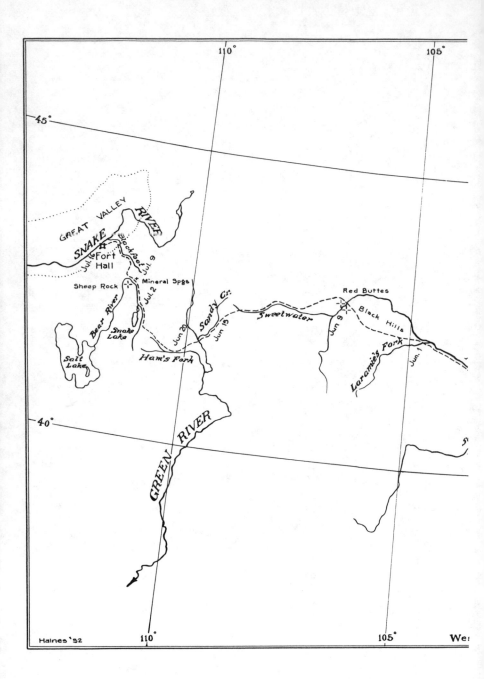

45°   110°   105°

GREAT VALLEY
SNAKE RIVER
Jul. 16 · Fort
Hall   Blackfoot   Jul. 9
Sheep Rock   ·   Mineral Spgs
Jul 2
Bear River   Sandy Cr.   Red Buttes
Snake   Jun 20   Jun 15   Sweetwater   Jun 9   Black Hills
Lake
Salt   Ham's Fork   Laramie's Fork   Jun 1
Lake

40°   GREEN RIVER

Haines '52   110°   105°   We

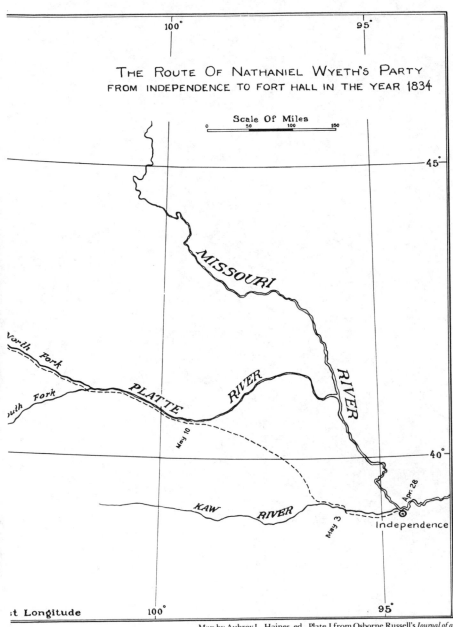

The Route Of Nathaniel Wyeth's Party
From Independence To Fort Hall In The Year 1834

Scale Of Miles

Map by Aubrey L. Haines, ed., Plate I from Osborne Russell's *Journal of a Trapper*, published by the Oregon Historical Society, 1955.

TOWNSEND'S NARRATIVE OF A JOURNEY ACROSS THE
ROCKY MOUNTAINS, TO THE COLUMBIA RIVER

———

Reprint of pp. 1-186, 217-264, of original edition: Philadelphia,
1839. "A Visit to the Sandwich Islands, Chili, &c., with a Scientific
Appendix," also contained in this edition, is here omitted as irrelevant
to the scope of the present series.

1

Hunting the Buffalo

ENTERED according to Act of Congress, in the year 1839, by
JOHN K. TOWNSEND,
in the Office of the Clerk of the District Court of the Eastern District of
Pennsylvania.

ADVERTISEMENT

THE Columbia River Fishing and Trading Company was formed in 1834, by several individuals in New York and Boston. Capt. WYETH, having an interest in the enterprise, collected a party of men to cross the continent to the Pacific, with the purpose chiefly of establishing trading posts beyond the Rocky Mountains and on the coast.

The idea of making one of Capt. Wyeth's party was suggested to the author by the eminent botanist, Mr. NUTTALL, who had himself determined to join the expedition across the North American wilderness. Being fond of Natural History, particularly the science of Ornithology, the temptation to visit a country hitherto unexplored by naturalists was irresistible; and the following pages, originally penned for the family-circle, and without the slightest thought of publication, will furnish some account of his travels.

4

CONTENTS

CHAPTER I

CHAPTER II

5

CHAPTER III

CHAPTER IV

CHAPTER V

CHAPTER IX

CHAPTER X

CHAPTER XV

CHAPTER XVI

NARRATIVE OF A JOURNEY ACROSS THE ROCKY MOUNTAINS, &c.

CHAPTER I

Arrival at St. Louis — Preparations for the journey — Sâque Indians — Their appearance, dress, and manners — Squaws — Commencement of a pedestrian tour — Sandhill cranes — Prairie settlers — Their hospitality — Wild pigeons, golden plovers and prairie hens — Mr. P. and his daughters — An abundant repast — Simplicity of the prairie maidens — A deer and turkey hunt — Loutre Lick hotel — Unwelcome bed-fellows — A colored Charon — Comfortable quarters — Young men of the west — Reflections on leaving home — Loquacity of the inhabitants — Gray squirrels — Boonville — Parroquets — Embarkation in a steamboat — Large catfish — Accident on board the boat — Arrival at Independence — Description of the town — Procure a supply of horses — Encampment of the Rocky Mountain company — Character of the men — Preparation for departure — Requisites of a leader — Backwoods familiarity — Milton Sublette and his band — Rev. Jason Lee, the missionary — A letter from home — Mormonites — Military discipline and its consequences.

ON the evening of the 24th of March, 1834, Mr. NUTTALL[1] and myself arrived at St. Louis, in the steamboat Boston, from Pittsburg.

On landing, we had the satisfaction to learn that Captain WYETH was already there, and on the afternoon of the next day we called upon him, and consulted him in reference to the outfit which it would be necessary to purchase for the journey. He accompanied us to a store in the town, and selected a number of articles for us, among which were several pairs of leathern [10] pantaloons, enormous overcoats, made of green blankets, and white wool hats, with

---

[1] For sketch of Thomas Nuttall, see preface to Nuttall's *Journal*, our volume xiii.— ED.

round crowns, fitting tightly to the head, brims five inches wide, and almost hard enough to resist a rifle ball.

The day following we saw about one hundred Indians of the Sâque tribe, who had left their native forests for the purpose of treating for the sale of some land at the Jefferson barracks.[2] They were dressed and decorated in the true primitive style; their heads shaved closely, and painted with alternate stripes of fiery red and deep black, leaving only the long scalping tuft, in which was interwoven a quantity of elk hair and eagle's feathers. Each man was furnished with a good blanket, and some had an under dress of calico, but the greater number were entirely naked to the waist. The faces and bodies of the men were, almost without an exception, fantastically painted, the predominant color being deep red, with occasionally a few stripes of dull clay white around the eyes and mouth. I observed one whose body was smeared with light colored clay, interspersed with black streaks. They were unarmed, with the exception of tomahawks and knives. The chief of the band,

---

[2] For the early history of the Sauk Indians, see J. Long's *Voyages*, in our volume ii, p.185, note 85. By the treaty of 1804 they ceded a large portion of their lands (in the present Wisconsin, Iowa, and Illinois) to the United States. Upon removing to the west of the Mississippi, as per agreement with the federal government, they broke into several well-defined and often quarrelsome bands. This division was intensified by the War of 1812-15, when part of the tribe aided the British against the American border. The so-called Missouri band, dwelling north of that river in the present state of the name, in 1815 made with the United States a treaty of friendship, which was kept with fidelity. In 1830 a second land cession was made by the Sauk, and after the Black Hawk War (1832), in which the Missouri band took no part, they were desirous of moving to some permanent home south of the Missouri River. It was in pursuit of this intention, doubtless, that the visit recorded by Townsend was made. The final treaty therefor was not drawn until 1836.

Jefferson Barracks, just south of St. Louis on the Mississippi River, were built for the federal government (1826) on a site secured from the village of Carondolet (1824). General Henry Atkinson was in charge of the erection of the fort to which the garrison was (August, 1826) transferred from Bellefontaine on the Missouri. The post has been in continuous occupation since its erection.— ED (who is said to be Black Hawk's father-in-law,[3]) was a large dignified looking man, of perhaps fifty-five years of age, distinguished from the rest, by his richer habiliments, a more profuse display of trinkets in his ears, (which were cut and gashed in a frightful manner to receive them,) and above all, by a huge necklace made of the claws of the grizzly bear. The squaws, of whom there were about twenty, were dressed very much like the men, and at a little distance could scarcely be distinguished from them. Among them was an old, superannuated crone, who, soon after her arrival, had been presented with a broken umbrella. The only use that she made of it was to wrench the plated ends from the whalebones, string them on a piece of wire, take her knife from her belt, with which she deliberately cut a slit of an inch in length [11] along the upper rim of her ear, and insert them in it. I saw her soon after this operation had been performed; her cheeks were covered with blood, and she was standing with a vast deal of assumed dignity among her tawny sisters, who evidently envied her the possession of the worthless baubles.

28th.— Mr. N. and myself propose starting to-morrow on foot towards the upper settlements, a distance of about three hundred miles. We intend to pursue our journey

[3] Black Hawk whose Indian name was Makataineshekiakiah (black sparrow-hawk) was born among the Sauk in 1767. A chief neither by heredity nor election, he became by superior ability leader of the so-called British band, with headquarters at Saukenak, near Rock Island, Illinois. He participated in Tecumseh's battle (1811), and those about Detroit in the War of 1812-15, and made many raids upon the American settlements, until 1816 when a treaty of amity was signed with the United States. The chief event of his career was the war of 1832, known by his name. Consult on this subject, Thwaites, "Black Hawk War," in *How George Rogers Clark won the Northwest* (Chicago, 1903). At its conclusion this picturesque savage leader was captured, sent a prisoner to Jefferson Barracks, and later confined at Fortress Monroe, Virginia. After an extended tour of the Eastern states, Black Hawk returned to Iowa, where he was placed under the guardianship of his rival Keokuk, and where in 1838 he died. His wife was Asshawequa (Singing Bird), who died in Kansas (1846).— ED.

leisurely, as we have plenty of time before us, and if we become tired, we can enter the stage which will probably overtake us.

29th.— This morning our Indians returned from the barracks, where I understand they transacted their business satisfactorily. I went on board the boat again to see them. I feel very much interested in them, as they are the first Indians I have ever seen who appear to be in a state of uncultivated nature, and who retain the savage garb and manners of their people. They had engaged the entire covered deck for their especial use, and were lolling about in groups, wrapped in their blankets. Some were occupied in conversation, others seemed more contemplative, and appeared to be thinking deeply, probably of the business which brought them amongst us. Here and there two might be seen playing a Spanish game with cards, and some were busily employed in rendering themselves more hideous with paint. To perform this operation, the dry paint is folded in a thin muslin or gauze cloth, tied tightly and beaten against the face, and a small looking-glass is held in the other hand to direct them where to apply it. Two middle-aged squaws were frying beef, which they distributed around to the company in wooden bowls, and several half loaves of bread were circulating rapidly amongst them, by being tossed from one to another, each taking a huge bite of it. There were among the company, several younger females, but they were all so *hard favored* that I could not feel much sympathy with them, and was therefore not anxious to cultivate [12] their acquaintance. There was another circumstance, too, that was not a very attractive one; I allude to the custom so universal amongst Indians, of seeking for vermin in each other's heads, and then *eating* them. The fair damsels were engaged in this way during most of the time that I remained on board, only suspending their delectable occupation to take their bites of bread as it passed them in rotation. The effect upon my person was what an Irishman would call the attraction of repulsion, as I found myself almost unconsciously edging away until I halted at a most respectable distance from the scene of slaughter.

At noon, Mr. N. and myself started on our pedestrian tour, Captain Wyeth offering to accompany us a few miles on the way. I was glad to get clear of St. Louis, as I felt uncomfortable in many respects while there, and the bustle and restraint of a town was any thing but agreeable to me. We proceeded over a road generally good, a low dry prairie, mostly heavily timbered, the soil underlaid with horizontal strata of limestone, abounding in organic remains, shells, coralines, &c., and arrived in the evening at Florisant, where we spent the night.⁴ The next day Captain Wyeth left us for St. Louis, and my companion and myself proceeded on our route. We observed great numbers of the brown, or sandhill crane, (*Grus canadensis*,) flying over us; some flocks were so high as to be entirely beyond the reach of vision, while their harsh, grating voices were very distinctly heard. We saw several flocks of the same cranes while ascending the Mississippi, several days since. At about noon, we crossed the river on a boat worked by horses, and stopped at a little town called St. Charles.⁵

We find it necessary, both for our comfort and convenience, to travel very slowly, as our feet are already becom-

---

⁴ Florissant is an old Spanish town not far from St. Louis, founded soon after the latter. At first it was a trading post and Jesuit mission station, whence it acquired the name of San Fernando, which still applies to the township. Later it was made the country residence of the Spanish governors, and in 1793 was by their authority incorporated and granted five thousand arpents of land for a common. The titles were confirmed by the United States in 1812. In 1823 there was established at Florissant a Jesuit novitiate, among whose founders was Father Pierre de Smet, who was buried there in 1873. Florissant had (1900) a population of 732.— ED.

⁵ For St. Charles, see Bradbury's *Travels*, in volume v of our series, p. 39, note 9.— ED.

ing tender, and that we may have an opportunity of observing the country, and collecting interesting specimens. Unfortunately for the pursuits of my companion, the plants (of which he finds a [13] number that are rare and curious) are not yet in flower, and therefore of little use to him. The birds are in considerable numbers, among the principal of which is the large pileated woodpecker, (*Picus pileatus.*)

Mr. N. and myself are both in high spirits. We travel slowly, and without much fatigue, and when we arrive at a house, stop and rest, take a drink of milk, and chat with those we see. We have been uniformly well treated; the living is good, and very cheap, and at any house at which we stop the inhabitants are sure to welcome us to their hospitality and good cheer. They live comfortably, and without much labor; possess a fruitful and easily tilled soil, for which they pay the trifling sum of one dollar and a quarter per acre; they raise an abundance of good Indian corn, potatoes, and other vegetables; have excellent beef and pork, and, in short, every thing necessary for good, wholesome living.

31*st.*— The road to-day was muddy and slippery, rendered so by a heavy rain which fell last night. This morning, we observed large flocks of wild pigeons passing over, and on the bare prairies were thousands of golden plovers; the ground was often literally covered with them for acres. I killed a considerable number. They were very fat, and we made an excellent meal of them in the evening. The prairie hen, or pinnated grouse, is also very numerous, but in these situations is shy, and difficult to be procured.

Towards evening we were overtaken by a bluff, jolly looking man, on horseback, who, as is usual, stopped, and entered into conversation with us. I saw immediately that he was superior to those we had been accustomed to meet. He did not ply us with questions so eagerly as most, and when he heard that we were naturalists, and were travelling in that capacity, he seemed to take considerable interest in us. He invited us to stop at his house, which was only a mile beyond, and as night was almost [14] upon us, we accepted the invitation with cheerfulness. Upon arriving at his mansion, our good host threw wide his hospitable doors, and then with a formal, and rather ultra-dignified politeness, making us a low bow, said, "Gentlemen, my name is P., and I am very happy of your company." We seated ourselves in a large, and well-furnished parlor. Mr. P. excused himself for a few minutes, and soon returned, bringing in three fine looking girls, whom he introduced as his daughters. I took a particular fancy to one of them, from a strong resemblance which she bore to one of my female friends at home. These girls were certainly very superior to most that I had seen in Missouri, although somewhat touched with the awkward bashfulness and prudery which generally characterizes the prairie maidens. They had lost their mother when young, and having no companions out of the domestic circle, and consequently no opportunity of aping the manners of the world, were perfect children of nature. Their father, however, had given them a good, plain education, and they had made some proficiency in needle work, as was evinced by numerous neatly worked *samplers* hanging in wooden frames around the room. Anon, supper was brought in. It consisted of pork chops, ham, eggs, Indian bread and butter, tea, coffee, milk, potatoes, *preserved ginger*, and though last, certainly not least in value, an enormous tin dish of plovers, (the contents of my game-bag,) *fricaseed*. Here was certainly a most abundant repast, and we did ample justice to it.

I endeavored to do the agreeable to the fair ones in the evening, and Mr. N. was monopolized by the father, who took a great interest in plants, and was evidently much gratified by the information my companion gave him on the subject.

The next morning when we rose, it was raining, and much had evidently fallen during the night, making the roads wet and muddy, and therefore unpleasant for pedestrians. I confess [15] I was not sorry for this, for I felt myself very comfortably situated, and had no wish to take to the road. Mr. P. urged the propriety of our stopping at least another day, and the motion being seconded by his fair daughter, (my favorite,) it was irresistible.

On the following morning the sun was shining brightly, the air was fresh and elastic, and the roads tolerably dry, so that there was no longer any excuse for tarrying, and we prepared for our departure. Our good host, grasping our hands, said that he had been much pleased with our visit, and hoped to see us again, and when I bid good bye to the pretty Miss P., I told her that if I ever visited Missouri again, I would go many miles out of my way to see her and her sisters. Her reply was unsophisticated enough. "Do come again, and come in May or June, for then there are plenty of prairie hens, and you can shoot as many as you want, and you must stay a long while with us, and we'll have nice times; good bye; I'm so sorry you're going."

April 4th.— I rose this morning at daybreak, and left Mr. N. dreaming of weeds, in a little house at which we stopped last night, and in company with a long, lanky boy, (a son of the poor widow, our hostess,) set to moulding bullets in an old iron spoon, and preparing for deer hunting. The boy shouldered a rusty rifle, that looked almost antediluvian, and off we plodded to a thicket, two miles from the house. We soon saw about a dozen fine deer, and the boy, clapping his old fire-lock to his shoulder, brought down a beautiful doe at the distance of a full hundred yards. Away sprang the rest of the herd, and I crept round the thicket to meet them. They soon came up, and I fired my piece at a large buck, and wounded the poor creature in the leg; he went limping away, unable to overtake his companions; I felt very sorry, but consoled myself with the reflection that he would soon get well again.

[16] We then gave up the pursuit, and turned our attention to the turkies, which were rather numerous in the thicket. They were shy, as usual, and, when started from their lurking places, ran away like deer, and hid themselves in the underwood. Occasionally, however, they would perch on the high limbs of the trees, and then we had some shots at them. In the course of an hour we killed four, and returned to the house, where, as I expected, Mr. N. was in a fever at my absence, and after a late, and very good breakfast, proceeded on our journey.

We find in this part of the country less timber in the same space than we have yet seen, and when a small belt appears, it is a great relief, as the monotony of a bare prairie becomes tiresome.

Towards evening we arrived at Loutre Lick.[6] Here there is a place called a *Hotel*. A Hotel, forsooth! a pig-stye would be a more appropriate name. Every thing about it was most exceedingly filthy and disagreeable, but no better lodging was to be had, for it might not be proper to apply for accommodation at a private house in the immediate vicinity of a public one. They gave us a wretched supper, not half so good as we had been accustomed to, and we were fain to spend the evening in a comfortless, unfurnished, nasty barroom, that smelt intolerably of rum and whiskey, to listen to the profane conversation of three or four uncouth individuals, (among whom were the host and his brother,) and

---

[6] Loutre Lick appears to be the hamlet now known as Big Spring, on Loutre Creek, in Loutre Township, Montgomery County. The settlement was made between 1808 and 1810, and was on the highway between St. Charles and Côte sans Dessein.— ED.

to hear long and disagreeably minute discussions upon horse-racing, gambling, and other vices equally unpleasant to us.

The host's brother had been to the Rocky Mountains, and soon learning *our* destination, gave us much unsought for advice regarding our method of journeying; painted in strong colors the many dangers and difficulties which we must encounter, and concluded by advising us to give up the expedition. My fast ebbing patience was completely exhausted. I told him that [17] nothing that he could say would discourage us,— that we went to that house in order to seek repose, and it was unfair to intrude conversation upon us unasked. The ruffian made some grumbling reply, and left us in quiet and undisturbed possession of our bench. We had a miserable time that night. The only spare bed in the house was so intolerably filthy that we dared not undress, and we had hardly closed our eyes before we were assailed by swarms of a vile insect, (the very name of which is offensive,) whose effluvia we had plainly perceived immediately as we entered the room. It is almost needless to say, that very early on the following morning, after paying our reckoning, and refusing the landlord's polite invitation to "*liquorize*," we marched from the house, shook the dust from our feet, and went elsewhere to seek a breakfast.

Soon after leaving, we came to a deep and wide creek, and strained our lungs for half an hour in vain endeavors to waken a negro boy who lived in a hut on the opposite bank, and who, we were told, would ferry us over. He came out of his den at last, half naked and rubbing his eyes to see who had disturbed his slumbers so early in the *marning*. We told him to hurry over, or we'd endeavor to assist him, and he came at last, with a miserable leaky little skiff that wet our feet completely. We gave him a *pickayune* for his trouble, and went on. We soon came to a neat little secluded cottage in the very heart of a thick forest, where we found a fine looking young man, with an interesting wife, and a very pretty child about six months old. Upon being told that we wanted some breakfast, the woman tucked up her sleeves, gave the child to her husband, and went to work in good earnest. In a very short time a capital meal was smoking on the board, and while we were partaking of the good cheer, we found our vexation rapidly evaporating. We complimented the handsome young hostess, [18] patted the chubby cheeks of the child, and were in a good humor with every body.

6th.— Soon after we started this morning, we were overtaken by a stage which was going to Fulton, seven miles distant, and as the roads were somewhat heavy, we concluded to make use of this convenience. The only passengers were three young men from the far west, who had been to the eastward purchasing goods, and were then travelling homeward. Two of them evidently possessed a large share of what is called *mother wit*, and so we had jokes without number. Some of them were not very refined, and perhaps did not suit the day very well, (it being the Sabbath,) yet none of them were really offensive, but seemed to proceed entirely from an exuberance of animal spirits.

In about an hour and a half we arrived at Fulton, a pretty little town, and saw the villagers in their holiday clothes parading along to church.[7] The bell at that moment sounded, and the peal gave rise to many reflections. It might be long ere I should hear the sound of the "church-going bell" again. I was on my way to a far, far country,

[7] Fulton is the seat of Callaway County, laid out in 1825, and originally christened Volney; but its appellation was soon changed in honor of Robert Fulton, inventor of the steamboat. The first settler and proprietor was George Nichols. In 1832 the population was about two hundred; by 1900 it had increased to nearly five thousand.— ED.

and I did not know that I should ever be permitted to revisit my own. I felt that I was leaving the scenes of my childhood; the spot which had witnessed all the happiness I ever knew, the home where all my affections were centered. I was entering a land of strangers, and would be compelled hereafter to mingle with those who might look upon me with indifference, or treat me with neglect.

These reflections were soon checked, however. We took a light lunch at the tavern where we stopped. I shouldered my gun, Mr. N. his stick and bundle, and off we trudged again, westward, ho! We soon lost sight of the prairie entirely, and our way lay through a country thickly covered with heavy timber, the roads very rough and stony, and we had frequently to ford [19] the creeks on our route, the late freshets having carried away the bridges.

Our accommodation at the farm houses has generally been good and comfortable, and the inhabitants obliging, and anxious to please. They are, however, exceedingly inquisitive, propounding question after question, in such quick succession as scarcely to allow you breathing time between them. This kind of catechising was at first very annoying to us, but we have now become accustomed to it, and have hit upon an expedient to avoid it in a measure. The first question generally asked, is, "where do you come from, gentlemen?" We frame our answer somewhat in the style of Dr. Franklin. "We come from Pennsylvania; our names, Nuttall and Townsend; we are travelling to Independence on foot, for the purpose of seeing the country to advantage, and we intend to proceed from thence across the mountains to the Pacific. Have you any mules to sell?" The last clause generally changes the conversation, and saves us trouble. To a stranger, and one not accustomed to the manners of the western people, this kind of interrogating seems to imply a lack of modesty and common decency, but it is certainly not so intended, each one appearing to think himself entitled to gain as much intelligence regarding the private affairs of a stranger, as a very free use of his lingual organ can procure for him.

We found the common gray squirrel very abundant in some places, particularly in the low bottoms along water courses; in some situations we saw them skipping on almost every tree.   On last Christmas day, at a squirrel hunt in this neighborhood, about thirty persons killed the astonishing number of *twelve hundred*, between the rising and setting of the sun.

This may seem like useless barbarity, but it is justified by the consideration that all the crops of corn in the country are frequently [20] destroyed by these animals.   This extensive extermination is carried on every year, and yet it is said that their numbers do not appear to be much diminished.

About mid-day on the 7th, we passed through a small town called Columbia, and stopped in the evening at Rocheport, a little village on the Missouri river.[8]   We were anxious to find a steam-boat bound for Independence, as we feared we might linger too long upon the road to make the necessary preparations for our contemplated journey.

On the following day, we crossed the Missouri, opposite Rocheport, in a small skiff.   The road here, for several miles, winds along the bank of the river, amid fine groves of sycamore and Athenian poplars, then stretches off for about three miles, and does not again approach it until you arrive at Boonville.   It is by far the most hilly road that we

---

[8] Columbia, seat of Boone County and of the Missouri State University, was organized first as Smithton.   Later (1820), when made the county seat, the name was changed, and a period of prosperity began.   The location of the university was secured in 1839.   In 1900 the population was 5,651.

Rocheport, on the Missouri River, at the mouth of Moniteau Creek, was laid out in 1832 on land obtained on a New Madrid certificate.   At one time the place rivaled Columbia.   Its present population is about six hundred.— ED.

have seen, and I was frequently reminded, while travelling on it, of our Chester county. We entered the town of Boonville early in the afternoon, and took lodgings in a very clean, and respectably kept hotel. I was much pleased with Boonville. It is the prettiest town I have seen in Missouri; situated on the bank of the river, on an elevated and beautiful spot, and overlooks a large extent of lovely country. The town contains two good hotels, (but no *grog shops*, properly so called,) several well-furnished stores, and five hundred inhabitants. It was laid out thirty years ago by the celebrated western pioneer, whose name it bears.[9]

We saw here vast numbers of the beautiful parrot of this country, (the *Psittacus carolinensis*.) They flew around us in flocks, keeping a constant and loud screaming, as though they would chide us for invading their territory; and the splendid green and red of their plumage glancing in the sunshine, as they whirled and circled within a few feet of us, had a most magnificent appearance. They seem entirely unsuspicious of danger, and after being fired at, only huddle closer together, as if to obtain protection [21] from each other, and as their companions are falling around them, they curve down their necks, and look at them fluttering upon the ground, as though perfectly at a loss to account for so unusual an occurrence. It is a most inglorious sort of shooting; down right, cold-blooded murder.[10]

On the afternoon of the 9th, a steamboat arrived, on board of which we were surprised and pleased to find Captain Wyeth, and our "*plunder*." We embarked immediately, and soon after, were puffing along the Missouri, at the rate of seven miles an hour. When we stopped in the after-

---

[9] For Boonville, see note 59, p. 89, *ante*. Townsend is in error in attributing its founding to Daniel Boone, although named in his honor.— ED.

[10] For the appearance of paroquets in this latitude, see Cuming's *Tour* in our volume iv, p. 161, note 108.— ED.

noon to "wood," we were gratified by a sight of one of the enormous catfish of this river and the Mississippi, weighing full sixty pounds. It is said, however, that they are sometimes caught of at least double this weight. They are excellent eating, coarser, but quite as good as the common small catfish of our rivers. There is nothing in the scenery of the river banks to interest the traveller particularly. The country is generally level and sandy, relieved only by an occasional hill, and some small rocky acclivities.

A shocking accident happened on board during this trip. A fine looking black boy (a slave of one of the deck passengers) was standing on the platform near the fly-wheel. The steam had just been stopped off, and the wheel was moving slowly by the impetus it had acquired. The poor boy unwittingly thrust his head between the spokes; a portion of the steam was at that moment let on, and his head and shoulders were torn to fragments. We buried him on shore the same day; the poor woman, his mistress, weeping and lamenting over him as for her own child. She told me she had brought him up from an infant; he had been as an affectionate son to her, and for years her only support.

March 20th.—On the morning of the 14th, we arrived at Independence landing, and shortly afterwards, Mr. N. and [22] myself walked to the town, three miles distant. The country here is very hilly and rocky, thickly covered with timber, and no prairie within several miles.

The site of the town is beautiful, and very well selected, standing on a high point of land, and overlooking the surrounding country, but the town itself is very indifferent; [11] the houses, (about fifty,) are very much scattered, composed of logs and clay, and are low and inconvenient. There are six or eight stores here, two taverns, and a few tipling houses. As we did not fancy the town, nor the society

---

[11] For Independence, see our volume xix, p. 189, note 34 (Gregg).— ED.

that we saw there, we concluded to take up our residence at the house on the landing until the time of starting on our journey. We were very much disappointed in not being able to purchase any mules here, all the salable ones having been bought by the Santa Fee traders, several weeks since. Horses, also, are rather scarce, and are sold at higher prices than we had been taught to expect, the demand for them at this time being greater than usual. Mr. N. and myself have, however, been so fortunate as to find five excellent animals amongst the hundreds of wretched ones offered for sale, and have also engaged a man to attend to packing our loads, and perform the various duties of our camp.

The men of the party, to the number of about fifty, are encamped on the bank of the river, and their tents whiten the plain for the distance of half a mile. I have often enjoyed the view on a fine moonlight evening from the door of the house, or perched upon a high hill immediately over the spot. The beautiful white tents, with a light gleaming from each, the smouldering fires around them, the incessant hum of the men, and occasionally the lively notes of a bacchanalian song, softened and rendered sweeter by distance. I probably contemplate these and similar scenes with the more interest, as they exhibit the manner in which the next five months of my life are to be spent.

[23] We have amongst our men, a great variety of dispositions. Some who have not been accustomed to the kind of life they are to lead in future, look forward to it with eager delight, and talk of stirring incidents and hair-breadth 'scapes. Others who are more experienced seem to be as easy and unconcerned about it as a citizen would be in contemplating a drive of a few miles into the country. Some have evidently been reared in the shade, and not accustomed to hardships, but the majority are strong, able-bodied men, and many are almost as rough

as the grizzly bears, of their feats upon which they are fond
of boasting.

During the day the captain keeps all his men employed
in arranging and packing a vast variety of goods for car-
riage. In addition to the necessary clothing for the company, arms, ammunition, &c., there are thousands of
trinkets of various kinds, beads, paint, bells, rings, and
such trumpery, intended as presents for the Indians, as
well as objects of trade with them. The bales are usually
made to weigh about eighty pounds, of which a horse
carries two.

I am very much pleased with the manner in which Captain W. manages his men. He appears admirably calculated to gain the good will, and ensure the obedience of
such a company, and adopts the only possible mode of
accomplishing his end. They are men who have been
accustomed to act independently; they possess a strong
and indomitable spirit which will never succumb to authority, and will only be conciliated by kindness and
familiarity. I confess I admire this spirit. It is noble; it
is free and characteristic, but for myself, I have not been
accustomed to seeing it exercised, and when a rough fellow comes up without warning, and slaps me on the shoulder,
with, "stranger what for a gun is that you carry?" I
start, and am on the point of making an angry reply, but
I remember where I am, check the feeling instantly, and
submit the weapon to his inspection. Captain W. [24]
may frequently be seen sitting on the ground, surrounded
by a knot of his independents, consulting them as to his
present arrangements and future movements, and paying the
utmost deference to the opinion of the least among them.

We were joined here by Mr. Milton Sublette, a trader
and trapper of some ten or twelve years' standing. It is
his intention to travel with us to the mountains, and we

are very glad of his company, both on account of his inti-
mate acquaintance with the country, and the accession
to our band of about twenty trained hunters, "true as the
steel of their tried blades," who have more than once followed their brave and sagacious leader over the very track
which we intend to pursue. He appears to be a man of
strong sense and courteous manners, and his men are
enthusiastically attached to him.[12]

Five missionaries, who intend to travel under our escort,
have also just arrived. The principal of these is a Mr.
Jason Lee, (a tall and powerful man, who looks as though
he were well calculated to buffet difficulties in a wild country,)
his nephew, Mr. Daniel Lee, and three younger men of
respectable standing in society, who have arrayed themselves under the missionary banner, chiefly for the gratifi-
cation of seeing a new country, and participating in strange
adventures.[13]

---

[12] For Milton Sublette, see note 44, p. 67, *ante.*— ED.

[13] The establishment of the Oregon mission was due to the appeal published
in the East, of a deputation (1831) of Flathead chiefs to General William Clark
at St. Louis for the purpose of gaining religious instruction. The leaders of the
Methodist church, thus aroused, chose (1833) Jason Lee to found the mission to
the Western Indians, and made an appropriation for the purpose. Jason Lee was
born in Canada (1803), of American parents; he had already taught Indians in his
native village, and attended Wesleyan Seminary at Wilbraham, Massachusetts.
After several efforts to arrange the journey to Oregon, he heard of Wyeth's return,
and requested permission to join his outgoing party. Arrived at Vancouver, he
determined to establish his mission station in the Willamette valley, where he
labored for ten years, building a colony as well as a mission. Once he returned
to the United States (1838-40) for money and reinforcements. In 1844, while
visiting Honolulu, he learned that he had been superseded in the charge of the
mission, and returned to the United States to die the following year, near his birth-
place in Lower Canada.

Daniel Lee, who accompanied his uncle, seconded the latter's efforts in the
mission establishment. In 1835 he voyaged to Hawaii for his health, and in 1838
established the Dalles mission, where he labored until his return to the United
States in 1843. The other missionaries were Cyrus Shepard, a lay helper and
teacher — who died at the Willamette mission, January 1, 1840 — C. M. Walker,
and A. L. Edwards, who joined the party in Missouri.— ED.

My favorites, the birds, are very numerous in this vicinity, and I am therefore in my element. Parroquets are plentiful in the bottom lands, the two species of squirrel are abundant, and rabbits, turkies, and deer are often killed by our people.

I was truly rejoiced to receive yesterday a letter from my family. I went to the office immediately on my arrival here, confidently expecting to find one lying there for me; I was told there was none, and I could not believe it, or would not; I took all the letters in my hand, and examined each of them myself, and I suppose that during the process my expressions of disappointment were "loud and deep," as I observed the eyes of a number [25] of persons in the store directed towards me with manifest curiosity and surprise. The obtuse creatures could not appreciate my feelings. I was most anxious to receive intelligence from home, as some of the members of the family were indisposed when I left, and in a few days more I should be traversing the uncultivated prairie and the dark forest, and perhaps never hear from my home again. The letter came at last, however, and was an inexpressible consolation to me.

The little town of Independence has within a few weeks been the scene of a brawl, which at one time threatened to be attended with serious consequences, but which was happily settled without bloodshed. It had been for a considerable time the stronghold of a sect of fanatics, called Mormons, or Mormonites, who, as their numbers increased, and they obtained power, showed an inclination to lord it over the less assuming inhabitants of the town. This was a source of irritation which they determined to rid themselves of in a summary manner, and accordingly the whole town rose, *en masse*, and the poor followers of the prophet were forcibly ejected from the community. They took refuge in the little town of Liberty, on the opposite side of the river, and the villagers here are now in a constant state of feverish alarm. Reports have been circulated that the Mormons are preparing to attack the town, and put the inhabitants to the sword, and they have therefore stationed sentries along the river for several miles, to prevent the landing of the enemy.[14] The troops parade and study military tactics every day, and seem determined to repel, with spirit, the threatened invasion. The probability is, that the report respecting the attack, is, as John Bull says, "all humbug," and this training and marching has already been a source of no little annoyance to us, as the miserable little skeleton of a saddler who is engaged to work for our party, has neglected his business, and must go a soldiering in stead. A day or two ago, I tried to convince the little man that he was of no use to the army, [26] for if a Mormon were to say *pooh* at him, it would blow him away beyond the reach of danger or of glory; but he thought not, and no doubt concluded that he was a "marvellous proper man," so we were put to great inconvenience waiting for our saddles.

---

[14] For these Mormon troubles, see Gregg's *Commerce of the Prairies,* in our volume xx, pp. 93-99.— ED.

[27] CHAPTER II

Departure of the caravan — A storm on the prairie — Arrangement of the camp — The cook's desertion — Kanzas Indians — Kanzas river — Indian lodges — Passage of the river — Buffalo canoes — Kanzas chief — Costume of the Indians — Upper Kaw village — Their wigwams — Catfish and ravens — Return of Mr. Sublette — Pawnee trace — Desertion of three men — Difficulties occasioned by losing the trail — Intelligence of Mr. Sublette's party— Escape of the band of horses — Visit of three Otto Indians — Anecdote of Richardson, the chief hunter — His appearance and character — White wolves and antelopes — Buffalo bones — Sublette's deserted camp — Lurking wolves.

ON the 28th of April, at 10 o'clock in the morning, our caravan, consisting of seventy men, and two hundred and fifty horses, began its march; Captain Wyeth and Milton Sublette took the lead, Mr. N. and myself rode beside them; then the men in double file, each leading, with a line, two horses heavily laden, and Captain Thing (Captain W.'s assistant) brought up the rear. The band of missionaries, with their horned cattle, rode along the flanks.

I frequently sallied out from my station to look at and admire the appearance of the cavalcade, and as we rode out from the encampment, our horses prancing, and neighing, and pawing the ground, it was altogether so exciting that I could scarcely contain myself. Every man in the company seemed to feel a portion of the same kind of enthusiasm; uproarious bursts of merriment, and gay and lively songs, were constantly echoing along the line. We were certainly a most merry and happy company. What cared we for the future? We had reason to expect that ere long difficulties and dangers, in various shapes, [28] would assail us, but no anticipation of reverses could check the happy exuberance of our spirits.

Our road lay over a vast rolling prairie, with occasional

small spots of timber at the distance of several miles apart, and this will no doubt be the complexion of the track for some weeks.

In the afternoon we crossed the *Big Blue* river at a shallow ford.[15] Here we saw a number of beautiful yellow-headed troopials, (*Icterus zanthrocephalus*,) feeding upon the prairie in company with large flocks of black birds, and like these, they often alight upon the backs of our horses.

29th.— A heavy rain fell all the morning, which had the effect of calming our transports in a great measure, and in the afternoon it was succeeded by a tremendous hail storm. During the rain, our party left the road, and proceeded about a hundred yards from it to a range of bushes, near a stream of water, for the purpose of encamping. We had just arrived here, and had not yet dismounted, when the hail storm commenced. It came on very suddenly, and the stones, as large as musket balls, dashing upon our horses, created such a panic among them, that they plunged, and kicked, and many of them threw their loads, and fled wildly over the plain. They were all overtaken, however, and as the storm was not of long duration, they were soon appeased, and *staked* for the night.

To stake or fasten a horse for the night, he is provided with a strong leathern halter, with an iron ring attached to the chin strap. To this ring, a rope of hemp or plaited leather, twenty-two feet in length, is attached, and the opposite end of the line made fast with several clove hitches around an oak or hickory pin, two and a half feet long. The top of this pin or stake is ringed with iron to prevent its being

---

[15] Townsend is here in error. It would be impossible to reach the Big Blue River the first day out from Independence, and before crossing the Kansas. The former stream is a northern tributary of the latter, over a hundred miles from its mouth. The Oregon Trail led along its banks for some distance, crossing at the entrance of the Little Blue.— Ed.

bruised, and it is then driven to the head in the ground. For greater security, hopples made of stout leather are buckled around the fore legs; and then, [29] if the tackling is good, it is almost impossible for a horse to escape. Care is always taken to stake him in a spot where he may eat grass all night. The animals are placed sufficiently far apart to prevent them interfering with each other.

Camping out to-night is not so agreeable as it might be, in consequence of the ground being very wet and muddy, and our blankets (our only bedding) thoroughly soaked; but we expect to encounter greater difficulties than these ere long, and we do not murmur.

A description of the formation of our camp may, perhaps, not be amiss here. The party is divided into messes of eight men, and each mess is allowed a separate tent. The captain of a mess, (who is generally an "old hand," *i. e.* an experienced forester, hunter, or trapper,) receives each morning the rations of pork, flour, &c. for his people, and they choose one of their body as cook for the whole. Our camp now consists of nine messes, of which Captain W.'s forms one, although it only contains four persons besides the cook.

When we arrive in the evening at a suitable spot for an encampment, Captain W. rides round a space which he considers large enough to accommodate it, and directs where each mess shall pitch its tent. The men immediately unload their horses, and place their bales of goods in the direction indicated, and in such manner, as in case of need, to form a sort of fortification and defence. When all the messes are arranged in this way, the camp forms a hollow square, in the centre of which the horses are placed and staked firmly to the ground. The guard consists of from six to eight men, and is relieved three times each night, and so arranged that each gang may serve alternate nights. The captain of a guard (who is generally also the captain of a mess) collects his people at the appointed hour, and posts them around outside the camp in such situations that they may command [30] a view of the environs, and be ready to give the alarm in case of danger.

The captain cries the hour regularly by a watch, and *all's well*, every fifteen minutes, and each man of the guard is required to repeat this call in rotation, which if any one should fail to do, it is fair to conclude that he is asleep, and he is then immediately visited and stirred up. In case of defection of this kind, our laws adjudge to the delinquent the hard sentence of walking three days. As yet none of our poor fellows have incurred this penalty, and the probability is, that it would not at this time be enforced, as we are yet in a country where little molestation is to be apprehended; but in the course of another week's travel, when thieving and ill-designing Indians will be outlying on our trail, it will be necessary that the strictest watch be kept, and, for the preservation of our persons and property, that our laws shall be rigidly enforced.

May 1st.— On rising this morning, and inquiring about our prospects of a breakfast, we discovered that the cook of our mess (a little, low-browed, ill-conditioned Yankee) had decamped in the night, and left our service to seek for a better. He probably thought the duties too hard for him, but as he was a miserable cook, we should not have much regretted his departure, had he not thought proper to take with him an excellent rifle, powder-horn, shot-pouch, and other matters that did not belong to him. It is only surprising that he did not select one of our best horses to carry him; but as he had the grace to take his departure on foot, and we have enough men without him, we can wish him God speed, and a fair run to the settlements.

We encamped this evening on a small branch of the Kanzas

river.   As we approached our stopping place, we were joined
by a band of Kanzas Indians, (commonly called *Kaw* Indians.)[16]   They are encamped in a neighboring copse, where
they have [31] six lodges.   This party is a small division
of a portion of this tribe, who are constantly wandering; but
although their journeys are sometimes pretty extensive, they
seldom approach nearer to the settlements than they are at
present.   They are very friendly, are not so tawdrily decorated as those we saw below, and use little or no paint.   This
may, however, be accounted for by their not having the cus-
tomary ornaments, &c., as their ears are filled with trinkets
of various kinds, and are horribly gashed in the usual manner.   The dress of most that we have seen, has consisted of
ordinary woollen pantaloons received from the whites, and
their only covering, from the waist up, is a blanket or buffalo
robe.   The head is shaved somewhat in the manner of the
Sâques and Foxes, leaving the well known scalping tuft; but
unlike the Indians just mentioned, the hair is allowed to
grow upon the middle of the head, and extends backwards in
a longitudinal ridge to the occiput.   It is here gathered into
a kind of queue, plaited, and suffered to hang down the
back.   There were amongst them several squaws, with
young children tied to their backs, and a number of larger
urchins ran about our camp wholly naked.

The whole of the following day we remained in camp,
trading buffalo robes, *apishemeaus*,[17] &c., of the Indians.
These people became at length somewhat troublesome to us
who were not traders, by a very free exercise of their begging

---

[16] For the first stretches of the Oregon Trail and the crossing of the Kansas,
see note 30, p. 49, *ante,*   The Kansa Indians are noticed in Bradbury's *Travels,*
our volume v, p. 67, note 37.— ED.

[17] These are mats made of rushes, used for building wigwams, carpets, beds,
and coverings of all sorts.   The early Algonquian term was "apaquois;" see
Wisconsin Historical Collections, xvi, index.   "Apichement" is the usual form of
the word.— ED.

propensities. They appear to be exceedingly poor and needy, and take the liberty of asking unhesitatingly, and without apparent fear of refusal, for any articles that happen to take their fancy.

I have observed, that among the Indians now with us, none but the chief uses the pipe. He smokes the article called *kanikanik*,— a mixture of tobacco and the dried leaves of the poke plant, (*Phytolacca decandra.*) I was amused last evening by the old chief asking me in his impressive manner, (first by pointing with his finger towards the sunset, and then raising his [32] hands high over his head,) if I was going to the mountains. On answering him in the affirmative, he depressed his hands, and passed them around his head in both directions, then turned quickly away from me, with a very solemn and significant *ugh!* He meant, doubtless, that my brain was turned; in plain language, that I was a fool. This may be attributed to his horror of the Blackfeet Indians, with whom a portion of his tribe was formerly at war. The poor Kaws are said to have suffered dreadfully in these savage conflicts, and were finally forced to abandon the country to their hereditary foes.

We were on the move early the next morning, and at noon arrived at the Kanzas river, a branch of the Missouri.[18] This is a broad and not very deep stream, with the water dark and turbid, like that of the former. As we approached it, we saw a number of Indian lodges, made of saplings driven into the ground, bent over and tied at top, and covered with bark and buffalo skins. These lodges, or wigwams, are numerous on both sides of the river. As we passed them, the inhabitants, men, women, and children, flocked out to see us, and almost prevented our progress by their eager greetings. Our party stopped on the bank of the river,

---

[18] For the Kansas River, see James's *Long's Expedition*, in our volume xiv, p. 174, note 140.— ED.

and the horses were unloaded and driven into the water. They swam beautifully, and with great regularity, and arrived safely on the opposite shore, where they were confined in a large lot, enclosed with a fence. After some difficulty, and considerable detention, we succeeded in procuring a large flat bottomed boat, embarked ourselves and goods in it, and landed on the opposite side near our horse pen, where we encamped. The lodges are numerous here, and there are also some good frame houses inhabited by a few white men and women, who subsist chiefly by raising cattle, which they drive to the settlements below. They, as well as the Indians, raise an abundance of good corn; potatoes and other vegetables are also plentiful, and they can therefore live sufficiently well.

[33] The canoes used by the Indians are mostly made of buffalo skins, stretched, while recent, over a light frame work of wood, the seams sewed with sinews, and so closely, as to be wholly impervious to water. These light vessels are remarkably buoyant, and capable of sustaining very heavy burthens.[19]

In the evening the principal Kanzas chief paid us a visit in our tent. He is a young man about twenty-five years of age, straight as a poplar, and with a noble countenance and bearing, but he appeared to me to be marvellously deficient in most of the requisites which go to make the character of a *real* Indian chief, at least of such Indian chiefs as we read of in our popular books. I begin to suspect, in truth, that these lofty and dignified attributes are more apt to exist in the fertile brain of the novelist, than in reality. Be this as it may, *our* chief is a very lively, laughing, and rather playful personage; perhaps he may put on his dignity, like a glove, when it suits his convenience.

---

[19] For these skin canoes, see illustration in Maximilian's *Travels*, atlas, our volume xxv.— ED.

We remained in camp the whole of next day, and traded with the Indians for a considerable number of robes, *apishemeaus*, and halter ropes of hide. Our fat bacon and tobacco were in great demand for these useful commodities.

The Kaws living here appear to be much more wealthy than those who joined our camp on the prairie below. They are in better condition, more richly dressed, cleaner, and more comfortable than their wandering brothers. The men have generally fine countenances, but all the women that I have seen are homely. I cannot admire them. Their dress consists, universally of deer skin leggings, belted around the loins, and over the upper part of the body a buffalo robe or blanket.

On the 20th in the morning, we packed our horses and rode out of the Kaw settlement, leaving the river immediately, and making a N. W. by W. course — and the next day came to another village of the same tribe, consisting of about thirty lodges, and situated in the midst of a beautiful level prairie.

[34] The Indians stopped our caravan almost by force, and evinced so much anxiety to trade with us, that we could not well avoid gratifying them. We remained with them about two hours, and bought corn, moccasins and leggings in abundance. The lodges here are constructed very differently from those of the lower village. They are made of large and strong timbers, a ridge pole runs along the top, and the different pieces are fastened together by leathern thongs. The roofs,—which are single, making but one angle,—are of stout poplar bark, and form an excellent defence, both against rain and the rays of the sun, which must be intense during midsummer in this region. These prairies are often visited by heavy gales of wind, which would probably demolish the huts, were they built of frail materials like those below. We encamped in the evening on a small

stream called Little Vermillion creek,[20] where we found an abundance of excellent catfish, exactly similar to those of the Schuylkill river. Our people caught them in great numbers. Here we first saw the large ravens, (*Corvus corax*.) They hopped about the ground all around our camp; and as we left it, they came in, pell-mell, croaking, fighting, and scrambling for the few fragments that remained.

8th.—This morning Mr. Sublette left us to return to the settlements. He has been suffering for a considerable time with a fungus in one of his legs, and it has become so much worse since we started, in consequence of irritation caused by riding, that he finds it impossible to proceed. His departure has thrown a gloom over the whole camp. We all admired him for his amiable qualities, and his kind and obliging disposition. For myself, I had become so much attached to him, that I feel quite melancholy about his leaving us.[21]

[35] The weather is now very warm, and there has been a dead calm all day, which renders travelling most uncomfortable. We have frequently been favored with fresh breezes, which make it very agreeable, but the moment these fail us we are almost suffocated with intense heat. Our rate of travelling is about twenty miles per day, which, in this warm weather, and with heavily packed horses, is as much as we can accomplish with comfort to ourselves and animals.

On the afternoon of the next day, we crossed a broad Indian trail, bearing northerly, supposed to be about five days old, and to have been made by a war party of Pawnees. We are now in the country traversed by these Indians, and are daily expecting to see them, but Captain W. seems very desirous to avoid them, on account of their well known

---

[20] Now usually known as the Red Vermilion, a northern tributary of Kansas River in Pottawatomie County, Kansas.— ED.

[21] I have since learned that his limb was twice amputated; but notwithstanding this, the disease lingered in the system, and about a year ago, terminated his life. — TOWNSEND.

thieving propensities, and quarrelsome disposition. These Indians go every year to the plains of the Platte, where they spend some weeks in hunting the buffalo, jerking their meat, and preparing their skins for robes; they then push on to the Black Hills, and look out for the parties of Blackfeet, which are also bound to the Platte river plains. When the opposing parties come in collision, (which frequently happens,) the most cruel and sanguinary conflicts ensue. In the evening, three of our men deserted. Like our quondam cook, they all took rifles, &c., that did not belong to them, and one of these happened to be a favorite piece of Captain W.'s, which had done him good service in his journey across this country two years ago. He was very much attached to the gun, and in spite of his calm and cool philosophy in all vexatious matters, he cannot altogether conceal his chagrin.

The little streams of this part of the country are fringed with a thick growth of pretty trees and bushes, and the buds are now swelling, and the leaves expanding, to "welcome back the spring." The birds, too, sing joyously amongst them, grosbeaks, thrushes, and buntings, a merry and musical band. I am particularly [36] fond of sallying out early in the morning, and strolling around the camp. The light breeze just bends the tall tops of the grass on the boundless prairie, the birds are commencing their matin carollings, and all nature looks fresh and beautiful. The horses of the camp are lying comfortably on their sides, and seem, by the glances which they give me in passing, to know that their hour of toil is approaching, and the patient kine are ruminating in happy unconsciousness.

11th.—We encountered some rather serious difficulties today in fording several wide and deep creeks, having muddy and miry bottoms. Many of our horses, (and particularly those that were packed,) fell into the water, and it was with the greatest difficulty and labor that they were extricated. Some of the scenes presented were rather ludicrous to those who were not actors in them. The floundering, kicking, and falling of horses in the heavy slough, man and beast rolling over together, and *squattering* amongst the black mud, and the wo-begone looks of horse, rider, and horse-furniture, often excited a smile, even while we pitied their begrimed and miserable plight. All these troubles are owing to our having lost the trail yesterday, and we have been travelling to-day as nearly in the proper course as our compass indicated, and hope soon to find it.

12th.— Our scouts came in this morning with the intelligence that they had found a large trail of white men, bearing N. W. We have no doubt that this is Wm. Sublette's party, and that it passed us last evening.[22] They must have travelled very rapidly to overtake us so soon, and no doubt had men ahead watching our motions. It seems rather unfriendly, perhaps, to run by us in this furtive way, without even stopping to say good morning, but Sublette is attached to a rival company, and all stratagems are deemed allowable when interest is concerned. It is a matter of some moment to be the first at the mountain rendezvous, [37] in order to obtain the furs brought every summer by the trappers.

Last night, while I was serving on guard, I observed an unusual commotion among our band of horses, a wild neighing, snorting, and plunging, for which I was unable to account. I directed several of my men to go in and appease them, and endeavor to ascertain the cause. They had scarcely started, however, when about half of the band broke their fastenings, snapped the hopples on their legs, and

---

[22] For biographical sketch of William Sublette, see our volume xix, p. 221, note 55 (Gregg). His haste to reach the rendezvous in the mountains before the arrival of Wyeth's party, was connected with the arrangements for supplies; see preface to the present volume.— ED.

went dashing right through the midst of the camp. Down went several of the tents, the rampart of goods was cleared in gallant style, and away went the frightened animals at full speed over the plain. The whole camp was instantly aroused. The horses that remained, were bridled as quickly as possible; we mounted them without saddles, and set off in hard pursuit after the fugitives. The night was pitch dark, but we needed no light to point out the way, as the clattering of hoofs ahead on the hard ground of the prairie, sounded like thunder. After riding half an hour, we overtook about forty of them, and surrounding them with difficulty, succeeded in driving them back, and securing them as before. Twenty men were then immediately despatched to scour the country, and bring in the remainder. This party was headed by Mr. Lee, our missionary, (who, with his usual promptitude, volunteered his services,) and they returned early this morning, bringing nearly sixty more. We find, however, upon counting the horses in our possession, that there are yet three missing.

While we were at breakfast, three Indians of the Otto tribe, came to our camp to see, and smoke with us.[23] These were men of rather short stature, but strong and firmly built. Their countenances resemble in general expression those of the Kanzas, and their dresses are very similar. We are all of opinion, that it is to these Indians we owe our difficulties of last night, and we have no doubt that the three missing horses are now in their [38] possession, but as we cannot prove it upon them, and cannot even converse with them, (having no interpreters,) we are compelled to submit to our loss in silence. Perhaps we should even be thankful that we have not lost more.

While these people were smoking the pipe of peace with us, after breakfast, I observed that Richardson, our chief hunter,

---

[23] For the Oto, see Bradbury's *Travels*, in our volume v, p. 74, note 42.— ED.

(an experienced man in this country, of a tall and iron frame, and almost child-like simplicity of character, in fact an exact counterpart of *Hawk-eye* in his younger days,) stood aloof, and refused to sit in the circle, in which it was always the custom of the *old hands* to join.

Feeling some curiosity to ascertain the cause of this unusual diffidence, I occasionally allowed my eyes to wander to the spot where our sturdy hunter stood looking moodily upon us, as the calamet passed from hand to hand around the circle, and I thought I perceived him now and then cast a furtive glance at one of the Indians who sat opposite to me, and sometimes his countenance would assume an expression almost demoniacal, as though the most fierce and deadly passions were raging in his bosom. I felt certain that hereby hung a tale, and I watched for a corresponding expression, or at least a look of consciousness, in the face of my opposite neighbor, but expression there was none. His large features were settled in a tranquillity which nothing could disturb, and as he puffed the smoke in huge volumes from his mouth, and the fragrant vapor wreathed and curled around his head, he seemed the embodied spirit of meekness and taciturnity.

The camp moved soon after, and I lost no time in overhauling Richardson, and asking an explanation of his singular conduct.

"Why," said he, "that *Injen* that sat opposite to you, is my bitterest enemy. I was once going down alone from the rendezvous with letters for St. Louis, and when I arrived on the lower [39] part of the Platte river, (just a short distance beyond us here,) I fell in with about a dozen Ottos. They were known to be a friendly tribe, and I therefore felt no fear of them. I dismounted from my horse and sat with them upon the ground. It was in the depth of winter; the ground was covered with snow, and the river was frozen solid. While I was thinking of nothing but my dinner, which I was then about preparing, four or five of the cowards jumped on me, mastered my rifle, and held my arms fast, while they took from me my knife and tomahawk, my flint and steel, and all my ammunition. They then loosed me, and told me to be off. I begged them, for the love of God, to give me my rifle and a few loads of ammunition, or I should starve before I could reach the settlements. No—I should have nothing, and if I did not start off immediately, they would throw me under the ice of the river. And," continued the excited hunter,—while he ground his teeth with bitter, and uncontrollable rage,—"that man that sat opposite to you was the chief of them. He recognised me, and knew very well the reason why I would not smoke with him. I tell you, sir, if ever I meet that man in any other situation than that in which I saw him this morning, I'll shoot him with as little hesitation as I would shoot a deer. Several years have passed since the perpetration of this outrage, but it is still as fresh in my memory as ever, and I again declare, that if ever an opportunity offers, I will kill that man." "But, Richardson, did they take your horse also?" "To be sure they did, and my blankets, and every thing I had, except my clothes." "But how did you subsist until you reached the settlements? You had a long journey before you." "Why, set to *trappin'* prairie squirrels with little nooses made out of the hairs of my head." I should remark that his hair was so long, that it fell in heavy masses on his shoulders. "But squirrels in winter, Richardson, I never heard of squirrels in winter." "Well but there was plenty of them, though; little white ones, that lived among the [40] snow." "Well, really, this was an unpleasant sort of adventure enough, but let me suggest that you do very wrong to remember it with such blood-thirsty feelings." He shook his head with a dogged and determined air, and rode off as if anxious to escape a lecture.

A little sketch of our hunter may perhaps not be uninteresting, as he will figure somewhat in the following pages, being one of the principal persons of the party, the chief hunter, and a man upon whose sagacity and knowledge of the country we all in a great measure depended.

In height he is several inches over six feet, of a spare but remarkably strong and vigorous frame, and a countenance of almost infantile simplicity and openness. In disposition he is mild and affable, but when roused to indignation, his keen eyes glitter and flash, the muscles of his large mouth work convulsively, and he looks the very impersonation of the spirit of evil. He is implacable in anger, and bitter in revenge; never forgetting a kindness, but remembering an injury with equal tenacity. Such is the character of our hunter, and none who have known him as I have, will accuse me of delineating from fancy. His native place is Connecticut, which he left about twelve years ago, and has ever since been engaged in roaming through the boundless plains and rugged mountains of the west, often enduring the extremity of famine and fatigue, exposed to dangers and vicissitudes of every kind, all for the paltry, and often uncertain pittance of a Rocky Mountain hunter. He says he is now tired of this wandering and precarious life, and when he shall be enabled to save enough from his earnings to buy a farm in Connecticut, he intends to settle down a quiet tiller of the soil, and enjoy the sweets of domestic felicity. But this day will probably never arrive. Even should he succeed in realizing a little fortune, and the farm should be taken, the monotony and tameness of the scene will weary his free spirit; he will often sigh for a habitation [41] on the broad prairie, or a ramble over the dreary mountains where his lot has so long been cast.

15*th*.— We saw to-day several large white wolves, and two herds of antelopes. The latter is one of the most beautiful animals I ever saw. When full grown, it is nearly as large as a deer. The horns are rather short, with a single prong near the top, and an abrupt backward curve at the summit like a hook. The ears are very delicate, almost as thin as paper, and hooked at the tip like the horns. The legs are remarkably light and beautifully formed, and as it bounds over the plain, it seems scarcely to touch the ground, so exceedingly light and agile are its motions. This animal is the *Antelope furcifer* of zoologists, and inhabits the western prairies of North America exclusively. The ground here is strewn with great quantities of buffalo bones; the skulls of many of them in great perfection. I often thought of my friend Doctor M. and his *golgotha*, while we were kicking these fine specimens about the ground. We are now travelling along the banks of the Blue river,—a small fork of the Kanzas. The grass is very luxuriant and good, and we have excellent and beautiful camps every night.

This morning a man was sent ahead to see W. Sublette's camp, and bear a message to him, who returned in the evening with the information that the company is only one day's journey beyond, and consists of about thirty-five men. We see his deserted camps every day, and, in some cases, the fires are not yet extinguished. It is sometimes amusing to see the wolves lurking like guilty things around these camps seeking for the fragments that may be left; as our party approaches, they sneak away with a mean, hang-dog air which often coaxes a whistling bullet out of the rifle of the wayfarer.

[42] CHAPTER III

ON the 18th of May we arrived at the Platte river. It is
from one and a half to two miles in width, very shoal; large
sand flats, and small, verdant islands appearing in every part.
Wolves and antelopes were in great abundance here, and the
latter were frequently killed by our men. We saw, also, the
sandhill crane, great heron, (*Ardea heroidas*,) and the long-
billed curlew, stalking about through the shallow water, and
searching for their aquatic food.

The prairie is here as level as a race course, not the slightest
undulation appearing throughout the whole extent of vision,
in a north and westerly direction; but to the eastward of the
river, and about eight miles from it, is seen a range of high
bluffs or sand banks, stretching away to the south-east until
they are lost in the far distance.

The ground here is in many places encrusted with an im-
pure salt, which by the taste appears to be a combination of
the sulphate and muriate of soda; there are also a number of
little pools, of only a few inches in depth, scattered over the
plain, the water of which is so bitter and pungent, that it
seems to penetrate [43] into the tongue, and almost to produce decortication of the mouth.

We are now within about three days' journey of the usual

haunts of the buffalo, and our men (particularly the unin-
itiated) look forward to our arrival amongst them with considerable anxiety. They have listened to the garrulous
hunter's details of "*approaching*," and "*running*," and
"*quartering*," until they fancy themselves the very actors
in the scenes related, and are fretting and fuming with
impatience to draw their maiden triggers upon the unoffending rangers of the plain.

The next morning, we perceived two men on horseback, at
a great distance; and upon looking at them with our telescope,
discovered them to be Indians, and that they were approaching us. When they arrived within three or four hundred
yards, they halted, and appeared to wish to communicate
with us, but feared to approach too nearly. Captain W.
rode out alone and joined them, while the party proceeded
slowly on its way. In about fifteen minutes he returned
with the information that they were of the tribe called Grand
Pawnees.[24] They told him that a war party of their people,
consisting of fifteen hundred warriors, was encamped about
thirty miles below; and the captain inferred that these men
had been sent to watch our motions, and ascertain our
place of encampment; he was therefore careful to impress
upon them that we intended to go but a few miles further,
and pitch our tents upon a little stream near the main river.
When we were satisfied that the messengers were out of
sight of us, on their return to their camp, our whole caravan
was urged into a brisk trot, and we determined to steal a
march upon our neighbors. The little stream was soon
passed, and we went on, and on, without slackening our pace,
until 12 o'clock at night. We then called a halt on the bank
of the river, made a hasty meal, threw ourselves down in our
blankets, without pitching the tents, and slept soundly for

---

[24] On the different branches of Pawnee, see James's *Long's Expedition*, in
our volume xiv, p. 233, note 179.— ED.

three hours. We were [44] then aroused, and off we went again, travelling steadily the whole day, making about thirty-five miles, and so got quite clear of the Grand Pawnees.

The antelopes are very numerous here. There is not half an hour during the day in which they are not seen, and they frequently permit the party to approach very near them. This afternoon, two beautiful does came bounding after us, bleating precisely like sheep. The men imitated the call, and they came up to within fifty yards of us, and stood still; two of the hunters fired, and both the poor creatures fell dead. We can now procure as many of these animals as we wish, but their flesh is not equal to common venison, and is frequently rejected by our people. A number are, however, slaughtered every day, from mere wantonness and love of killing, the greenhorns glorying in the sport, like our striplings of the city, in their annual murdering of robins and sparrows.

20th.—This afternoon, we came in sight of a large *gang* of the long-coveted buffalo. They were grazing on the opposite side of the Platte, quietly as domestic cattle, but as we neared them, the foremost *winded* us, and started back, and the whole herd followed in the wildest confusion, and were soon out of sight. There must have been many thousands of them. Towards evening, a large band of elk came towards us at full gallop, and passed very near the party. The appearance of these animals produced a singular effect upon our horses, all of which became restive, and about half the loose ones broke away, and scoured over the plain in full chase after the elk. Captain W. and several of his men went immediately in pursuit of them, and returned late at night, bringing the greater number. Two have, however, been lost irrecoverably. Our observed latitude, yesterday, was 40° 31′, and our computed distance from the Missouri settlements, about 360 miles.

[45] The day following, we saw several small herds of buffalo on our side of the river. Two of our hunters started out after a huge bull that had separated himself from his companions, and gave him chase on fleet horses.

Away went the buffalo, and away went the men, hard as they could dash; now the hunters gained upon him, and pressed him hard; again the enormous creature had the advantage, plunging with all his might, his terrific horns often ploughing up the earth as he spurned it under him. Sometimes he would double, and rush so near the horses as almost to gore them with his horns, and in an instant would be off in a tangent, and throw his pursuers from the track. At length the poor animal came to bay, and made some unequivocal demonstrations of combat; raising and tossing his head furiously, and tearing up the ground with his feet. At this moment a shot was fired. The victim trembled like an aspen, and fell to his knees, but recovering himself in an instant, started again as fast as before. Again the determined hunters dashed after him, but the poor bull was nearly exhausted, he proceeded but a short distance and stopped again. The hunters approached, rode slowly by him, and shot two balls through his body with the most perfect coolness and precision. During the race,— the whole of which occurred in full view of the party,— the men seemed wild with the excitement which it occasioned; and when the animal fell, a shout rent the air, which startled the antelopes by dozens from the bluffs, and sent the wolves howling like demons from their lairs.

This is the most common mode of killing the buffalo, and is practised very generally by the travelling hunters; many are also destroyed by approaching them on foot, when, if the bushes are sufficiently dense, or the grass high enough to afford concealment, the hunter,— by keeping carefully to leeward of his game,— may sometimes approach so near as

almost to touch [46] the animal. If on a plain, without grass or
bushes, it is necessary to be very circumspect; to approach
so slowly as not to excite alarm, and, when observed by the
animal, to imitate dexterously, the clumsy motions of a
young bear, or assume the sneaking, prowling attitude of
a wolf, in order to lull suspicion.

The Indians resort to another stratagem, which is, perhaps, even more successful. The skin of a calf is properly
dressed, with the head and legs left attached to it. The
Indian envelopes himself in this, and with his short bow and
a brace of arrows, ambles off into the very midst of a herd.
When he has selected such an animal as suits his fancy, he
comes close alongside of it, and without noise, passes an arrow through its heart. One arrow is always sufficient, and
it is generally delivered with such force, that at least half the
shaft appears through the opposite side. The creature
totters, and is about to fall, when the Indian glides around,
and draws the arrow from the wound lest it should be broken.
A single Indian is said to kill a great number of buffaloes in
this way, before any alarm is communicated to the herd.

Towards evening, on rising a hill, we were suddenly greeted
by a sight which seemed to astonish even the oldest amongst
us. The whole plain, as far as the eye could discern, was
covered by one enormous mass of buffalo. Our vision, at
the very least computation, would certainly extend ten
miles, and in the whole of this great space, including about
eight miles in width from the bluffs to the river bank, there
was apparently no vista in the incalculable multitude. It
was truly a sight that would have excited even the dullest
mind to enthusiasm. Our party rode up to within a few
hundred yards of the edge of the herd, before any alarm was
communicated; then the bulls,—which are always stationed
around as sentinels,—began pawing the ground, and [47]
throwing the earth over their heads; in a few moments they

started in a slow, clumsy canter; but as we neared them, they quickened their pace to an astonishingly rapid gallop, and in a few minutes were entirely beyond the reach of our guns, but were still so near that their enormous horns, and long shaggy beards, were very distinctly seen. Shortly after we encamped, our hunters brought in the choice parts of five that they had killed.

For the space of several days past, we have observed an inclination in five or six of our men to leave our service. Immediately as we encamp, we see them draw together in some secluded spot, and engage in close and earnest conversation. This has occurred several times, and as we are determined, if possible, to keep our horses, &c., for our own use, we have stationed a sentry near their tent, whose orders are peremptory to stop them at any hazard in case of an attempt on their part, to appropriate our horses. The men we are willing to lose, as they are of very little service, and we can do without them; but horses here are valuable, and we cannot afford to part with them without a sufficient compensation.

22d.— On walking into our tent last night at eleven o'clock, after the expiration of the first watch, (in which I had served as supernumerary, to prevent the desertion of the men,) and stooping to lay my gun in its usual situation near the head of my pallet, I was startled by seeing a pair of eyes, wild and bright as those of a tiger, gleaming from a dark corner of the lodge, and evidently directed upon me. My first impression, was that a wolf had been lurking around the camp, and had entered the tent in the prospect of finding meat. My gun was at my shoulder instinctively, my aim was directed between the eyes, and my finger pressed the trigger. At that moment a tall Indian sprang before me with a loud *wah!* seized the gun, and elevated the muzzle above my head; in another instant, a second Indian was by my side, and I saw his keen knife glitter as it left the [48] scabbard. I had not time for thought, and was struggling with all my might with the first savage for the recovery of my weapon, when Captain W., and the other inmates of the tent were aroused, and the whole matter was explained, and set at rest in a moment. The Indians were chiefs of the tribe of Pawnee Loups,[25] who had come with their young men to shoot buffalo: they had paid an evening visit to the captain, and as an act of courtesy had been invited to sleep in the tent. I had not known of their arrival, nor did I even suspect that Indians were in our neighborhood, so could not control the alarm which their sudden appearance occasioned me.

As I laid myself down, and drew my blanket around me, Captain W. touched me lightly with his finger, and pointed significantly to his own person, which I perceived,— by the fire light at the mouth of the tent,— to be garnished with his knife and pistols; I observed also that the muzzle of his rifle laid across his breast, and that the breech was firmly grasped by one of his legs. I took the hint; tightened my belt, drew my gun closely to my side, and composed myself to sleep. But the excitement of the scene through which I had just passed, effectually banished repose. I frequently directed my eyes towards the dark corner, and in the midst of the shapeless mass which occupied it, I could occasionally see the glittering orbs of our guest shining amidst the surrounding obscurity. At length fatigue conquered watchfulness, and I sank to sleep, dreaming of Indians, guns, daggers, and buffalo.

Upon rising the next morning, all had left the tent: the men were busied in cooking their morning meal; kettles were hanging upon the rude cranes, great ribs of meat were roast-

---

[25] For the Pawnee Loup (Wolf) Indians, consult Bradbury's *Travels*, in our volume v, p. 78, note 44.— ED.

ing before the fires, and loading the air with fragrance, and my dreams and midnight reveries, and apprehensions of evil, fled upon the wings of the bright morning, and nought remained but a feeling of surprise that the untoward events of the night should have disturbed my equanimity.

[49] While these thoughts were passing in my mind, my eye suddenly encountered the two Indians. They were squatting upon the ground near one of the fires, and appeared to be surveying, with the keenness of morning appetite, the fine *"hump ribs"* which were roasting before them. The moment they perceived me, I received from them a quick glance of recognition: the taller one,—my opponent of the previous night,—rose to his feet, walked towards me, and gave me his hand with great cordiality; then pointed into the tent, made the motions of raising a gun to his shoulder, taking aim, and in short repeated the entire pantomime with great fidelity, and no little humor, laughing the whole time as though he thought it a capital joke. Poor fellow! it was near proving a dear joke for him, and I almost trembled as I recollected the eager haste with which I sought to take the life of a fellow creature. The Indian evidently felt no ill will towards me, and as a proof of it, proposed an exchange of knives, to which I willingly acceded. He deposited mine,—which had my name engraved upon the handle,— in the sheath at his side, and walked away to his *hump ribs* with the air of a man who is conscious of having done a good action. As he left me, one of our old trappers took occasion to say, that in consequence of this little act of savage courtesy, the Indian became my firm friend; and that if I ever met him again, I should be entitled to share his hospitality, or claim his protection.

While the men were packing the horses, after breakfast, I was again engaged with my Indian friend. I took his bow and arrows in my hand, and remarked that the latter were

smeared with blood throughout: upon my expressing surprise at this he told me, by signs, that they had passed through
the body of the buffalo. I assumed a look of incredulity;
the countenance of the savage brightened, and his peculiar
and strange eyes actually flashed with eagerness, as he
pointed to a dead antelope lying upon the ground about forty
feet from us, and which one of [50] the guard had shot near the
camp in the morning. The animal lay upon its side with the
breast towards us: the bow was drawn slightly, without any
apparent effort, and the arrow flew through the body of the
antelope, and skimmed to a great distance over the plain.

These Indians were the finest looking of any I have seen.
Their persons were tall, straight, and finely formed; their
noses slightly aqualine, and the whole countenance expressive of high and daring intrepidity. The face of the
taller one was particularly admirable; and Gall or Spurzheim, at a single glance at his magnificent head, would have
invested him with all the noblest qualities of the species.[26] I
know not what a physiognomist would have said of his eyes,
but they were certainly the most wonderful eyes I ever looked
into; glittering and scintillating constantly, like the mirror-
glasses in a lamp frame, and rolling and dancing in their
orbits as though possessed of abstract volition.

The tribe to which these Indians belong, is a division of the
great Pawnee nation. There are four of these divisions or
tribes, known by the names of Grand Pawnees, Pawnee
Loups, Pawnee Republicans, and Pawnee Picts. They are
all independent of each other, governed exclusively by chiefs
chosen from among their own people, and although they
have always been on terms of intimacy and friendship, never

[26] Noted German phrenologists. Franz Joseph Gall (1758-1828) was founder
of the school of phrenology; his chief work was *Anatomie et Physiologie du système
nerveux* (1810-20). Kasper Spurzheim (1776-1832) was a disciple of Gall's,
publishing *Physiognomical System of Drs. Gall and Spurzheim* (1815). He died
in Boston.— ED.

intermarry, nor have other intercourse than that of trade, or a conjunction of their forces to attack the common enemy. In their dealings with the whites, they are arbitrary and over-bearing, chaffering about the price of a horse, or a beaver skin, with true huckster-like eagerness and mendacity, and seizing with avidity every unfair advantage, which circumstances or their own craft may put in their power.

The buffalo still continue immensely numerous in every direction around, and our men kill great numbers, so that we are in truth living upon the fat of the land, and better feeding need [51] no man wish. The savory buffalo hump has suffered no depreciation since the "man without a cross" vaunted of its good qualities to "the stranger;" and in this, as in many other particulars, we have realized the truth and fidelity of Cooper's admirable descriptions.

23*d.*—When we rose this morning, not a single buffalo, of the many thousands that yesterday strewed the plain, was to be seen. It seemed like magic. Where could they have gone? I asked myself this question again and again, but in vain. At length I applied to Richardson, who stated that they had gone to the bluffs, but for what reason he could not tell; he, however, had observed their tracks bearing towards the bluffs, and was certain that they would be found there. He and Sandsbury (another hunter) were then about starting on a hunt to supply the camp, and I concluded to accompany them; Mr. Lee, the missionary, also joined us, and we all rode off together. The party got under way about the same time, and proceeded along the bank of the river, while we struck off south to look for the buffalo. About one hour's brisk trotting carried us to the bluffs, and we entered amongst large conical hills of yellow clay, intermixed with strata of limestone, but without the slightest vegetation of any kind. On the plains which we had left, the grass was in great luxuriance, but here not a blade of it was to be seen, and yet, as Richardson had predicted, here were the buffalo. We had not ridden a mile before we entered upon a plain of sand of great extent, and observed ahead vast clouds of dust rising and circling in the air as though a tornado or a whirlwind were sweeping over the earth. "Ha!" said Richardson, "there they are; now let us take the wind of them, and you shall see some sport." We accordingly went around to leeward, and, upon approaching nearer, saw the huge animals rolling over and over in the sand with astonishing agility enveloping themselves by the exercise in a perfect atmosphere of dust; occasionally two of the bulls would[52]spring from the ground and attack each other with amazing address and fury, retreating for ten or twelve feet, and then rushing suddenly forward, and dashing their enormous fronts together with a shock that seemed annihilating. In these rencontres, one of the combatants was often thrown back upon his haunches, and tumbled sprawling upon the ground; in which case, the victor, with true prize-fighting generosity, refrained from persecuting his fallen adversary, contenting himself with a hearty resumption of his rolling fit, and kicking up the dust with more than his former vigor, as if to celebrate his victory.

This appeared to be a good situation to approach and kill the buffalo, as, by reason of the plentiful distribution of the little clay hills, an opportunity would be afforded of successful concealment; we separated, therefore, each taking his own course. In a very few minutes I heard the crack of a rifle in the direction in which Richardson had gone, and immediately after saw the frightened animals flying from the spot. The sound reverberated among the hills, and as it died away the herd halted to watch and listen for its repetition. For myself, I strolled on for nearly an hour, leading my horse, and peering over every hill, in the hope of finding a buffalo within range, but not one could I see that was sufficiently near; and when I attempted the stealthy approach which I had seen Richardson practise with so much success, I felt compelled to acknowledge my utter insufficiency. I had determined to kill a buffalo, and as I had seen it several times done with so much apparent ease, I considered it a mere moonshine matter, and thought I could compass it without difficulty; but now I had attempted it, and was grievously mistaken in my estimate of the required skill. I had several times heard the guns of the hunters, and felt satisfied that we should not go to camp without meat, and was on the point of altering my course to join them, when, as I wound around the base of a little hill, I saw about twenty buffalo lying quietly on the ground within [53] thirty yards of me. Now was my time. I took my picket from my saddle, and fastened my horse to the ground as quietly as possible, but with hands that almost failed to do their office, from my excessive eagerness and trembling anxiety. When this was completed, I crawled around the hill again, almost suspending my breath from fear of alarming my intended victims, until I came again in full view of the unsuspecting herd. There were so many fine animals that I was at a loss which to select; those nearest me appeared small and poor, and I therefore settled my aim upon a huge bull on the outside. Just then I was attacked with the "*bull fever*" so dreadfully, that for several minutes I could not shoot. At length, however, I became firm and steady, and pulled my trigger at exactly the right instant. Up sprang the herd like lightning, and away they scoured, and my bull with them. I was vexed, angry, and discontented; I concluded that I could never kill a buffalo, and was about to mount my horse and ride off in despair, when I observed that one of the animals had stopped in the midst of his career. I rode towards him, and sure enough, there was my great bull trembling and swaying from side to side, and the clotted gore hanging like icicles from his nostrils. In a few minutes after, he fell heavily upon his side, and I dismounted and surveyed the unwieldy brute, as he panted and struggled in the death agony.

When the first ebullition of my triumph had subsided, I perceived that my prize was so excessively lean as to be worth nothing, and while I was exerting my whole strength in a vain endeavor to raise the head from the ground for the purpose of removing the tongue, the two hunters joined me, and laughed heartily at my achievement. Like all inexperienced hunters, I had been particular to select the largest bull in the gang, supposing it to be the best, (and it proved, as usual, the poorest,) while more than a dozen fat cows were nearer me, either of which I might have killed with as little trouble.

[54] As I had supposed, my companions had killed several animals, but they had taken the meat of only one, and we had, therefore, to be diligent, or the camp might suffer for provisions. It was now past mid-day; the weather was very warm, and the atmosphere was charged with minute particles of sand, which produced a dryness and stiffness of the mouth and tongue, that was exceedingly painful and distressing. Water was now the desideratum, but where was it to be found? The arid country in which we then were, produced none, and the Platte was twelve or fourteen miles from us, and no buffalo in that direction, so that we could not afford time for so trifling a matter. I found that Mr. Lee was suffering as much as myself, although he had not spoken of it, and I perceived that Richardson was masticating a leaden bullet, to excite the salivary glands. Soon afterwards, a bull was killed, and we all assembled around the carcass to assist in the manipulations. The animal was first raised from his side where he had lain, and supported upon his knees, with his hoofs turned under him; a longitudinal incis-

ion was then made from the nape, or anterior base of the hump, and continued backward to the loins, and a large portion of the skin from each side removed; these pieces of skin were placed upon the ground, with the under surface uppermost, and the *fleeces*, or masses of meat, taken from along the back, were laid upon them. These fleeces, from a large animal, will weigh, perhaps, a hundred pounds each, and comprise the whole of the hump on each side of the vertical processes, (commonly called the *hump ribs*,) which are attached to the vertebra. The fleeces are considered the choice parts of the buffalo, and here, where the game is so abundant, nothing else is taken, if we except the tongue, and an occasional marrow bone.

This, it must be confessed, appears like a useless and unwarrantable waste of the goods of Providence; but when are men economical, unless compelled to be so by necessity? Here are [55] more than a thousand pounds of delicious and savory flesh, which would delight the eyes and gladden the heart of any epicure in Christendom, left neglected where it fell, to feed the ravenous maw of the wild prairie wolf, and minister to the excesses of the unclean birds of the wilderness. But I have seen worse waste and havoc than this, and I feel my indignation rise at the recollection. I have seen dozens of buffalo slaughtered merely for the tongues, or for practice with the rifle; and I have also lived to see the very perpetrators of these deeds, lean and lank with famine, when the meanest and most worthless parts of the poor animals they had so inhumanly slaughtered, would have been received and eaten with humble thankfulness.

But to return to ourselves. We were all suffering from excessive thirst, and so intolerable had it at length become, that Mr. Lee and myself proposed a gallop over to the Platte river, in order to appease it; but Richardson advised us not to go, as he had just thought of a means of relieving us, which

he immediately proceeded to put in practice. He tumbled
our mangled buffalo over upon his side, and with his knife
opened the body, so as to expose to view the great stomach,
and still crawling and twisting entrails. The good missionary and myself stood gaping with astonishment, and no little
loathing, as we saw our hunter plunge his knife into the
distended paunch, from which gushed the green and gelati-
nous juices, and then insinuate his tin pan into the opening,
and by depressing its edge, strain off the water which was
mingled with its contents.

Richardson always valued himself upon his politeness, and
the cup was therefore first offered to Mr. Lee and myself, but
it is almost needless to say that we declined the proffer, and
our features probably expressed the strong disgust which we
felt, for our companion laughed heartily before he applied
the cup to his own mouth. He then drank it to the dregs,
smacking his lips, and drawing a long breath after it, with
the satisfaction of a man [56] taking his wine after dinner.
Sansbury, the other hunter, was not slow in following the
example set before him, and we, the audience, turned our
backs upon the actors.

Before we left the spot, however, Richardson induced me
to taste the blood which was still fluid in the heart, and immediately as it touched my lips, my burning thirst, aggravated by hunger, (for I had eaten nothing that day,) got the
better of my abhorrence; I plunged my head into the reeking
ventricles, and drank until forced to stop for breath. I felt
somewhat ashamed of assimilating myself so nearly to the
brutes, and turned my ensanguined countenance towards the
missionary who stood by, but I saw no approval there: the
good man was evidently attempting to control his risibility,
and so I smiled to put him in countenance; the roar could
no longer be restrained, and the missionary laughed until
the tears rolled down his cheeks. I did not think, until

afterwards, of the horrible ghastliness which must have characterized my smile at that particular moment.

When we arrived at the camp in the evening, and I enjoyed the luxury of a hearty draft of water, the effect upon my stomach was that of a powerful emetic: the blood was violently ejected without nausea, and I felt heartily glad to be rid of the disgusting encumbrance. I never drank blood from that day.

[57] CHAPTER IV

ON the morning of the 24th of May we forded the Platte
river, or rather its south fork, along which we had been
travelling during the previous week.[27]   On the northern side,
we found the country totally different in its aspect.   Instead
of the extensive and apparently interminable green plains,
the monotony of which had become so wearisome to the eye,
here was a great sandy waste, without a single green thing to
vary and enliven the dreary scene.   It was a change, however, and we were therefore enjoying it, and remarking to
each other how particularly agreeable it was, when we were
suddenly assailed by vast swarms of most ferocious little
black gnats; the whole atmosphere seemed crowded with
them, and they dashed into our faces, assaulted our eyes,
ears, nostrils, and mouths, as though they were determined to
bar our passage through their territory.   These little creatures were so exceedingly minute that, singly, they were
scarcely visible; and yet their sting caused such excessive
pain, that for [58] the rest of the day our men and horses were

---

[27] There were two fords to the South Platte, both of which led toward the
North Platte at Ash Creek.   Wyeth's party took the lower ford, eight miles above
the forks.— ED.

rendered almost frantic, the former bitterly imprecating, and the latter stamping, and kicking, and rolling in the sand, in tremendous, yet vain, efforts to rid themselves of their pertinacious little foes. It was rather amusing to see the whole company with their handkerchiefs, shirts, and coats, thrown over their heads, stemming the animated torrent, and to hear the greenhorns cursing their tormenters, the country, and themselves, for their foolhardiness in venturing on the journey. When we encamped in the evening, we built fires at the mouths of the tents, the smoke from which kept our enemies at a distance, and we passed a night of tolerable comfort, after a day of most peculiar misery.

The next morning I observed that the faces of all the men were more or less swollen, some of them very severely, and poor Captain W. was totally blind for two days afterwards.

25th.—We made a noon camp to-day on the north branch or fork of the river, and in the afternoon travelled along the bank of the stream.[28] In about an hour's march, we came to rocks, precipices, and cedar trees, and although we anticipated some difficulty and toil in the passage of the heights, we felt glad to exchange them for the vast and wearisome prairies we had left behind. Soon after we commenced the ascent, we struck into an Indian path very much worn, occasionally mounting over rugged masses of rock, and leaping wide fissures in the soil, and sometimes picking our way over the jutting crags, directly above the river. On the top of one of the stunted and broad spreading cedars, a bald eagle had built its enormous nest; and as we descended the mountain, we saw the callow young lying within it, while the anxious parents hovered over our heads, screaming their alarm.

In the evening we arrived upon the plain again; it was thickly covered with ragged and gnarled bushes of a species of wormwood, (*Artemesia*,) which perfumed the air, and at

---

[28] See note 32 (Wyeth), *ante*, p. 52.— ED.

first was [59] rather agreeable. The soil was poor and sandy, and the straggling blades of grass which found their way to the surface were brown and withered. Here was a poor prospect for our horses; a sad contrast indeed to the rich and luxuriant prairies we had left. On the edges of the little streams, however, we found some tolerable pasture, and we frequently stopped during the day to bait our poor animals in these pleasant places.

We observed here several species of small marmots, (*Arctomys,*) which burrowed in the sand, and were constantly skipping about the ground in front of our party. The short rattlesnake of the prairies was also abundant, and no doubt derived its chief subsistence from foraging among its playful little neighbors. Shortly before we halted this evening, being a considerable distance in advance of the caravan, I observed a dead gopher, (*Diplostoma,*) — a small animal about the size of a rat, with large external cheek pouches, — lying upon the ground; and near it a full grown rattlesnake, also dead. The gopher was yet warm and pliant, and had evidently been killed but a few minutes previously; the snake also gave evidence of very recent death, by a muscular twitching of the tail, which occurs in most serpents, soon after life is extinct. It was a matter of interest to me to ascertain the mode by which these animals were deprived of life. I therefore dismounted from my horse, and examined them carefully, but could perceive nothing to furnish even a clue. Neither of them had any external or perceptible wound. The snake had doubtless killed the quadruped, but what had killed the snake? There being no wound upon its body was sufficient proof that the gopher had not used his teeth, and in no other way could he cause death.

I was unable to solve the problem to my satisfaction, so I pocketed the animal to prepare its skin, and rode on to the camp.

The birds thus far have been very abundant. There is a considerable [60] variety, and many of them have not before been seen by naturalists. As to the plants, there seems to be no end to them, and Mr. N. is finding dozens of new species daily. In the other branches of science, our success has not been so great, partly on account of the rapidity and steadiness with which we travel, but chiefly from the difficulty, and almost impossibility, of carrying the subjects. Already we have cast away all our useless and superfluous clothing, and have been content to mortify our natural pride, to make room for our specimens. Such things as spare waistcoats, shaving boxes, soap, and stockings, have been ejected from our trunks, and we are content to dress, as we live, in a style of primitive simplicity. In fact, the whole appearance of our party is sufficiently primitive; many of the men are dressed entirely in deerskins, without a single article of civilized manufacture about them; the old trappers and hunters wear their hair flowing on their shoulders, and their large grizzled beards would scarcely disgrace a Bedouin of the desert.

The next morning the whole camp was suddenly aroused by the falling of all the tents. A tremendous blast swept as from a funnel over the sandy plain, and in an instant precipitated our frail habitations like webs of gossamer. The men crawled out from under the ruins, rubbing their eyes, and, as usual, muttering imprecations against the country and all that therein was; it was unusually early for a start, but we did not choose to pitch the tents again, and to sleep without them here was next to impossible; so we took our breakfast in the open air, devouring our well sanded provisions as quickly as possible, and immediately took to the road.

During the whole day a most terrific gale was blowing directly in our faces, clouds of sand were driving and hurtling by us, often with such violence as nearly to stop our progress; and when we halted in the evening, we could scarcely recognise each other's faces beneath their odious mask of dust and dirt.

[61] There have been no buffalo upon the plain to-day, all the game that we have seen, being a few elk and antelopes; but these of course we did not attempt to kill, as our whole and undivided attention was required to assist our progress.

28th.—We fell in with a new species of game to-day; — a large band of wild horses. They were very shy, scarcely permitting us to approach within rifle distance, and yet they kept within sight of us for some hours. Several of us gave them chase, in the hope of at least being able to approach sufficiently near to examine them closely, but we might as well have pursued the wind; they scoured away from us with astonishing velocity, their long manes and tails standing out almost horizontally, as they sprang along before us. Occasionally they would pause in their career, turn and look at us as we approached them, and then, with a neigh that rang loud and high above the clattering of the hoofs, dart their light heels into the air, and fly from us as before. We soon abandoned this wild chase, and contented ourselves with admiring their sleek beauty at a distance.

In the afternoon, I committed an act of cruelty and wantonness, which distressed and troubled me beyond measure, and which I have ever since recollected with sorrow and compunction. A beautiful doe antelope came running and bleating after us, as though she wished to overtake the party; she continued following us for nearly an hour, at times approaching within thirty of forty yards, and standing to gaze at us as we moved slowly on our way. I several times raised my gun to fire at her, but my better nature as often gained the ascendency, and I at last rode into the midst of the party to escape the temptation. Still the doe followed us, and I finally fell into the rear, but without intending it, and again looked at her as she trotted behind us. At that moment, my evil genius and love of sport triumphed; I slid down from my horse, aimed at the poor antelope, and shot a ball through her side. Under other circumstances, [62] there would have been no cruelty in this; but here, where better meat was so abundant, and the camp was so plentifully supplied, it was unfeeling, heartless murder. It was under the influence of this too late impression, that I approached my poor victim. She was writhing in agony upon the ground, and exerting herself in vain efforts to draw her mangled body farther from her destroyer; and as I stood over her, and saw her cast her large, soft, black eyes upon me with an expression of the most touching sadness, while the great tears rolled over her face, I felt myself the meanest and most abhorrent thing in creation. But now a finishing blow would be mercy to her, and I threw my arm around her neck, averted my face, and drove my long knife through her bosom to the heart. I did not trust myself to look upon her afterwards, but mounted my horse, and galloped off to the party, with feelings such as I hope never to experience again. For several days the poor antelope haunted me, and I shall never forget its last look of pain and upbraiding.

The bluffs on the southern shore of the Platte, are, at this point, exceedingly rugged, and often quite picturesque; the formation appears to be simple clay, intermixed, occasionally, with a stratum of limestone, and one part of the bluff bears a striking and almost startling resemblance to a dilapidated feudal castle. There is also a kind of obelisk, standing at a considerable distance from the bluffs, on a wide plain, towering to the height of about two hundred feet, and tapering to a small point at the top. This pillar is known to the hunters and trappers who traverse these regions, by the name of the "*chimney*." Here we diverged from the usual course, leaving the bank of the river, and entered a large and deep ravine between the enormous bluffs.[29]

[63] The road was very uneven and difficult, winding from amongst innumerable mounds six to eight feet in height, the space between them frequently so narrow as scarcely to admit our horses, and some of the men rode for upwards of a mile kneeling upon their saddles. These mounds were of hard yellow clay, without a particle of rock of any kind, and along their bases, and in the narrow passages, flowers of every hue were growing. It was a most enchanting sight; even the men noticed it, and more than one of our matter-of-fact people exclaimed, *beautiful, beautiful!* Mr. N. was here in his glory. He rode on ahead of the company, and cleared the passages with a trembling and eager hand, looking anxiously back at the approaching party, as though he feared it would come ere he had finished, and tread his lovely prizes under foot.

The distance through the ravine is about three miles. We then crossed several beautiful grassy knolls, and descending to the plain, struck the Platte again, and travelled along its bank. Here one of our men caught a young antelope, which he brought to the camp upon his saddle. It was a beautiful and most delicate little creature, and in a few days became so tame as to remain with the camp without being tied, and to drink, from a tin cup, the milk which our good missionaries spared from their own scanty meals. The men christened it " *Zip Coon,*" and it soon became familiar with its name, running to them when called, and exhibiting many evidences of affection and attachment. It became a

---

[29] These are called "Scott's Bluffs;" so named from an unfortunate trader, who perished here from disease and hunger, many years ago. He was deserted by his companions; and the year following, his crumbling bones were found in this spot.— TOWNSEND.

Comment by Ed. See this story in detail in Irving, *Rocky Mountains,* i, pp. 45, 46.

great favorite with every one. A little pannier of willows was made for it, which was packed on the back of a mule, and when the camp moved in the mornings, little *Zip* ran to his station beside his long-eared hack, bleating with impatience until some one came to assist him in mounting.

On the afternoon of the 31st, we came to green trees and bushes again, and the sight of them was more cheering than can [64] be conceived, except by persons who have travelled for weeks without beholding a green thing, save the grass under their feet. We encamped in the evening in a beautiful grove of cottonwood trees, along the edge of which ran the Platte, dotted as usual with numerous islands.

In the morning, Mr. N. and myself were up before the dawn, strolling through the umbrageous forest, inhaling the fresh, bracing air, and making the echoes ring with the report of our gun, as the lovely tenants of the grove flew by dozens before us. I think I never before saw so great a variety of birds within the same space. All were beautiful, and many of them quite new to me; and after we had spent an hour amongst them, and my game bag was teeming with its precious freight, I was still loath to leave the place, lest I should not have procured specimens of the whole.

None but a naturalist can appreciate a naturalist's feelings — his delight amounting to ecstacy — when a specimen such as he has never before seen, meets his eye, and the sorrow and grief which he feels when he is compelled to tear himself from a spot abounding with all that he has anxiously and unremittingly sought for.

This was peculiarly my case upon this occasion. We had been long travelling over a sterile and barren tract, where the lovely denizens of the forest could not exist, and I had been daily scanning the great extent of the desert, for some little *oasis* such as I had now found; here was my wish at length gratified, and yet the caravan would not halt for me; I must turn my back upon the *El Dorado* of my fond anticipations, and hurry forward over the dreary wilderness which lay beyond.

What valuable and highly interesting accessions to science might not be made by a party, composed exclusively of naturalists, on a journey through this rich and unexplored region! The botanist, the geologist, the mamalogist, the ornithologist, and [65] the entomologist, would find a rich and almost inexhaustible field for the prosecution of their inquiries, and the result of such an expedition would be to add most materially to our knowledge of the wealth and resources of our country, to furnish us with new and important facts relative to its structure, organization, and natural productions, and to complete the fine native collections in our already extensive museums.

On the 1st of June, we arrived at Laramie's fork of the Platte, and crossed it without much difficulty.[30]

Here two of our "free trappers" left us for a summer "hunt" in the rugged Black Hills. These men joined our party at Independence, and have been travelling to this point with us for the benefit of our escort. Trading companies usually encourage these free trappers to join them, both for the strength which they add to the band, and that they may have the benefit of their generally good hunting qualities. Thus are both parties accommodated, and no obligation is felt on either side.

I confess I felt somewhat sad when I reflected upon the possible fate of the two adventurous men who had left us in the midst of a savage wilderness, to depend entirely upon their unassisted strength and hardihood, to procure the

---

[30] Wyeth relates in his journal that he found thirteen of Sublette's men building a fort at this place. Such was the origin of the famous Fort Laramie, first known as Fort William, then Fort John, and in 1846, removed a mile farther up the stream, and re-christened Fort Laramie. It became a government post in 1849.— ED.

means of subsistence and repel the aggression of the Indian.

Their expedition will be fraught with stirring scenes, with peril and with strange adventure; but they think not of this, and they care not for it. They are ohly two of the many scores who annually subject themselves to the same difficulties and dangers; they see their friends return unscathed, and laden with rich and valuable furs, and if one or two should have perished by Indian rapacity, or fallen victims to their own daring and fool-hardy spirit, they mourn the loss of their ₅brethren who have not returned, and are only the more anxious to pursue the same track in order to avenge them.

On the 2d, we struck a range of high and stony mountains, [66] called the Black Hills. The general aspect here, was dreary and forbidding; the soil was intersected by deep and craggy fissures; rock jutted over rock, and precipice frowned over precipice in frightful, and apparently endless, succession. Soon after we commenced the ascent, we experienced a change in the temperature of the air; and towards mid-day, when we had arrived near the summit, our large blanket *capeaus*, — which in the morning had been discarded as uncomfortable, — were drawn tightly around us, and every man was shivering in his saddle as though he had an ague fit. The soil here is of a deep reddish or ferruginous hue, intermixed with green sand; and on the heights, pebbles of chalcedony and agate are abundant.

We crossed, in the afternoon, the last and steepest spur of this chain, winding around rough and stony precipices, and along the extreme verges of tremendous ravines, so dangerous looking that we were compelled to dismount and lead our horses.

On descending to the plain, we saw again the north fork of the Platte, and were glad of an opportunity of encamping.

Our march to-day has been an unusually wearisome one, and many of our loose horses are bruised and lame.

7th. — The country has now become more level, but the prairie is barren and inhospitable looking to the last degree. The twisted, aromatic wormwood covers and extracts the strength from the burnt and arid soil. The grass is dry and brown, and our horses are suffering extremely for want of food. Occasionally, however, a spot of lovely green appears, and here we allow our poor jaded friends to halt, and roam without their riders, and their satisfaction and pleasure is expressed by many a joyous neigh, and many a heart-felt roll upon the verdant sward.

In the afternoon, we arrived at the "Red Butes," two or three brown-red cliffs, about two thousand feet in height." This is a remarkable point in the mountain route. One of these cliffs terminates a long, lofty, wooded ridge, which has bounded our [67] southern view for the past two days. The summits of the cliffs are covered with patches of snow, and the contrast of the dazzling white and brick-red produces a very pretty effect.

The next day, we left the Platte river, and crossed a wide, sandy desert, dry and desolate; and on the 9th, encamped at noon on the banks of the Sweet-water. Here we found a large rounded mass of granite, about fifty feet high, called Rock Independence." Like the Red Butes, this rock is also a rather remarkable point in the route. On its smooth, perpendicular sides, we see carved the names of most of the mountain *bourgeois*," with the dates of their arrival. We

[31] The trail continued along the North Platte until it reached Red Buttes, described by Townsend. They form the western end of what is known as Caspar range, in Natrona County, Wyoming.— ED.

[32] For Sweetwater River and Independence Rock, see notes 33, 34 (Wyeth), *ante*, p. 53.— ED.

[33] In fur-trade parlance the *bourgeois* was the leader or commander of an expedition or a trading post. See J. Long's *Voyages* in our volume ii, p. 75, note 35.— ED.

observed those of the two Sublette's, Captains Bonneville, Serre, Fontinelle, &c.,[34] and after leaving our own, and taking a hearty, but hasty lunch in the shade of a rock, and a draught from the pure and limpid stream at its base, we pursued our journey.

The river is here very narrow, often only twelve or fifteen feet wide, shallow, and winding so much, that during our march, to-day, we crossed it several times, in order to pursue a straight course. The banks of the stream are clothed with the most luxuriant pasture, and our invaluable dumb friends appear perfectly happy.

We saw here great numbers of a beautiful brown and white avocet, (the *Recurvirostra americana* of ornithologists.) These fine birds were so tame as to allow a very near approach, running slowly before our party, and scarcely taking wing at the report of a gun. They frequent the marshy plains in the neighborhood of the river, and breed here.

On the 10th, about ninety miles to the west, we had a striking view of the Wind-river mountains. They are almost wholly of a dazzling whiteness, being covered thickly with snow, and the lofty peaks seem to blend themselves with the dark clouds which hang over them.[35] This chain gives rise to the sources of the Missouri, the Colorado of the west,

---

[34] For Captain Bonneville, see Gregg's *Commerce of the Prairies*, in our volume xx, p. 267, note 167.

Michael Lamie Cerré belonged to a French family of note in the annals of the West. His grandfather, Gabriel, was an early merchant at Kaskaskia, and acquired a fortune in the fur-trade. Later he removed to St. Louis, where one of his daughters married Auguste Chouteau. Pascal Cerré, father of Michael, was also a fur-trader of note. The son had been employed in the Santa Fé trade, and was persuaded to act as Bonneville's business agent in his expeditions of 1832-35.

For Lucien Fontenelle, see our volume xiv, p. 275, note 196.— ED.

[35] The Wind River Mountains, in Fremont County, Wyoming, trend nearly north from South Pass to the Yellowstone. They are covered with snow during all the year, and were credited by the early explorers with being the highest chain of the Rockies. In 1843 Frémont ascended the peak named for him, which has an altitude of 13,790 feet.— ED.

and Lewis' river of the [68] Columbia, and is the highest land on the continent of North America.

We saw, to-day, a small flock of the hairy sheep of the Rocky Mountains, the big horn of the hunters, (*Ovis montana*.) We exerted ourselves in vain to shoot them. They darted from us, and hid themselves amongst the inaccessible cliffs, so that none but a chamois hunter might pretend to reach them. Richardson says that he has frequently killed them, but he admits that it is dangerous and wearisome sport; and when good beef is to be found upon the plains, men are not anxious to risk their necks for a meal of mutton.

In the afternoon, one of our men had a somewhat perilous adventure with a grizzly bear. He saw the animal crouching his huge frame in some willows which skirted the river, and approaching on horseback to within twenty yards, fired upon him. The bear was only slightly wounded by the shot, and with a fierce growl of angry malignity, rushed from his cover, and gave chase. The horse happened to be a slow one, and for the distance of half a mile, the race was hard contested; the bear frequently approaching so near the terrified animal as to snap at his heels, while the equally terrified rider, — who had lost his hat at the start, — used whip and spur with the most frantic diligence, frequently looking behind, from an influence which he could not resist, at his rugged and determined foe, and shrieking in an agony of fear, "shoot him, shoot him?" The man, who was one of the greenhorns, happened to be about a mile behind the main body, either from the indolence of his horse, or his own carelessness; but as he approached the party in his desperate flight, and his lugubrious cries reached the ears of the men in front, about a dozen of them rode to his assistance, and soon succeeded in diverting the attention of his pertinacious foe. After he had received the contents of all the guns, he fell, and was soon dispatched. The man rode in among his fellows, pale and

[69] haggard from overwrought feelings, and was probably effectually cured of a propensity for meddling with grizzly bears.

A small striped rattlesnake is abundant on these plains: — it is a different species from our common one at home, but is equally malignant and venomous. The horses are often startled by them, and dart aside with intuitive fear when their note of warning is sounded in the path.

12*th*. — The plains of the Sweet-water at this point, — latitude 43° 6′, longitude 110° 30′, — are covered with little salt pools, the edges of which are encrusted with alkaline efflorescences, looking like borders of snow. The rocks in the vicinity are a loose, fine-grained sandstone, the strata nearly horizontal, and no organic remains have been discovered. We have still a view of the lofty Wind-river mountains on our right hand, and they have for some days served as a guide to determine our course. On the plain, we passed several huge rhomboidal masses of rock, standing alone, and looking, at a little distance, like houses with chimneys. The freaks of nature, as they are called, have often astonished us since we have been journeying in the wilderness. We have seen, modeled without art, representations of almost all the most stupendous works of man; and how do the loftiest and most perfect creations of his wisdom and ingenuity sink into insignificance by the comparison. Noble castles, with turrets, embrazures, and loop holes, with the drawbridge in front, and the moat surrounding it: behind, the humble cottages of the subservient peasantry, and all the varied concomitants of such a scene, are so strikingly evident to the view, that it requires but little stretch of fancy to imagine that a race of antediluvian giants may here have swayed their iron sceptre, and left behind the crumbling palace and the tower, to tell of their departed glory.

On the 14th, we left the Sweet-water, and proceeded in a

south-westerly direction to Sandy river, a branch of the Colorado of the west.[36]   We arrived here at about 9 o'clock in the evening, [70] after a hard and most toilsome march for both man and beast.   We found no water on the route, and not a single blade of grass for our horses.   Many of the poor animals stopped before night, and resolutely refused to proceed; and others with the remarkable sagacity, peculiar to them, left the track in defiance of those who drove and guided them, sought and found water, and spent the night in its vicinity.   The band of missionaries, with their horses and horned cattle, halted by the way, and only about half the men of the party accompanied us to our encampment on Sandy.   We were thus scattered along the route for several miles; and if a predatory band of Indians had then found us, we should have fallen an easy prey.

The next morning by about 10 o'clock all our men and horses had joined us, and, in spite of the fatigues of the previous day, we were all tolerably refreshed, and in good spirits.   Towards noon we got under way, and proceeded seven or eight miles down the river to a spot where we found a little poor pasture for our horses.   Here we remained until the next morning, to recruit.   I found here a beautiful new species of mocking bird,[37] which I shot and prepared.   Birds are, however, generally scarce, and there is here very little of interest in any department of natural history.   We are also beginning to suffer somewhat for food: buffalo are rarely seen, the antelopes are unusually shy, and the life of our little favorite, "Zip," has been several times menaced.   I be-

---

[36] Sandy River is a northern affluent of the Green, rising just beyond South Pass and flowing southwest into the main stream, through Fremont and Sweetwater counties, Wyoming.   The Little Sandy was the first stream beyond the divide, but eight miles from the pass.   The trail followed the Big Sandy almost its entire length.— ED.

[37] This is the mountain mocking bird, (*Orpheus montanus*), described in the Appendix [not included in our reprint].— TOWNSEND.

lieve, however, that his keeper, from sheer fondness, would witness much greater suffering in the camp, ere he would consent to the sacrifice of his playful little friend.

16*th*. — We observed a hoar frost and some thin ice, this morning at sunrise; but at mid-day, the thermometer stood at 82°. We halted at noon, after making about fifteen miles, and dined. Saw large herds of buffalo on the plains of Sandy river, [71] grazing in every direction on the short and dry grass. Domestic cattle would certainly starve here, and yet the bison exists, and even becomes fat; a striking instance of the wonderful adaptation of Providence.

17*th*. — We had yesterday a cold rain, the first which has fallen in our track for several weeks. Our vicinity to the high mountains of Wind river will perhaps account for it. To-day at noon, the mercury stood at 92° in the shade, but there being a strong breeze, we did not suffer from heat.

Our course was still down the Sandy river, and we are now looking forward with no little pleasure to a rest of two or more weeks at the mountain rendezvous on the Colorado. Here we expect to meet all the mountain companies who left the States last spring, and also the trappers who come in from various parts, with the furs collected by them during the previous year. All will be mirth and jollity, no doubt, but the grand desideratum with some of us, is to allow our horses to rest their tired limbs and exhausted strength on the rich and verdant plains of the Siskadee. At our camp this evening, our poor horses were compelled to fast as heretofore, there being absolutely nothing for them to eat. Some of the famished animals attempted to allay their insatiable cravings, by cropping the dry and bitter tops of the wormwood with which the plain is strewed.

We look forward to brighter days for them ere long; soon shall they sport in the green pastures, and rest and plenty shall compensate for their toils and privations.

[72] CHAPTER V

Arrival at the Colorado — The author in difficulty — Loss of a journal, and advice to travelling tyros — The rendezvous — Motley groups infesting it — Rum drinking, swearing, and other accomplishments in vogue — Description of the camp — Trout and grayling — Abundance of game — Cock of the plains — Departure from the rendezvous — An accession to the band — A renegado Blackfoot chief — Captain Stewart and Mr. Ashworth — Muddy creek — More carousing — Abundance of trout — Bear river — A hard day's march — Volcanic country — White clay pits and "Beer spring" — Rare birds and common birds — Mr. Thomas McKay — Rough and arid country — Meeting with Captain Bonneville's party — Captains Stewart and Wyeth's visit to the lodge of the "bald chief" — Blackfoot river — Adventure with a grizzly bear — Death of "Zip Koon" — Young grizzly bears and buffalo calves — A Blackfoot Indian — Dangerous experiment of McKay — the three "Tetons" — Large trout — Departure of our Indian companions — Shoshoné river — Site of "Fort Hall" — Preparations for a buffalo hunt.

June 19th. — We arrived to-day on the Green river, Siskadee[38] or Colorado of the west, — a beautiful, clear, deep, and rapid stream, which receives the waters of Sandy, — and encamped upon its eastern bank. After making a hasty meal, as it was yet early in the day, I sallied forth with my gun, and roamed about the neighborhood for several hours in quest of birds. On returning, towards evening, I found that the whole company had left the spot, the place being occupied only by a few hungry wolves, ravens, and magpies, the invariable gleaners of a forsaken camp.

I could not at first understand the meaning of all I saw. I thought the desertion strange, and was preparing to make the best of it, when a quick and joyful neigh sounded in the bushes near me, and I recognized the voice of my favorite horse. I found him carefully tied, with the saddle, &c., lying near him. I had not the least idea where the com-

[38] For this river see note 38 (Wyeth), *ante*, p. 60. The term "Siskadee" signified Prairie Hen River.— ED.

pany had gone, but I knew that on the rich, alluvial banks of the river, the trail of the horses would be distinct enough, and I determined to place my dependence, in a great measure, upon the sagacity of my excellent dumb friend, satisfied that he would take me the right course. I accordingly mounted, and off we went at a speed which I found some difficulty in restraining. About half an hour's hard riding brought us to the edge of a large branch of the stream, and I observed that the horses had here entered. I noticed other tracks lower down, but supposed them to have been made by the wanderings of the loose animals. Here then seemed the proper fording place, and with some little hesitation, I allowed my nag to enter the water; we had proceeded but a few yards, however, when down he went off a steep bank, far beyond his depth. This was somewhat disconcerting; but there was but one thing to be done, so I turned my horse's head against the swift current, and we went snort'ng and blowing for the opposite shore. We arrived at length, though in a sadly wet and damaged state, and in a few minutes after, came in view of the new camp.

Captain W. explained to me that he had heard of good pasture here, and had concluded to move immediately, on account of the horses; he informed me, also, that he had crossed the stream about fifty yards below the point where I had entered, and had found an excellent ford. I did not regret my adventure, however, and was congratulating myself upon my good fortune in arriving so seasonably, when, upon looking to my saddle, I discovered that my coat was missing. I had felt uncomfortably warm when I mounted, and had removed the coat and attached it carelessly to the saddle; the rapidity of the current had disengaged it, and it was lost forever. The coat itself was not of much consequence after the hard service it had seen, but it contained the [74] second volume of my journal, a pocket compass, and other articles of essential value to me. I would gladly have relinquished every thing the garment held, if I could have recovered the book; and although I returned to the river, and searched assiduously until night, and offered large rewards to the men, it could not be found.

The journal commenced with our arrival at the Black Hills, and contained some observations upon the natural productions of the country, which to me, at least, were of some importance; as well as descriptions of several new species of birds, and notes regarding their habits, &c., which cannot be replaced.

I would advise all tourists, who journey by land, never to carry their itineraries upon their persons; or if they do, let them be attached by a cord to the neck, and worn under the clothing. A convenient and safe plan would probably be, to have the book deposited in a close pocket of leather, made on the inner side of the saddle-wing; it would thus be always at hand, and if a deep stream were to be passed the trouble of drying the leaves would not be a very serious matter.

In consequence of remaining several hours in wet clothes, after being heated by exercise, I rose the next morning with so much pain, and stiffness of the joints, that I could scarcely move. But notwithstanding this, I was compelled to mount my horse with the others, and to ride steadily and rapidly for eight hours. I suffered intensely during this ride; every step of my horse seemed to increase it, and induced constant sickness and retching.

When we halted, I was so completely exhausted, as to require assistance in dismounting, and shortly after, sank into a state of insensibility from which I did not recover for several hours. Then a violent fever commenced, alternating for two whole days, with sickness and pain. I think I never was more unwell in my [75] life; and if I had been at home, lying on a feather bed instead of the cold ground, I should probably have fancied myself an invalid for weeks.[39]

22d. — We are now lying at the rendezvous. W. Sublette, Captains Serre, Fitzpatrick, and other leaders, with their companies, are encamped about a mile from us, on the same plain, and our own camp is crowded with a heterogeneous assemblage of visitors.[40] The principal of these are Indians, of the Nez Percé, Banneck and Shoshoné tribes, who come with the furs and peltries which they have been collecting at the risk of their lives during the past winter and spring, to trade for ammunition, trinkets, and "fire water."[41] There is, in addition to these, a great

[39] I am indebted to the kindness of my companion and friend, Professor Nuttall, for supplying, in a great measure, the deficiency occasioned by the loss of my journal.— TOWNSEND.

[40] The rendezvous for 1834 changed sites several times; see Wyeth's *Oregon Expeditions*, p. 225. The Rocky Mountain men were first met on Green River; the twentieth, they moved over to Ham's Fork, which was on the twenty-seventh again ascended a short distance for forage.

Thomas Fitzpatrick was one of the partners in the Rocky Mountain Fur Company, whose daring exploits and explorations of the mountains filled the thoughts of the men of his day. He was known to the Indians as "Broken Hand," from having shattered one of those members. He joined Ashley on his early expeditions, and was in the Arikara campaign of 1823; but his chief operations were between 1830 and 1836. In 1831, he went out on the Santa Fé trail, barely escapng when Jedidiah S. Smith was killed. From 1832 to 1835, he conducted the trade at the mountain rendezvous, once (1832) being lost some days in the mountains. In 1833 he was robbed by the Crows, probably at the instigation of a rival fur company. Upon the decline of the fur-trade, he continued to dwell on the frontier, acting as guide for government exploring expeditions, being commissioned captain, and later major. In 1850 he was agent for all the upper region of the Platte, and of great use in Indian negotiations.— ED

[41] For the Shoshoni, see Bradbury's *Travels*, in our volume v, p. 227, note 123; for the Nez Percés, Franchère's *Narrative*, vi, p. 340, note 145.

The Bannock are a Shoshonean tribe, whose habitat was midway between that of the Shoshoni proper and the Comanche, about the upper Lewis River and Great Salt Lake. They had the reputation of being fierce and treacherous, and next to the Blackfeet, were dreaded by white travelers. Lying athwart both the California and Oregon trails, they occasionally were formidable, although usually on trading terms with the trappers. They are now concentrated on the Fort Hall and Lemhi reservations in Idaho, intermingled with Shoshoni.— ED.

variety of personages amongst us; most of them calling themselves white men, French-Canadians, half-breeds, &c., their color nearly as dark, and their manners wholly as wild, as the Indians with whom they constantly associate. These people, with their obstreperous mirth, their whooping, and howling, and quarrelling, added to the mounted Indians, who are constantly dashing into and through our camp, yelling like fiends, the barking and baying of savage wolf-dogs, and the incessant cracking of rifles and carbines, render our camp a perfect bedlam. A more unpleasant situation for an invalid could scarcely be conceived. I am confined closely to the tent with illness, and am compelled all day to listen to the hiccoughing jargon of drunken traders, the *sacré* and *foutre* of Frenchmen run wild, and the swearing and screaming of our own men, who are scarcely less savage than the rest, being heated by the detestable liquor which circulates freely among them.

It is very much to be regretted that at times like the present, there should be a positive necessity to allow the men as much rum as they can drink, but this course has been sanctioned and [76] practised by all leaders of parties who have hitherto visited these regions, and reform cannot be thought of now. The principal liquor in use here is alcohol diluted with water. It is sold to the men at *three dollars* the pint! Tobacco, of very inferior quality, such as could be purchased in Philadelphia at about ten cents per pound, here brings two dollars! and everything else in proportion. There is no coin in circulation, and these articles are therefore paid for by the independent mountain-men, in beaver skins, buffalo robes, &c.; and those who are hired to the companies, have them charged against their wages.

I was somewhat amused to-day by observing one of

our newly hired men enter the tent, and order, with the air of a man who knew he would not be refused, *twenty dollars' worth of rum, and ten dollars worth of sugar*, to treat two of his companions who were about leaving the rendezvous!

30th.— Our camp here is a most lovely one in every respect, and as several days have elapsed since we came, and I am convalescent, I can roam about the country a little and enjoy it. The pasture is rich and very abundant, and it does our hearts good to witness the satisfaction and comfort of our poor jaded horses. Our tents are pitched in a pretty little valley or indentation in the plain, surrounded on all sides by low bluffs of yellow clay. Near us flows the clear deep water of the Siskadee, and beyond, on every side, is a wide and level prairie, interrupted only by some gigantic peaks of mountains and conical *butes* in the distance. The river, here, contains a great number of large trout, some grayling, and a small narrow-mouthed white fish, resembling a herring. They are all frequently taken with the hook, and, the trout particularly, afford excellent sport to the lovers of angling. Old Izaac Walton would be in his glory here, and the precautionary measures which he so strongly recommends in approaching a trout stream, he would not need to practise, as the fish is not [77] shy, and bites quickly and eagerly at a grasshopper or minnow.

Buffalo, antelopes, and elk are abundant in the vicinity, and we are therefore living well. We have seen also another kind of game, a beautiful bird, the size of a half grown turkey, called the cock of the plains, (*Tetrao urophasianus.*) We first met with this noble bird on the plains, about two days' journey east of Green river, in flocks, or *packs*, of fifteen or twenty, and so exceedingly tame as to allow an approach to within a few feet, run-

ning before our horses like domestic fowls, and not unfrequently hopping under their bellies, while the men
amused themselves by striking out their feathers with
their riding whips. When we first saw them, the temptation
to shoot was irresistible; the guns were cracking all around
us, and the poor grouse falling in every direction; but
what was our disappointment, when, upon roasting them
nicely before the fire, we found them so strong and bitter
as not to be eatable. From this time the cock of the plains
was allowed to roam free and unmolested, and as he has
failed to please our palates, we are content to admire the
beauty of his plumage, and the grace and spirit of his attitudes.

July 2d.—We bade adieu to the rendezvous this morning;
packed up our moveables, and journied along the bank
of the river. Our horses are very much recruited by the
long rest and good pasture which they have enjoyed, and,
like their masters, are in excellent spirits.

During our stay at the rendezvous, many of us looked
anxiously for letters from our families, which we expected
by the later caravans, but we were all disappointed. For
myself, I have received but one since I left my home, but
this has been my solace through many a long and dreary
journey. Many a time, while pacing my solitary round
as night-guard in the wilderness, have I [78] sat myself
down, and stirring up the dying embers of the camp fire,
taken the precious little memento from my bosom, un-
drawn the string of the leathern sack which contained
it, and poured over the dear characters, till my eyes would
swim with sweet, but sad recollections, then kissing the
inanimate paper, return it to its sanctuary, tighten up my
pistol belt, shoulder my gun, and with a quivering voice,
swelling the " *all's well* " upon the night breeze, resume my
slow and noiseless tramp around my sleeping companions.

Many of our men have left us, and joined the returning

companies, but we have had an accession to our party of about thirty Indians; Flat-heads, Nez Percés, &c., with their wives, children, and dogs. Without these our camp would be small; they will probably travel with us until we arrive on Snake river, and pass over the country where the most danger is to be apprehended from their enemies, the Black-feet.

Some of the women in this party, particularly those of the Nez Percé nation, are rather handsome, and their persons are decked off in truly savage taste. Their dresses of deer skin are profusely ornamented with beads and porcupine quills; huge strings of beads are hung around their necks, and their saddles are garnished with dozens of little hawk's bells, which jingle and make music for them as they travel along. Several of these women have little children tied to their backs, sewed up papoose fashion, only the head being seen; as they jolt along the road, we not unfrequently hear their voices ringing loud and shrill above the music of the bells. Other little fellows who have ceased to require the maternal contributions, are tied securely on other horses, and all their care seems to be to sleep, which they do most pertinaciously in spite of jolting, noise, and clamor. There is among this party, a Blackfoot chief; a renegado from his tribe, who sometime since killed the principal chief of his nation, and was [79] in consequence under the necessity of absconding. He has now joined the party of his hereditary foes, and is prepared to fight against his own people and kindred. He is a fine, warlike looking fellow, and although he takes part in all the war-songs, and sham-battles of his adopted brothers, and whoops, and howls as loud as the best of them, yet it is plain to perceive that he is distrusted and disliked. All men, whether, civilized or savage, honorable, or otherwise, detest and scorn a traitor!

We were joined at the rendezvous by a Captain Stewart, an English gentleman of noble family, who is travelling for amusement, and in search of adventure. He has already been a year in the mountains, and is now desirous of visiting the lower country, from which he may probably take passage to England by sea. Another Englishman, a young man, named Ashworth, also attached himself to our party, for the same purpose.[42]

Our course lay along the bank of Ham's fork, through a hilly and stony, but not a rocky country; the willow flourished on the margin of the stream, and occasionally the eye was relieved, on scanning the plain, by a pretty clump of cottonwood or poplar trees. The cock of the plains is very abundant here, and our pretty little summer yellow bird, (*Sylvia œstiva*,) one of our most common birds at home, is our constant companion. How natural sounds his little monotonous stave, and how it seems to carry us back to the dear scenes which we have exchanged for the wild and pathless wilderness!

4th.—We left Ham's fork this morning,—now diminished to a little purling brook,—and passed across the hills in a north-westerly direction for about twenty miles, when we struck Muddy creek.[43] This is a branch of Bear river,

---

[42] Sir William Drummond Stuart, Bart., of Perthshire, Scotland, who was rumored to have served under Wellington, came to the United States (1833) to hunt big game in the Rockies. He sustained his share of the caravan's work, mounting guard and serving in the skirmishes against the Indians, and was highly respected by the mountain men. He went as far as the Columbia, on this expedition. See also Elliott Coues, *Forty Years a Fur-Trader on the Upper Missouri* (New York, 1898), index. Townsend is, so far as we are aware, the only contemporary traveller who mentions Ashworth in a published work.— ED.

[43] Ham's Fork is a western affluent of Black Fork of Green River, in southwestern Wyoming. It was an important stream on the Oregon Trail, which later bent southward from this point to Fort Bridger, going by Muddy Creek, another affluent of the Green. The Muddy Creek of Townsend, however, is a different stream, flowing into Bear River; it is not now known by this name. The Oregon Short Line railway, which follows Ham's Fork and crosses to the Bear, approximating Townsend's route, follows the valley of Rock Creek to the latter river.— ED.

which empties into the Salt lake, or "lake Bonneville,"
as it has been lately named, for what reason I know not.
Our camp here, is a beautiful and most delightful one.
A large plain, like a meadow, of rich, waving [80] grass,
with a lovely little stream running through the midst,
high hills, capped with shapely cedars on two sides, and
on the others an immense plain, with snow clad mountains
in the distance. This being a memorable day, the liquor
kegs were opened, and the men allowed an abundance.
We, therefore, soon had a renewal of the coarse and brutal
scenes of the rendezvous. Some of the bacchanals called
for a volley in honor of the day, and in obedience to the
order, some twenty or thirty "happy" ones reeled into line
with their muzzles directed to every point of the compass, and when the word "fire" was given, we who were
not "happy" had to lie flat upon the ground to avoid the
bullets which were careering through the camp.

In this little stream, the trout are more abundant than
we have yet seen them. One of our *sober* men took, this
afternoon, upwards of thirty pounds. These fish would
probably average fifteen or sixteen inches in length, and
weigh three-quarters of a pound; occasionally, however,
a much larger one is seen.

5th. — We travelled about twenty miles this day, over
a country abounding in lofty hills, and early in the afternoon arrived on Bear river, and encamped. This is a
fine stream of about one hundred and fifty feet in width,
with a moveable sandy bottom. The grass is dry and
poor, the willow abounds along the banks, and at a distance marks the course of the stream, which meanders
through an alluvial plain of four to six miles in width.
At the distance of about one hundred miles from this
point, the Bear river enters the Salt lake, a large body
of salt water, without outlet, in which there is so large

an island as to afford streams of fresh water for goats and other animals living upon it.[44]

On the next day we crossed the river, which we immediately left, to avoid a great bend, and passed over some lofty ranges of hills and through rugged and stony valleys between them; the wind was blowing a gale right ahead, and clouds of dust were flying in our faces, so that at the end of the day, our countenances [81] were disguised as they were on the plains of the Platte. The march today has been a most laborious and fatiguing one both for man and beast; we have travelled steadily from morning till night, not stopping at noon; our poor horses' feet are becoming very much worn and sore, and when at length we struck Bear river again and encamped, the wearied animals refused to eat, stretching themselves upon the ground and falling asleep from very exhaustion.

Trout, grayling, and a kind of char are very abundant here — the first very large. The next day we travelled but twelve miles, it being impossible to urge our worn-out horses farther. Near our camp this evening we found some large gooseberries and currants, and made a hearty meal upon them. They were to us peculiarly delicious. We have lately been living entirely upon dried buffalo, without vegetables or bread; even this is now failing us,

---

[44] Bear River rises in the Uintah Mountains of northeastern Utah, and flows north and slightly northwest along the borders of Utah, Wyoming, and Idaho; until in Idaho, it takes a sudden bend southwest and south, and after a course of more than a hundred miles, enters Great Salt Lake. The trail struck this river near the southeastern corner of Idaho, following its course northwest to its bend — almost the identical route of the present Oregon Short Line railway.

Great Salt Lake had probably been seen by white men before the explorations of Ashley's party; but no authentic account of its discovery has been found before that of James Bridger, who in the winter of 1824–25 followed Bear River to its outlet. Finding the water salt he concluded it to be an arm of the ocean; but the following spring some of the party explored its coast line in skin-boats, finding no outlet. Captain Bonneville gave it his own name, but this is applied only to the geological area occupied by the lake in the quaternary era.— ED.

and we are upon short allowance. Game is very scarce, our hunters cannot find any, and our Indians have killed but two buffalo for several days. Of this small stock they would not spare us a mouthful, so it is probable we shall soon be hungry.

The alluvial plain here presents many unequivocal evidences of volcanic action, being thickly covered with masses of lava, and high walls and regular columns of basalt appear in many places. The surrounding country is composed, as usual, of high hills and narrow, stony valleys between them; the hills are thickly covered with a growth of small cedars, but on the plain, nothing flourishes but the everlasting wormwood, or *sage* as it is here called.

Our encampment on the 8th, was near what are called the " White-clay pits," still on Bear river. The soil is soft chalk, white and tenacious; and in the vicinity are several springs of strong supercarbonated water, which bubble up with all the activity of artificial fountains. The taste was very agreeable [82] and refreshing, resembling Saratoga water, but not so saline.[45] The whole plain to the hills, is covered with little mounds formed of calcareous sinter, having depressions on their summits, from which once issued streams of water. The extent of these eruptions, at some former period, must have been very great. At about half a mile distant, is an eruptive thermal spring of the temperature of 90°, and near this is an opening in the earth from which a stream of gas issues without water.

In a thicket of common red cedars, near our camp, I

---

[45] This is what is now known as Soda Springs, at the upper bend of Bear River. Irving describes it (*Rocky Mountains*, ii, p. 31) as an area of half a mile, with a dazzling surface of white clay, on which the springs have built up their mounds It is, in miniature, what is found on a large scale in Yellowstone Park. One geyser exists in the form that Townsend describes. See Palmer's account, in our volume xxx.— ED.

found, and procured several specimens of two beautiful and rare birds which I had never before seen — the Lewis' woodpecker and Clark's crow, (*Picus torquatus* and *Corvus columbianus.*)

We remained the whole of the following day in camp to recruit our horses, and a good opportunity was thus afforded me of inspecting all the curiosities of this wonderful region, and of procuring some rare and valuable specimens of birds. Three of our hunters sallied forth in pursuit of several buffalo whose tracks had been observed by some of the men, and we were overjoyed to see them return in the evening loaded with the meat and marrow bones of two animals which they had killed.

We saw here the whooping crane, and white pelican, numerous; and in the small streams near the bases of the hills, the common canvass-back duck, shoveller, and black duck, (*Anas obscura,*) were feeding their young.

We were this evening visited by Mr. Thomas McKay,[46] an Indian trader of some note in the mountains. He is a step-son of Dr. McLaughlin, the chief factor at Fort Vancouver, on the [83] Columbia, and the leader of a

---

[46] This is the son of Mr. Alexander McKay, who was massacred by the Indians of the N. W. Coast on board the ship "Tonquin," an account of which is given in Irving's "Astoria." I have often heard McKay speak of the tragica fate of his parent, and with the bitter animosity and love of revenge inherited from his Indian mother, I have heard him declare that he will yet be known on the coast as the avenger of blood.— TOWNSEND.

Comment by Ed. For Alexander McKay, consult Franchère's *Narrative* in our volume vi, p. 186, note 9..

Thomas McKay was born at Sault Ste. Marie, and when a lad (1811) came with his father to Oregon. After the failure of the Astoria enterprise, he entered the North West Company, and fought under their banner in the battle on Red River in 1816. Returning to Oregon, he became an important agent of the Hudson's Bay Company, under his step-father's management, usually in charge of the Snake River brigade. He was brave, dashing, a sure shot, and the idol of the half-breeds. He had a farm in Multnomah valley, and became a United States citizen, raising a company of militia which did active service in the Cayuse War of 1848.

party of Canadians and Indians, now on a hunt in the vicinity. This party is at present in our rear, and Mr. McKay has come ahead in order to join us, and keep us company until we reach Portneuf river, where we intend building a fort.

10*th.*— We were moving early this morning: our horses were very much recruited, and seemed as eager as their masters to travel on. It is astonishing how soon a horse revives, and overcomes the lassitude consequent upon fatigue, when he is allowed a day's rest upon tolerable pasture. Towards noon, however, after encountering the rough lava-strewn plain for a few hours, they became sufficiently sobered to desist from all unnecessary curvetting and prancing, and settled down into a very matter-of-fact trudge, better suited to the country and to the work which they have yet to do.

Soon after we left, we crossed one of the high and stony hills by which our late camp is surrounded; then making a gentle descent, we came to a beautiful and very fertile plain. This is, however, very different from the general face of the country; in a short time, after passing over the rich prairie, the same dry aridity and depauperation prevailed, which is almost universal west of the mountains. On the wide plain, we observed large sunken spots, some of them of great extent, surrounded by walls of lava, indicating the existence, at some very ancient date, of active craters. These eruptions have probably been antediluvian, or have existed at a period long anterior to the present order of creation. On the side of the hills are high walls of lava and basaltic dykes, and many large and dark caves are formed by the juxtaposition of the enormous masses.

Early in the afternoon we passed a large party of white men, encamped on the lava plain near one of the small streams. Horses were tethered all around, and men were lolling about playing games of cards, and loitering through the camp, as [84] though at a loss for employment. We soon ascertained it to be Captain Bonneville's company resting after the fatigues of a long march.[47] Mr. Wyeth and Captain Stewart visited the lodge of the" bald chief," and our party proceeded on its march. The difficulties of the route seemed to increase as we progressed, until at length we found ourselves wedged in among huge blocks of lava and columns of basalt, and were forced, most reluctantly, to retrace our steps for several miles, over the impediments which we had hoped we were leaving forever behind us. We had nearly reached Bonneville's camp again, when Captains Wyeth and Stewart joined us, and we struck into another path which proved more tolerable. Wyeth gave us a rather amusing account of his visit to the worthy captain. He and Captain Stewart were received very kindly by the veteran, and every delicacy that the lodge afforded was brought forth to do them honor. Among the rest, was some *metheglen* or diluted alcohol sweetened with honey, which the good host had concocted; this dainty beverage was set before them, and the thirsty guests were not slow in taking advantage of the invitation so obligingly given. Draught after draught of the precious liquor disappeared down the throats of the visitors, until the anxious, but still complaisant captain, began tc grow uneasy.

" I beg you will help yourselves, gentlemen," said the host, with a smile which he intended to express the utmost urbanity, but which, in spite of himself, had a certain ghastliness about it.

"Thank you, sir, we will do so freely," replied the two worthies, and away went the metheglen as before.

---

[47] Compare Irving's account of this meeting, in *Rocky Mountains*, ii, pp. 175–182.— ED.

Cup after cup was drained, until the hollow sound of the keg indicated that its contents were nearly exhausted, when the company rose, and thanking the kind host for his noble entertainment, were bowed out of the tent with all the polite formality which the accomplished captain knows so well how to assume.

Towards evening, we struck Blackfoot river, a small, sluggish, [85] stagnant stream, heading with the waters of a rapid rivulet passed yesterday, which empties into the Bear river.[48] This stream passes in a north-westerly direction through a valley of about six miles in width, covered with quagmires, through which we had great difficulty in making our way. As we approached our encampment, near a small grove of willows, on the margin of the river, a tremendous grizzly bear rushed out upon us. Our horses ran wildly in every direction, snorting with terror, and became nearly unmanageable. Several balls were instantly fired into him, but they only seemed to increase his fury. After spending a moment in rending each wound, (their invariable practice,) he selected the person who happened to be nearest, and darted after him, but before he proceeded far, he was sure to be stopped again by a ball from another quarter. In this way he was driven about amongst us for perhaps fifteen minutes, at times so near some of the horses, that he received several severe kicks from them. One of the pack horses was fairly fastened upon by the terrific claws of the brute, and in the terrified animal's efforts to escape the dreaded gripe, the pack and saddle were broken to pieces and disengaged. One of our mules also lent him a kick in the head while pursuing it up an adjacent hill, which sent him rolling to the bottom. Here he was finally brought to a stand.

---

[48] Blackfoot River is an eastern affluent of Lewis (or Snake) River, next above Portneuf. Its general course is northwest, entering the main river at Blackfoot, Idaho. Wyeth passed only along its upper reaches.— ED.

The poor animal was so completely surrounded by enemies that he became bewildered. He raised himself upon his hind feet, standing almost erect, his mouth partly open, and from his protruding tongue the blood fell fast in drops. While in this position, he received about six more balls, each of which made him reel. At last, as in complete desperation, he dashed into the water, and swam several yards with astonishing strength and agility, the guns cracking at him constantly; but he was not to proceed far. Just then, Richardson, who had been absent, rode up, and fixing his deadly aim upon him, fired a ball into the back [86] of his head, which killed him instantly. The strength of four men was required to drag the ferocious brute from the water, and upon examining his body, he was found completely riddled; there did not appear to be four inches of his shaggy person, from the hips upward, that had not received a ball. There must have been at least thirty shots made at him, and probably few missed him; yet such was his tenacity of life, that I have no doubt he would have succeeded in crossing the river, but for the last shot in the brain. He would probably weigh, at the least, six hundred pounds, and was about the height of an ordinary steer. The spread of the foot, laterally, was ten inches, and the claws measured seven inches in length. This animal was remarkably lean; when in good condition, he would, doubtless, much exceed in weight the estimate I have given. Richardson, and two other hunters, in company, killed two in the course of the afternoon, and saw several others.

This evening, our pet antelope, poor little " Zip Koon," met with a serious accident. The mule on which he rode, got her feet fastened in some lava blocks, and, in the struggle to extricate herself, fell violently on the pointed fragments. One of the delicate legs of our favorite was broken, and he was otherwise so bruised and hurt, that, from sheer mercy, we ordered him killed. We had hoped to be able to take him to the fort which we intend building on the Portneuf river, where he could have been comfortably cared for. This is the only pet we have had in the camp, which continued with us for more than a few days. We have sometimes taken young grizzly bears, but these little fellows, even when not larger than puppies, are so cross and snappish, that it is dangerous to handle them, and we could never become attached to any animal so ungentle, and therefore young "*Ephraim*," (to give him his mountain cognomen,) generally meets with but little mercy from us when his evil genius throws him in our way. The young buffalo calf is also very [87] often taken, and if removed from the mother, and out of sight of the herd, he will follow the camp as steadily as a dog; but his propensity for keeping close to the horse's heels often gets him into trouble, as he meets with more kicks than caresses from them. He is considered an interloper, and treated accordingly. The bull calf of a month or two old, is sometimes rather difficult to manage; he shows no inclination to follow the camp like the younger ones, and requires to be dragged along by main force. At such times, he watches for a good opportunity, and before his captor is aware of what is going on, he receives a *butt* from the clumsy head of the intractable little brute, which, in most cases, lays him sprawling upon the ground.

I had an adventure of this sort a few days before we arrived at the rendezvous. I captured a large bull calf, and with considerable difficulty, managed to drag him into the camp, by means of a rope noosed around his neck, and made fast to the high pommel of my saddle. Here I attached him firmly by a cord to a stake driven into the ground, and considered him secure. In a few minutes, however, he succeeded in breaking his fastenings, and away he scoured out of the camp. I lost no time in giving chase, and although I fell flat into a ditch, and afforded no little amusement to our people thereby, I soon overtook him, and was about seizing the stranded rope, which was still around his neck, when, to my surprise, the little animal showed fight; he came at me with all his force, and dashing his head into my breast, bore me to the ground in a twinkling. I, however, finally succeeded in recapturing him, and led and pushed him back into the camp; but I could make nothing of him; his stubbornness would neither yield to severity or kindness, and the next morning I loosed him and let him go.

11*th.*— On ascending a hill this morning, Captain Wyeth, who was at the head of the company, suddenly espied an Indian stealing cautiously along the summit, and evidently endeavoring [88] to conceal himself. Captain W. directed the attention of McKay to the crouching figure, who, the moment he caught a glimpse of him, exclaimed, in tones of joyful astonishment, " a Blackfoot, by —— !" and clapping spurs to his horse, tore up the hill with the most frantic eagerness, with his rifle poised in his hand ready for a shot. The Indian disappeared over the hill like a lightning flash, and in another second, McKay was also out of sight, and we could hear the rapid clatter of his horse's hoofs, in hot pursuit after the fugitive. Several of the men, with myself, followed after at a rapid gait, with, however, a very different object. Mine was simply curiosity, mingled with some anxiety, lest the wily Indian should lead our impetuous friend into an ambushment, and his life thus fall a sacrifice to his temerity. When we arrived at the hill-top, McKay was gone, but we saw the track of his horse passing down the side of it, and we traced him into a dense thicket about a quarter of a mile distant. Several of our hardy fellows entered this thicket, and beat about for some time in various directions, but nothing could they see either of McKay or the Indian. In the mean time, the party passed on, and my apprehensions were fast settling into a certainty that our bold companion had found the death he had so rashly courted, when I was inexpressibly relieved by hearing the crackling of the bushes near, which was immediately followed by the appearance of the missing man himself.

He was in an excessively bad humor, and grumbled audibly about the " Blackfoot rascal getting off in that cowardly fashion," without at all heeding the congratulations which I was showering upon him for his almost miraculous escape. He was evidently not aware of having been peculiarly exposed, and was regretting, like the hunter who loses his game by a sudden shift of wind, that his human prey had escaped him.

The appearance of this Indian is a proof that others are lurking near; and if the party happens to be large, they may give us [89] some trouble. We are now in a part of the country which is almost constantly infested by the Blackfeet; we have seen for several mornings past, the tracks of moccasins around our camp, and not unfrequently the prints of unshod horses, so that we know we are narrowly watched; and the slumbering of one of the guard, or the slightest appearance of carelessness in the conduct of the camp, may bring the savages whooping upon us like demons.

Our encampment this evening is on one of the head branches of the Blackfoot river, from which we can see the three remarkable conic summits known by the name of the *"Three Butes"* or *"Tetons."* Near these flows the

Portneuf, or south branch of Snake or Lewis' river.[49]
Here is to be another place of rest, and we look forward
to it with pleasure both on our own account and on that
of our wearied horses.

12th.— In the afternoon we made a camp on Ross's
creek, a small branch of Snake river.[50] The pasture is
better than we have had for two weeks, and the stream
contains an abundance of excellent trout. Some of these
are enormous, and very fine eating. They bite eagerly
at a grasshopper or minnow, but the largest fish are shy,
and the sportsman requires to be carefully concealed in
order to take them. We have here none of the fine tackle,
jointed rods, reels, and silkworm gut of the accomplished
city sportsman; we have only a piece of common cord,
and a hook seized on with half-hitches, with a willow rod
cut on the banks of the stream; but with this rough
equipment we take as many trout as we wish, and who
could do more, even with all the curious contrivances of
old Izaac Walton or Christopher North?

The band of Indians which kept company with us from
the rendezvous, left us yesterday, and fell back to join
Captain Bonneville's party, which is travelling on behind. We do not regret their absence; for although they
added strength to our band, and [90] would have been
useful in case of an attack from Blackfeet, yet they added
very materially to our cares, and gave us some trouble
by their noise, confusion, and singing at night.

[49] Townsend probably refers to the Three Buttes of the Lewis River plain
about forty miles west of their camp. The Three Tetons — a magnificent group
of snow-clad mountains — were sixty miles northeast, in the present Teton Forest
Reservation, Wyoming.

Portneuf is an eastern affluent of Lewis River, and a well-known halting pace
on the Oregon Trail.— ED.

[50] Ross's Creek is in reality an affluent of Portneuf. The usual route from
Soda Springs, on Bear River, was by way of the Portneuf; the route by Blackfoot and Ross's Creek was somewhat shorter, although rougher.— ED.

On the 14th, we travelled but about six miles, when a halt was called, and we pitched our tents upon the banks of the noble Shoshoné or Snake river. It seems now, as though we were really nearing the western extremity of our vast continent. We are now on a stream which pours its waters directly into the Columbia, and we can form some idea of the great Oregon river by the beauty and magnitude of its tributary. Soon after we stopped, Captain W., Richardson, and two others left us to seek for a suitable spot for building a fort, and in the evening they returned with the information that an excellent and convenient place had been pitched upon, about five miles from our present encampment. On their route, they killed a buffalo, which they left at the site of the fort, suitably protected from wolves, &c. This is very pleasing intelligence to us, as our stock of dried meat is almost exhausted, and for several days past we have been depending almost exclusively upon fish.

The next morning we moved early, and soon arrived at our destined camp. This is a fine large plain on the south side of the Portneuf, with an abundance of excellent grass and rich soil. The opposite side of the river is thickly covered with large timber of the cottonwood and willow, with a dense undergrowth of the same, intermixed with service-berry and currant bushes.[51]

Most of the men were immediately put to work, felling trees, making horse-pens, and preparing the various requisite

[51] This statement concerning the site of Fort Hall does not agree with that of later writers; possibly the fort was removed later, for Frémont in 1844 describes it as being nine miles above the mouth of Portneuf, on the narrow plain between that and Lewis River. The fort was named for Henry Hall, senior member of the firm furnishing Wyeth's financial backing. Wyeth sold this fort to the Hudson's Bay Company in 1836. The present Fort Hall, a government post, is forty miles northeast of the old fort, on Lincoln Creek, an affluent of Blackfoot River. It was built in May, 1870, and there, since that time, a garrison has been maintained.— ED.

materials for the building, while others were ordered to get themselves in readiness for a start on the back track, in order to make a hunt, and procure meat for the camp. To this party I have attached myself, and all my leisure time to-day is employed in preparing for it.

Our number will be twelve, and each man will lead a mule with [91] a pack-saddle, in order to bring in the meat that we may kill. Richardson is the principal of this party, and Mr. Ashworth has also consented to join us, so that I hope we shall have an agreeable trip. There will be but little hard work to perform; our men are mostly of the best, and no rum or cards are allowed.

[92] CHAPTER VI

July 16*th*.— Our little hunting party of twelve men, rode out of the encampment this morning, at a brisk trot, which gait was continued until we arrived at our late en-campment on Ross' creek, having gone about thirty miles. Here we came to a halt, and made a hearty meal on a buffalo which we had just killed. While we were eating, a little Welshman, whom we had stationed outside our camp to watch the horses, came running to us out of breath, crying in a terrified falsetto, " *Indians, Indians*! " In a moment every man was on his feet, and his gun in his hand; the horses were instantly surrounded, by Richard-son's direction, and driven into the bushes, and we were pre-paring ourselves for the coming struggle, when our hunter, peering out of the thick copse to mark the approach of the enemy, burst at once into a loud laugh, and muttering something about a Welsh coward, stepped boldly from his place of concealment, and told us to follow him. When we had done so, we perceived the band approaching steadily, and it seemed warily, along the path directly in our front. Richardson said something to them an an unknown tongue, which immediately brought several of the strangers towards [93] us at full gallop. One of these was a Canadian, as his peculiar physiognomy, scarlet sash, and hat ribbons of gaudy colors, clearly proved, and the two who accompanied him, were Indians. These people greeted us with great cordiality, the more so, perhaps, as they had supposed, on seeing the smoke from our fire, that we were a band of Blackfeet, and that, therefore, there was no alternative for them but to fight. While we were conversing, the whole party, of about thirty, came up, and it needed but a glance at the motley group of tawdrily dressed hybrid boys, and blanketted Indians, to convince us that this was McKay's company travelling on to join him at Fort Hall.

They inquired anxiously about their leader, and seemed pleased on being informed that he was so near; the prospect of a few days' rest at the fort, and the *regale* by which their arrival was sure to be commemorated, acted upon the spirits of the mercurial young half-breeds, like the potent liquor which they expected soon to quaff in company with the kindred souls who were waiting to receive them.

They all seemed hungry, and none required a second invitation to join us at our half finished meal. The huge masses of savoury fleece meat, hump-ribs, and side-ribs disappeared, and were polished with wonderful dispatch; the Canadians ate like half famished wolves, and the sombre Indians, although slower and more sedate in their movements, were very little behind their companions in the agreeable process of mastication.

The next day we rode thirty-four miles, and encamped on a pretty little stream, fringed with willows, running through the midst of a large plain. Within a few miles, we saw a small herd of buffalo, and six of our company left the camp for a hunt. In an hour two of them returned, bringing the meat of one animal. We all commenced work immediately, cutting it in thin slices, and hanging it on the bushes to dry. By sundown, our work was finished, and soon after dark, the remaining hunters [94] came in, bringing the best parts of three more. This will give us abundance of work for to-morrow, when the hunters will go out again.

Richardson and Sansbury mention having seen several Blackfeet Indians to-day, who, on observing them, ran rapidly away, and, as usual, concealed themselves in the bushes. We are now certain that our worst enemies are around us, and that they are only waiting for a favorable time and opportunity to make an attack. They are not here for nothing, and have probably been dogging us, and reconnoitering our outposts, so that the greatest caution and watchfulness will be required to prevent a surprise. We are but a small company, and there may be at this very moment hundreds within hearing of our voices.

The Blackfoot is a sworn and determined foe to all white men, and he has often been heard to declare that he would rather hang the scalp of a " pale face " to his girdle, than kill a buffalo to prevent his starving.

The hostility of this dreaded tribe is, and has for years been, proverbial. They are, perhaps, the only Indians who do not fear the power, and who refuse to acknowledge the superiority of the white man; and though so often beaten in conflicts with them, even by their own mode of warfare, and generally with numbers vastly inferior, their indomitable courage and perseverance still urges them on to renewed attempts; and if a single scalp is taken, it is considered equal to a great victory, and is hailed as a presage of future and more extensive triumphs.

It must be acknowledged, however, that this determined hostility does not originate solely in savage malignity, or an abstract thirst for the blood of white men; it is fomented and kept alive from year to year by incessant provocatives on the part of white hunters, trappers, and traders, who are at best but intruders on the rightful domains of the red man of the wilderness. [95] Many a night have I sat at the camp-fire, and listened to the recital of bloody and ferocious scenes, in which the narrators were the actors, and the poor Indians the victims, and I have felt my blood tingle with shame, and boil with indignation, to hear the diabolical acts applauded by those for whose amusement they were related. Many a precious villain, and merciless marauder, was made by these midnight tales of rapine, murder, and robbery; many a stripling, in whose tender mind the seeds of virtue and honesty had never germinated, burned for an opportunity of loading his pack-horse with the beaver skins of some solitary Blackfoot trapper, who was to be murdered and despoiled of the property he had acquired by weeks, and perhaps months, of toil and danger.

Acts of this kind are by no means unfrequent, and the subjects of this sort of atrocity are not always the poor and despised Indians: white men themselves often fall by the hands of their companions, when by good fortune and industry they have succeeded in loading their horses with fur. The fortunate trapper is treacherously murdered by one who has eaten from the same dish and drank from the same cup, and the homicide returns triumphantly to his camp with his ill gotten property. If his companion be inquired for, the answer is that some days ago they parted company, and he will probably soon join them.

The poor man never returns — no one goes to search for him — he is soon forgotten, or is only remembered by one more steadfast than the rest, who seizes with avidity the first opportunity which is afforded, of murdering an unoffending Indian in revenge for the death of his friend.

On the 20th, we moved our camp to a spot about twelve miles distant, where Richardson, with two other hunters, stopped yesterday and spent the night. They had killed several buffalo here, and were busily engaged in preparing the meat when we joined them. They gave us a meal of excellent cow's flesh, and [96] I thought I never had eaten anything so delicious. Hitherto we have had only the bulls which are at this season poor and rather unsavory, but now we are feasting upon the *best food in the world*.

It is true we have nothing but meat and good cold water, but this is all we desire: we have excellent appetites, no dyspepsia, clear heads, sharp ears, and high spirits, and what more does a man require to make him happy?

We rise in the morning with the sun, stir up our fires, and *roast* our breakfast, eating usually from one to two pounds of meat at a morning meal. At ten o'clock we lunch, dine at two, sup at five, and lunch at eight, and during the night-watch commonly provide ourselves with two or three " hump-ribs " and a marrow bone, to furnish employment and keep the drowsy god at a distance.

Our present camp is a beautiful one. A rich and open plain of luxuriant grass, dotted with buffalo in all directions, a high picturesque hill in front, and a lovely stream of cold mountain water flowing at our feet. On the borders of this stream, as usual, is a dense belt of willows, and under the shade of these we sit and work by day, and sleep soundly at night. Our meat is now dried upon scaffolds constructed of old timber which we find in great abundance upon the neighboring hill. We keep a fire going constantly, and when the meat is sufficiently dried, it is piled on the ground, preparatory to being baled.

21st.— The buffalo appear even more numerous than when we came, and much less suspicious than common. The bulls frequently pass slowly along within a hundred yards of us, and toss their shaggy and frightful looking heads as though to warn us against attacking or approaching them.

Towards evening, to-day, I walked out with my gun, in the direction of one of these prowling monsters, and the ground in his vicinity being covered densely with bushes, I determined to [97] approach as near him as possible, in order to try the efficacy of a ball planted directly in the centre of the forehead. I had heard of this experiment having been tried without success and I wished to ascertain the truth for myself.

"Taking the wind" of the animal, as it is called, (that is, keeping to leeward, so that my approach could not be perceived by communicating a taint to the air,) I crawled on my hands and knees with the utmost caution towards my victim. The unwieldy brute was quietly and unsuspiciously cropping the herbage, and I had arrived to within feet of him, when a sudden flashing of the eye, and an impatient motion, told me that I was observed. He raised his enormous head, and looked around him, and so truly terrible and grand did he appear, that I must confess, (in your ear,) I felt awed, almost frightened, at the task I had undertaken. But I had gone too far to retreat; so, raising my gun, I took deliberate aim at the bushy centre of the forehead, and fired. The monster shook his head, pawed up the earth with his hoofs, and making a sudden spring, accompanied by a terrific roar, turned to make his escape. At that instant, the ball from the second barrel penetrated his vitals, and he measured his huge length upon the ground. In a few seconds he was dead. Upon examining the head, and cutting away the enormous mass of matted hair and skin which enveloped the skull, my large bullet of twenty to the pound, was found completely flattened against the bone, having carried with

it, through the interposing integument, a considerable
portion of the cŏarse hair, but without producing the smallest fracture.   I was satisfied; and taking the tongue, (the
hunter's perquisite,) I returned to my companions.

This evening the roaring of the bulls in the *gang* near
us is terrific, and these sounds are mingled with the howling of large packs of wolves, which regularly attend upon
them, and the hoarse screaming of hundreds of ravens
flying over head.   The dreaded [98] grizzly bear is also
quite common in this neighborhood; two have just been
seen in some bushes near, and they visit our camr almost
every night, attracted by the piles of meat which are heaped
all around us.   The first intimation we have of his approach is a great *grunt* or *snort*, unlike any sound I ever
heard, but much more querulous than fierce; then we
hear the scraping and tramping of his huge feet, and the
snuffing of his nostrils, as the savory scent of the meat
is wafted to them.   He approaches nearer and nearer,
with a stealthy and fearful pace, but just as he is about to
accomplish the object of his visit, he suddenly stops short;
the snuffing is repeated at long and trembling intervals,
and if the slightest motion is then made by one of the party,
away goes " *Ephraim*," like a cowardly burglar as he is,
and we hear no more of him that night.

On the 23d a Nez Percé Indian, belonging to Mr. McKay's
company visited us.   He is one of several hundred who
have been sent from the fort on the same errand as ourselves.   This was a middle aged man, with a countenance
in which shrewdness or cunning, and complaisance, appeared singularly blended.   But his person was a perfect
wonder, and would have served admirably for the study
of a sculptor.   The form was perfection itself.   The lower
limbs were entirely naked, and the upper part of the person was only covered by a short checked shirt.   His blanket

lay by his side as he sat with us, and was used only while moving. I could not but admire the ease with which the man squatted on his haunches immediately as he alighted, and the position both of body and limbs was one that, probably, no white man unaccustomed to it, could have endured for many minutes together. The attitude, and indeed the whole figure was graceful and easy in the extreme ; and on criticising his person, one was forcibly reminded of the Apollo Belvidere of Canova. His only weapons were a short bow and half a dozen arrows, a scalping knife and tomahawk; with these, however, weak and inefficient [99] as they seemed, he had done good service, every arrow being smeared with blood to the feathers. He told Richardson that he and his three or four companions had killed about sixty buffalo, and that now, having meat enough, they intended to return to their camp to-morrow.

This afternoon I observed a large flock of wild geese passing over; and upon watching them, perceived that they alighted about a mile and a half from us, where I knew there was a lake. Concluding that a little change of diet might be agreeable, I sallied forth with my gun across the plain in quest of the birds. I soon arrived at a thick copse of willow and currant bushes, which skirted the water, and was about entering, when I heard a sort of angry growl or grunt directly before me — and instantly after, saw a grizzly bear of the largest kind erect himself upon his hind feet within a dozen yards of me, his savage eyes glaring with horrible malignity, his mouth wide open, and his tremendous paws raised as though ready to descend upon me. For a moment, I thought my hour had come, and that I was fated to die an inglorious death away from my friends and my kindred; but after waiting a moment in agonizing suspense, and the bear showing no inclination to advance, my lagging courage returned, and cocking both barrels of my gun, and presenting it as steadily as my nerves would allow, full at the shaggy breast of the creature, I retreated slowly backwards. Bruin evidently had no notion of braving gunpowder, but I did not know whether, like a dog, if the enemy retreated he would not yet give me a chase; so when I had placed about a hundred yards between us, I wheeled about and flew, rather than ran, across the plain towards the camp. Several times during this run for life, (as I considered it,) did I fancy that I heard the bear at my heels; and not daring to look over my shoulder to ascertain the fact, I only increased my speed, until the camp was nearly gained, when, from sheer exhaustion I relaxed my efforts, fell flat upon the ground, and [100] looked behind me. The whole space between me and the copse was untenanted, and I was forced to acknowledge, with a feeling strongly allied to shame, that my fears alone had represented the bear in chase of me.

When I arrived in camp, and told my break-neck adventure to the men, our young companion, Mr. Ashworth, expressed a wish to go and kill the bear, and requested the loan of my double-barrelled gun for this purpose. This I at first peremptorily refused, and the men, several of whom were experienced hunters, joined me in urging him not to attempt the rash adventure. At length, however, finding him determined on going, and that rather than remain, he would trust to his own single gun, I was finally induced to offer him mine, with a request, (which I had hoped would check his daring spirit,) that he would leave the weapon in a situation where I could readily find it; for after he had made one shot, he would never use a gun again.

He seemed to heed our caution and advice but little, and, with a dogged and determined air, took the way across the plain to the bushes, which we could see in the distance. I watched him for some time, until I saw him enter them, and then, with a sigh that one so young and talented should be lost from amongst us, and a regret that we did not forcibly prevent his going, I sat myself down, distressed and melancholy. We all listened anxiously to hear the report of the gun; but no sound reaching our ears, we began to hope that he had failed in finding the animal, and in about fifteen minutes, to my inexpressible relief, we saw him emerge from the copse, and bend his steps slowly towards us. When he came in, he seemed disappointed, and somewhat angry. He said he had searched the bushes in every direction, and although he had found numerous footprints, no bear was to be seen. It is probable that when I commenced my retreat in one direction, bruin made off in the other, and that although he was willing to dispute the ground with me, and prevent my [101] passing his lair, he was equally willing to back out of an engagement in which his fears suggested that he might come off the loser.

This evening, as we sat around the camp fire, cozily wrapped in our blankets, some of our old hunters became garrulous, and we had several good *"yarns,"* as a sailor would say. One told of his having been shot by a Blackfoot Indian, who was disguised in the skin of an elk, and exhibited, with some little pride, a great cicatrix which disfigured his neck. Another gave us an interesting account of an attack made by the Comanche Indians upon a party of Santa-Fee traders, to which he had been attached. The white men, as is usual in general engagements with Indians, gained a signal victory, not, however, without the loss of several of their best hunters; and the old man who told the story, — "uncle John," as he was usually called, — shed tears at the recollection of the death of his friends; and during that part of his narrative, was several times so much affected as to be unable to speak.[52]

The best story, however, was one told by Richardson, of a meeting he once had with three Blackfeet Indians. He had been out alone hunting buffalo, and towards the end of the day was returning to the camp with his meat, when he heard the clattering of hoofs in the rear, and, upon looking back, observed three Indians in hot pursuit of him.

He immediately *discharged his cargo* of meat to lighten his horse, and then urged the animal to his utmost speed, in an attempt to distance his pursuers. He soon discovered, however, that the enemy was rapidly gaining upon him, and that in a few [102] minutes more, he would be completely at their mercy, when he hit upon an expedient, as singular as it was bold and courageous. Drawing his long scalping knife from the sheath at his side, he plunged the keen weapon through his horse's neck, and severed the spine. The animal dropped instantly dead, and the determined hunter, throwing himself behind the fallen carcass, waited calmly the approach of his sanguinary pursuers. In a few moments, one Indian was within range of the fatal rifle, and at its report, his horse galloped riderless over the plain. The remaining two then thought to take him at advantage by approaching simultaneously on both sides of his rampart; but one of them, happening to venture too near in order to be sure of his aim, was shot to the heart by the long pistol of the white man, at the very instant that the ball from the Indian's gun whistled harmlessly by. The third savage, being wearied of the

---

[52] I have repeatedly observed these exhibitions of feeling in some of our people upon particular occasions, and I have been pleased with them, as they seemed to furnish an evidence, that amid all the mental sterility, and absence of moral rectitude, which is so deplorably prevalent, there yet lingers some kindliness of heart, some sentiments which are not wholly depraved.— TOWNSEND.

dangerous game, applied the whip vigorously to the flanks of his horse, and was soon out of sight, while Richardson set about collecting the trophies of his singular victory.

He caught the two Indians' horses; mounted one, and loaded the other with the meat which he had discarded, and returned to his camp with two spare rifles, and a good stock of ammunition.

On the morning of the 25th, we commenced baling up our meat in buffalo skins dried for the purpose. Each bale contains about a hundred pounds, of which a mule carries two; and when we had finished, our twelve long-eared friends were loaded. Our limited term of absence is now nearly expired, and we are anxious to return to the fort in order to prepare for the journey to the lower country.

At about 10 o'clock, we left our pleasant encampment, and bade adieu to the cold spring, the fat buffalo, and grizzly bears, and urging our mules into their fastest walk, we jolted along with our *provant* towards the fort.

[103] In about an hour after, an unpleasant accident happened to one of our men, named McCarey. He had been running a buffalo, and was about reloading the gun, which he had just discharged, when the powder in his horn was ignited by a burning wad remaining in the barrel; the horn was burst to fragments, the poor man dashed from his horse, and his face, neck, and hands, burnt in a shocking manner. We applied, immediately, the simple remedies which our situation and the place afforded, and in the course of an hour he was somewhat relieved, and travelled on with us, though in considerable suffering. His eyes were entirely closed, the lids very much swollen, and his long, flowing hair, patriarchal beard and eye-brows, had all vanished in smoke. It will be long ere he gets another such crop.

The weather here is generally uncomfortably warm,

so much so, that we discard, while travelling, all such encumbrances as coats, neckcloths, &c., but the nights are excessively cold, ice often forming in the camp kettles, of the thickness of half an inch, or more. My custom has generally been to roll myself in my blanket at night, and use my large coat as a pillow; but here the coat must be worn, and my saddle has to serve the purpose to which the coat is usually applied.

We travelled, this day, thirty miles, and the next afternoon, at 4 o'clock, arrived at the fort. On the route we met three hunters, whom Captain W. had sent to kill game for the camp. They informed us that all hands have been for several days on short allowance, and were very anxious for our return.

When we came in sight of the fort, we gave them a mountain salute, each man firing his gun in quick succession. They did not expect us until to-morrow, and the firing aroused them instantly. In a very few minutes, a score of men were armed and mounted, and dashing out to give battle to the advancing Indians, as they thought us. The general supposition was, that [104] their little hunting party had been attacked by a band of roving Blackfeet, and they made themselves ready for the rescue in a space of time that did them great credit.

It was perhaps "*bad medicine*," (to use the mountain phrase,) to fire a salute at all, inasmuch as it excited some unnecessary alarm, but it had the good effect to remind them that danger might be near when they least expected it, and afforded them an opportunity of showing the promptness and alacrity with which they could meet and brave it.

Our people were all delighted to see us arrive, and I could perceive many a longing and eager gaze cast upon the well filled bales, as our mules swung their little bodies through the camp. My companion, Mr. N., had become so exceedingly thin that I should scarcely have known him; and upon my expressing surprise at the great change in his appearance, he heaved a sigh of inanity, and remarked that I "would have been as thin as he if I had lived on old *Ephraim* for two weeks, and short allowance of that." I found, in truth, that the whole camp had been subsisting, during our absence, on little else than two or three grizzly bears which had been killed in the neighborhood; and with a complacent glance at my own rotund and *cow-fed* person, I wished my *poor* friend better luck for the future.

We found Mr. McKay's company encamped on the bank of the river within a few hundred yards of our tents. It consists of thirty men, thirteen of whom are Indians, Nez Percés, Chinooks and Kayouse,[53] with a few squaws. The remainder are French-Canadians, and half-breeds. Their lodges,— of which there are several,— are of a conical form, composed of ten long poles, the lower ends of which are pointed and driven into the ground; the upper blunt, and drawn together at the top by thongs. Around these poles, several dressed buffalo skins, sewed together, are stretched, a hole being left on one side for entrance.

These are the kind of lodges universally used by the mountain [105] Indians while travelling: they are very comfortable and commodious, and a squaw accustomed to it, will erect and prepare one for the reception of her husband, while he is removing the trapping, from his horse. I have seen an expert Indian woman stretch a lodge in half the time that was required by four white men to perform the same operation with another in the neighborhood.

At the fort, affairs look prosperous: the stockade is finished; two bastions have been erected, and the work is singularly good, considering the scarcity of proper build-

---

[53] For the Chinook, see Franchère's *Narrative* in our volume vi, p. 240, note 40; for the Cayuse, Ross's *Oregon Settlers*, our volume vii, p. 137, note 37.— ED.

ing tools. The house will now soon be habitable, and the structure can then be completed at leisure by men who will be left here in charge, while the party travels on to its destination, the Columbia.

On the evening of the 26th, Captain W., Mr. Nuttall and myself supped with Mr. McKay in his lodge. I am much pleased with this gentleman: he unites the free, frank and open manners of the mountain man, with the grace and affability of the Frenchman. But above all, I admire the order, decorum, and strict subordination which exists among his men, so different from what I have been accustomed to see in parties composed of Americans. Mr. McKay assures me that he had considerable difficulty in bringing his men to the state in which they now are. The free and fearless Indian was particularly difficult to subdue; but steady, determined perseverance, and bold measures, aided by a rigid self-example, made them as clay in his hand, and has finally reduced them to their present admirable condition. If they misbehaved, a commensurate punishment is sure to follow: in extreme cases, flagellation is resorted to, but it is inflicted only by the hand of the Captain; were any other appointed to perform this office *on an Indian*, the indignity would be deemed so great, that nothing less than the blood of the individual could appease the wounded feelings of the savage.

[106] After supper was concluded, we sat ourselves down on a buffalo robe at the entrance of the lodge, to see the Indians at their devotions. The whole thirteen were soon collected at the call of one whom they had chosen for their chief, and seated with sober, sedate countenances around a large fire. After remaining in perfect silence for perhaps fifteen minutes, the chief commenced an harangue in a solemn and impressive tone, reminding them of the object for which they were thus assembled, that of wor-

shipping the "Great Spirit who made the light and the darkness, the fire and the water," and assured them that if they offered up their prayers to him with but "one tongue," they would certainly be accepted. He then rose from his squatting position to his knees, and his example was followed by all the others. In this situation he commenced a prayer, consisting of short sentences uttered rapidly but with great apparent fervor, his hands clasped upon his breast, and his eyes cast upwards with a beseeching look towards heaven. At the conclusion of each sentence, a choral response of a few words was made, accompanied frequently by low moaning. The prayer lasted about twenty minutes. After its conclusion, the chief, still maintaining the same position of his body and hands, but with his head bent to his breast, commenced a kind of psalm or sacred song, in which the whole company presently joined. The song was a simple expression of a few sounds, no intelligible words being uttered. It resembled the words, *Ho-hă-ho-hă-ho-hă-hā-ā*, commencing in a low tone, and gradually swelling to a full, round, and beautifully modulated chorus. During the song, the clasped hands of the worshippers were moved rapidly across the breast, and their bodies swung with great energy to the time of the music. The chief ended the song that he had commenced, by a kind of swelling groan, which was echoed in chorus. It was then taken up by another, and the same routine was gone [107] through. The whole ceremony occupied perhaps one and a half hours; a short silence then succeeded, after which each Indian rose from the ground, and disappeared in the darkness with a step noiseless as that of a spectre.

I think I never was more gratified by any exhibition in my life. The humble, subdued, and beseeching looks of the poor untutored beings who were calling upon their heavenly father to forgive their sins, and continue his mercies to them, and the evident and heart-felt sincerity which characterized the whole scene, was truly affecting, and very impressive.

The next day being the Sabbath, our good missionary, Mr. Jason Lee, was requested to hold a meeting, with which he obligingly complied. A convenient, shady spot was selected in the forest adjacent, and the greater part of our men, as well as the whole of Mr. McKay's company, including the Indians, attended. The usual forms of the Methodist service, (to which Mr. L. is attached,) were gone through, and were followed by a brief, but excellent and appropriate exhortation by that gentleman, The people were remarkably quiet and attentive, and the Indians sat upon the ground like statues. Although not one of them could understand a word that was said, they nevertheless maintained the most strict and decorous silence, kneeling when the preacher kneeled, and rising when he rose, evidently with a view of paying him and us a suitable respect, however much their own notions as to the proper and most acceptable forms of worship, might have been opposed to ours.

A meeting for worship in the Rocky mountains is almost as unusual as the appearance of a herd of buffalo in the settlements. A sermon was perhaps never preached here before; but for myself, I really enjoyed the whole scene; it possessed the charm [108] of novelty, to say nothing of the salutary effect which I sincerely hope it may produce.

Mr. Lee is a great favorite with the men, deservedly so, and there are probably few persons to whose preaching they would have listened with so much complaisance. I have often been amused and pleased by Mr. L.'s manner of reproving them for the coarseness and profanity of expression which is so universal amongst them. The reproof, although decided, clear, and strong, is always characterized by the mildness and affectionate manner peculiar to the man; and although the good effect of the advice may not be discernible, yet it is always treated with respect, and its utility acknowledged.

In the evening, a fatal accident happened to a Canadian belonging to Mr. McKay's party. He was running his horse, in company with another, when the animals were met in full career by a third rider, and horses and men were thrown with great force to the ground. The Canadian was taken up completely senseless, and brought to Mr. McKay's lodge, where we were all taking supper. I perceived at once that there was little chance of his life being saved. He had received an injury of the head which had evidently caused concussion of the brain. He was bled copiously, and various local remedies were applied, but without success; the poor man died early next morning.

He was about forty years of age, healthy, active, and shrewd, and very much valued by Mr. McKay as a leader in his absence, and as an interpreter among the Indians of the Columbia.

At noon the body was interred. It was wrapped in a piece of coarse linen, over which was sewed a buffalo robe. The spot selected, was about a hundred yards south of the fort, and the funeral was attended by the greater part of the men of both camps. Mr. Lee officiated in performing the ordinary church [109] ceremony, after which a hymn for the repose of the soul of the departed, was sung by the Canadians present. The grave is surrounded by a neat palisade of willows, with a black cross erected at the head, on which is carved the name " *Casseau.*" [54]

---

[54] According to Wyeth's journal his name was Kanseau, and the services were Protestant, Catholic, and Indian —" as he had an Indian family; he at least was well buried."— ED.

[110] CHAPTER VII

Departure of Mr. McKay's party, Captain Stewart, and the missionaries — Debauch at the fort — Departure of the company — Poor provision — Blackfeet hunting ground — A toilsome journey, and sufferings from thirst — Goddin's creek — Antoine Goddin, the trapper — Scarcity of game — A buffalo — Rugged mountains — Comforting reflections of the traveller — More game — Unusual economy — Habits of the white wolf — " Thornburg's pass " — Difficult travelling — The captain in jeopardy among the snow — A countermarch — Deserted Banneck camp — Toilsome and dangerous passage of the mountain — Mallade river — Beaver dams, and beaver — A party of Snake Indians — Scarcity of pasture — Another Banneck camp — " Kamas prairie " — Indian mode of preparing the kamas — Racine blanc, or biscuit root — Travelling over the hills — Loss of horses by fatigue — Boisée or Big-wood river — Salmon — Choke-cherries, &c.

ON the 30th of July, Mr. McKay and his party left us for Fort Vancouver, Captain Stewart and our band of missionaries accompanying them. The object of the latter in leaving us, is, that they may have an opportunity of travelling more slowly than we should do, on account, and for the benefit of the horned cattle which they are driving to the lower country. We feel quite sad in the prospect of parting from those with whom we have endured some toil and danger, and who have been to some of us as brothers, throughout our tedious journey; but, if no unforeseen accident occurs, we hope to meet them all again at Walla-Walla, the upper fort on the Columbia. As the party rode off, we fired three rounds, which were promptly answered, and three times three cheers wished the travellers success.

August 5th.— At sunrise this morning, the "star-spangled banner" was raised on the flag-staff at the fort, and a salute [111] fired by the men, who, according to orders, assembled around it. All in camp were then allowed the free and uncontrolled use of liquor, and, as usual, the consequence was a scene of rioting, noise, and fighting, during the whole day; some became so drunk that their senses fled them entirely, and they were therefore harmless; but by far the greater number were just sufficiently under the influence of the vile trash, to render them in their conduct disgusting and tiger-like. We had "gouging," biting, fisticuffing, and "stamping" in the most "scientific" perfection; some even fired guns and pistols at each other, but these weapons were mostly harmless in the unsteady hands which employed them. Such scenes I hope never to witness again; they are absolutely sickening, and cause us to look upon our species with abhorrence and loathing. Night at last came, and cast her mantle over our besotted camp; the revel was over, and the men retired to their pallets peaceably, but not a few of them will bear palpable evidence of the debauch of the 5th of August.

The next morning we commenced packing, and at 11 o'clock bade adieu to "Fort Hall." [55] Our company now consists of but thirty men, several Indian women, and one hundred and sixteen horses. We crossed the main Snake or Shoshoné river, at a point about three miles from the fort. It is here as wide as the Missouri at Independence, but, beyond comparison, clearer and more beautiful.

Immediately on crossing the river, we entered upon a wide, sandy plain, thickly covered with wormwood, and early in the afternoon, encamped at the head of a delightful spring, about ten miles from our starting place.

On the route, our hunters killed a young grizzly bear, which, with a few grouse, made us an excellent dinner.

---

[55] Upon leaving Fort Hall, the usual trail followed the valley of the Lewis (or Snake) to Fort Boise. Wyeth, however, struck directly northwest across the Snake River Desert, past the Three Buttes. Godin's Creek was what is now known as Lost River, from having no outlet.— ED.

Fresh meat is now very grateful to our palates, as we have
been living for weeks past on nothing but poor, dried buffalo,
the better, and [112] far the larger part, having been deposited in the fort for the subsistence of the men who remain. We have no flour, nor vegetables of any kind, and
our meat may be aptly compared to dry chips, breaking
short off in our fingers; and when boiled to soften it a little,
and render it fit for mastication, not a star appears in the
pot. It seems astonishing that life can be sustained upon
such miserable fare, and yet our men (except when under
the influence of liquor) have never murmured, but have
always eaten their crusty meal, and drunk their cold water
with light and excellent spirits. We hope soon to fall
in with the buffalo, and we shall then endeavor to prepare
some good provision to serve until we reach the salmon
region.

We shall now, for about ten days, be travelling through
the most dangerous country west of the mountains, the
regular hunting ground of the Blackfeet Indians, who are
said to be often seen here in parties of hundreds, or even
thousands, scouring the plains in pursuit of the buffalo.
Traders, therefore, seldom travel this route without meeting them, and being compelled to prove their valor upon
them; the white men are, however, generally the victors,
although their numbers are always vastly inferior.

7th.— We were moving this morning with the dawn,
and travelled steadily the whole day, over one of the most
arid plains we have seen, covered thickly with jagged
masses of lava, and twisted wormwood bushes. Both
horses and men were jaded to the last degree; the former
from the rough, and at times almost impassable nature of
the track, and the latter from excessive heat and parching
thirst. We saw not a drop of water during the day,
and our only food was the dried meat before spoken of,

which we carried and chewed like biscuits as we travelled. There are two reasons by which the extreme thirst which the way-farer suffers in these regions, may be accounted [113] for; first, the intense heat of the sun upon the open and exposed plains; and secondly, the desiccation to which every thing here is subject. The air feels like the breath of a sirocco, the tongue becomes parched and horny, and the mouth, nose, and eyes are incessantly assailed by the fine pulverized lava, which rises from the ground with the least breath of air. Bullets, pebbles of chalcedony, and pieces of smooth obsidian, were in great requisition to-day; almost every man was mumbling some of these substances, in an endeavor to assuage his burning thirst. The camp trailed along in a lagging and desponding line over the plain for a mile or more, the poor horses' heads hanging low, their tongues protruding to their utmost extent, and their riders scarcely less drooping and spiritless. We were a sad and most forlorn looking company, certainly; not a man of us had any thing to say, and none cared to be interrupted in his blissful dream of cool rivers and streams. Occasionally we would pass a ravine or gorge in the hills, by which one side of the plain was bounded, and up this some of the men would steer, leaping over blocks of lava, and breaking a path through the dense bushes; but the poor searcher soon returned, disheartened and wo-begone, and those who had waited anxiously to hear his cheering call, announcing success, passed onward without a word. One of our men, a mulatto, after failing in a forage of this sort, cast himself resolutely from his horse to the ground, and declared that he would lie there till he died; " there was no water in the cursed country and he might as well die here as go farther." Some of us tried to infuse a little courage into him, but it proved of no avail, and each was too much occupied with his own particular grief to use his tongue much in persuasion; so we left him to his fate.

Soon after night-fall, some signs of water were seen in a small valley to our left, and, upon ascending it, the foremost of the party found a delightful little cold spring; but they soon exhausted [114] it, and then commenced, with axes and knives, to dig it out and enlarge it. By the time that Mr. N., and myself arrived, they had excavated a large space which was filled to overflowing with muddy water. We did not wait for it to settle, however, but throwing ourselves flat upon the ground, drank until we were ready to burst. The tales which I had read of suffering travellers in the Arabian deserts, then recurred with some force to my recollection, and I thought I could,— though in a very small measure,— appreciate their sufferings by deprivation, and their unmingled delight and satisfaction in the opportunity of assuaging them.

Poor Jim, the mulatto man, was found by one of the people, who went back in search of him, lying where he had first fallen, and either in a real or pretended swoon, still obstinate about dying, and scarcely heeding the assurances of the other that water was within a mile of him. He was, however, at length dragged and carried into camp, and soused head foremost into the mud puddle, where he guzzled and guzzled until his eyes seemed ready to burst from his head, and he was lifted out and laid dripping and flaccid upon the ground.

The next morning we made an early start towards a range of willows which we could distinctly see, at the distance of fifteen or twenty miles, and which we knew indicated Goddin's creek, so called from a Canadian of that name who was killed in this vicinity by the Blackfeet. Goddin's son, a half-breed, is now with us as a trapper; he is a fine sturdy fellow, and of such strength of limb and wind, that he is said to be able to run down a buffalo on foot, and kill him with arrows.

Goddin's creek was at length gained, and after travelling a few miles along its bank we encamped in some excellent pasture. Our poor horses seemed inclined to make up for lost time here, as yesterday their only food was the straggling blades of a little [115] dry and parched grass growing among the wormwood on the hills.

We have been considerably disappointed in not seeing any buffalo to-day, and their absence here has occasioned some fear that we may not meet with them on our route. Should this be the case, we shall have to depend upon such small game, hares, grouse, &c., as may happen to lie in our path. In a short time, however, even this resource will fail; and if we do not happen to see Indians on the upper waters of the Columbia, from whom we can purchase dried salmon, we shall be under the necessity of killing our horses for food.

We perhaps derive one advantage, however, from the absence of game here, — that of there being less probability of lurking Blackfeet in the vicinity; but this circumstance, convenient as it is, does not compensate for empty stomachs, and I believe the men would rather fight for the privilege of obtaining food, than live without it.

The next morning we left Goddin's creek, and travelled for ten miles over a plain, covered as usual with wormwood bushes and lava. Early in the day, the welcome cry of "a buffalo! a buffalo!" was heard from the head of the company, and was echoed joyfully along the whole line. At the moment, a fine large bull was seen to bound from the bushes in our front, and tear off with all his speed over the plain. Several hunters gave him chase immediately, and in a few minutes we heard the guns that proclaimed his death. The killing of this animal is a most fortunate circumstance for us: his meat will probably sustain us for three or four days, and by that time we are sanguine of procuring other provision. The appearance of this buffalo is not considered indicative of the vicinity of others: he is probably a straggler from a travelling band, and has been unable to proceed with it, in consequence of sickness or wounds.

[116] On leaving the plain this morning, we struck into a defile between some of the highest mountains we have yet seen. In a short time we commenced ascending, and continued passing over them, until late in the afternoon, when we reached a plain about a mile in width, covered with excellent grass, and a delightful cool stream flowing through the middle of it. Here we encamped, having travelled twenty-seven miles.

Our journey, to-day, has been particularly laborious. We were engaged for several hours, constantly in ascending and descending enormous rocky hills, with scarcely the sign of a valley between them; and some of them so steep, that our horses were frequently in great danger of falling, by making a mis-step on the loose, rolling stones. I thought the Black Hills, on the Platte, rugged and difficult of passage, but they sink into insignificance when compared with these.[56]

We observed, on these mountains, large masses of greenstone, and beautiful pebbles of chalcedony and fine agate; the summits of the highest are covered with snow. In the mountain passes, we found an abundance of large, yellow currants, rather acid, but exceedingly palatable to men who have been long living on animal food exclusively. We all ate heartily of them; indeed, some of our

---

[56] These mountains — in Custer County, Idaho, between the different branches of Lost River — have apparently no local name that has been cartographically recorded; they lie between the Sawtooth and Lost River ranges.— ED.

people became so much attached to the bushes, that we had considerable difficulty to induce them to travel again.

10*th*.— We commenced our march at seven this morning, proceeding up a narrow valley, bordering our encampment in a north-easterly direction. The ravine soon widened, until it became a broad, level plain, covered by the eternal " sage " bushes, but was much less stony than usual. About mid-day, we left the plain, and shaped our course over a spur of one of the large mountains; then taking a ravine, in about an hour we came to the level land, and struck Goddin's creek again, late in the afternoon.

Our provision was all exhausted at breakfast, this morning, [117] (most of our bull meat having been given to a band of ten trappers, who left us yesterday,) we had seen no game on our route, and we were therefore preparing ourselves to retire supperless to our pallets, when Richardson and Sansbury were descried approaching the camp and, to our great comfort, we observed that they had meat on their saddles. When they arrived, however, we were somewhat disappointed to find that they had only killed a calf, but they had brought the entire little animal with them, the time for picking and choosing of choice pieces having passed with us; and after making a hearty meal, we wrapped ourselves in our blankets and slept soundly. Although but a scant breakfast was left for us in the morning, and we knew not if any dinner would fall in our way, yet "none of these things moved us;" we lived altogether upon the present, and heeded not the future. We had always been provided for; often, when we had despaired of procuring sustenance, and when the pangs of hunger had soured our temper, and made us quarrelsome, when we thought there was no prospect before us but to sacrifice our valuable horses, or die of starvation, have the means been provided for our relief. A buffalo, an elk, or an antelope, has appeared like the goat provided for the faithful Abraham, to save a more valuable life, and I hope that some of us have been willing, reverently to acknowledge from whom these benefits and blessings have been received.

On the day following, Richardson killed two buffalo, and brought his horse heavily laden with meat to the camp. Our good hunter walked himself, that the animal might be able to bear the greater burthen. After depositing the meat in the camp, he took a fresh horse, and accompanied by three men, returned to the spot where the game had been killed, (about four miles distant,) and in the evening, brought in every pound of it, leaving only the heavier bones. The wolves will be disappointed this evening; they are accustomed to dainty picking when they [118] glean after the hunters, but we have now abandoned the "wasty ways" which so disgraced us when game was abundant; the despised leg bone, which was wont to be thrown aside with such contempt, is now polished of every tendon of its covering, and the savory hump is used as a kind of *dessert* after a meal of coarser meat.

Speaking of wolves, I have often been surprised at the perseverance and tenacity with which these animals will sometimes follow the hunter for a whole day, to feed upon the carcass he may leave behind him. When an animal is killed, they seem to mark the operation, and stand still at a most respectful distance, with drooping tail and ears, as though perfectly indifferent to the matter in progress. Thus will they stand until the game is butchered, the meat placed upon the saddle, and the hunter is mounted and on his way; then, if he glances behind him, he will see the wily forager stealthily crawling and prowling along towards the smoking remains, and pouncing upon it, and tearing it with tooth and nail, immediately as he gets out of reach.

During the day, the wolves are shy, and rarely permit an approach to within gun-shot; but at night, (where game is abundant,) they are so fearless as to come quite within the purlieus of the camp, and there sit, a dozen together, and howl hideously for hours. This kind of serenading, it may be supposed, is not the most agreeable; and many a time when on guard, have I observed the unquiet tossing of the bundles of blankets near me, and heard issue from them, the low, husky voice of some disturbed sleeper, denouncing heavy anathemas on the unseasonable music.

12th.— We shaped our course, this morning, towards what appeared to us a gap in a high and rugged mountain, about twenty miles ahead. After proceeding eight or ten miles, the character of the country underwent a remarkable and sudden change. Instead of the luxuriant sage bushes, by which the [119] whole plains have hitherto been covered, and the compact and dense growth of willows which has uniformly fringed every stream and rivulet, the ground was completely denuded; not a single shrub was to be seen, nor the smallest appearance of vegetation, except in small patches near the water. The mountains, also, which had generally been rocky, and covered with low, tangled bushes, here abound in beautiful and shapely pine trees. Some of the higher peaks are, however, completely bare, and capped with enormous masses of snow.

After we had travelled about twelve miles, we entered a defile between the mountains, about five hundred yards wide, covered, like the surrounding country, with pines; and, as we proceeded, the timber grew so closely, added to a thick undergrowth of bushes, that it appeared almost impossible to proceed with our horses. The farther we advanced, the more our difficulties seemed to increase;

obstacles of various kinds impeded our progress; — fallen trees, their branches tangled and matted together, large rocks and deep ravines, holes in the ground, into which our animals would be precipitated without the possibility of avoiding them, and an hundred other difficulties which beggar description.

We travelled for six miles through such a region as I have attempted to describe, and at 2 o'clock encamped in a clear spot of ground, where we found excellent grass, and a cold, rapid stream. Soon after we stopped, Captain W. and Richardson left us, to look for a pass through the mountains, or for a spot where it would be possible to cross them. Strange as it may appear, yet in this desolate and almost impassable region we have observed, to-day, the tracks of a buffalo which must have passed here last night, or this morning; at least so our hunters say, and they are rarely deceived in such matters.

Captain W. and Richardson returned early next morning, with the mortifying intelligence that no practicable pass through the [120] mountain could be found. They ascended to the very summit of one of the highest peaks, above the snow and the reach of vegetation, and the only prospect which they had beyond, was a confused mass of huge angular rocks, over which even a wild goat could scarcely have made his way. Although they utterly failed in the object of their exploration, yet they were so fortunate as to kill a buffalo, (*the* buffalo,) the meat of which they brought on their horses.

Wyeth told us of a narrow escape he had while travelling on foot near the summit of one of the peaks. He was walking on a ridge which sloped from the top at an angle of about forty degrees, and terminated, at its lower part, in a perpendicular precipice of a thousand or twelve hundred feet. He was moving along in the snow cautiously, near the lower edge, in order to attain a more level spot beyond, when his feet slipped and he fell. Before he could attempt to fix himself firmly, he slid down the declivity till within a few feet of the frightful precipice. At the instant of his fall, he had the presence of mind to plant the rifle which he held in one hand, and his knife which he drew from the scabbard with the other, into the snow, and as he almost tottered on the verge, he succeeded in checking himself, and holding his body perfectly still. He then gradually moved, first the rifle and then the knife, backward up the slanting hill behind him, and fixing them firmly, drew up his body parallel to them. In this way he moved slowly and surely until he had gained his former station, when, without further difficulty, he succeeded in reaching the more level land.

After a good breakfast, we packed our horses, and struck back on our trail of yesterday, in order to try another valley which we observed bearing parallel with this, at about three miles distant, and which we conclude must of course furnish a path through the mountain. Although our difficulties in returning by the same wretched route were very considerable, yet they were [121] somewhat diminished by the road having been partially broken, and we were enabled also to avoid many of the sloughs and pitfalls which had before so much incommoded us. We have named this rugged valley, " Thornburg's *pass*," after one of our men of this name, (a tailor,) whom we have to thank for leading us into all these troubles. Thornburg crossed this mountain two years ago, and might therefore be expected to know something of the route, and as he was the only man in the company who had been here, Captain W. acted by his advice, in opposition to his own judgment, which had suggested the other valley as affording a more probable chance of success. As we are probably the only white men who have ever penetrated into this most vile and abominable region, we conclude that the name we have given it must stand, from priority.[57]

In the bushes, along the stream in this valley, the black-tailed deer (*Cervus macrourus*) is abundant. The beautiful creatures frequently bounded from their cover within a few yards of us, and trotted on before us like domestic animals; "they are so unacquainted with man" and his cruel arts, that they seem not to fear him.

We at length arrived on the open plain again, and in our route towards the other valley, we came to a large, recent Indian encampment, probably of Bannecks,[58] who are travelling down to [122] the fisheries on Snake river. We here took their trail which led up the valley to which we had been steering. The entrance was very similar in appearance to that of Thornburg's pass, and it is therefore not very surprising that our guide should have been deceived. We travelled rapidly along the level land at the base of the mountain, for about three miles; we then began to ascend, and our progress was necessarily slow and tedious. The commencement of the Alpine path was, however, far better than we had

---

[57] The expedition apparently followed the east fork of Lost River, into a maze of mountains known locally as the "Devil's Bedstead."— ED.

[58] We afterwards learned, that only three days before our arrival, a hard contested, and most sanguinary battle, had been fought on this spot, between the Bannecks and Blackfeet, in which the former gained a signal and most complete victory, killing upwards of forty of their adversaries, and taking about three dozen scalps. The Blackfeet, although much the larger party, were on foot, but the Bannecks, being all well mounted, had a very decided advantage; and the contest occurring on an open plain, where there was no chance of cover, the Blackfeet were run down with horses, and, without being able to load their guns, were trampled to death, or killed with salmon spears and axes.

This was not the first time that we narrowly escaped a contest with this savage and most dreaded tribe. If we had passed there but a few days earlier, there is every probability to suppose that we should have been attacked, as our party at that time consisted of but twenty-six men.— TOWNSEND.

expected, and we entertained the hope that the passage could be made without difficulty or much toil, but the farther we progressed, the more laborious the travelling became. Sometimes we mounted steep banks of intermingled flinty rock, and friable slate, where our horses could scarcely obtain a footing, frequently sliding down several feet on the loose, broken stones: — again we passed along the extreme verge of tremendous precipices at a giddy height, whereat almost every step the stones and earth would roll from under our horses' feet, and we could hear them strike with a dull, leaden sound on the craggy rocks below. The whole journey, to-day, from the time we arrived at the heights, until we had crossed the mountain, has been a most fearful one. For myself, I might have diminished the danger very considerably, by adopting the plan pursued by the rest of the company, that of walking, and leading my horse over the most dangerous places, but I have been suffering for several days with a lame foot, and am wholly incapable of such exertion. I soon discovered that an attempt to guide my horse over the most rugged and steepest ranges was worse than useless, so I dropped the rein upon the animal's neck, and allowed him to take his own course, closing my eyes, and keeping as quiet as possible in the saddle. But I could not forbear [123] starting occasionally, when the feet of my horse would slip on a stone, and one side of him would slide rapidly towards the edge of the precipice, but I always recovered myself by a desperate effort, and it was fortunate for me that I did so.

Late in the afternoon, we completed the passage across the mountain, and with thankful hearts, again trod the level land. We entered here a fine rich valley or plain, of about half a mile in width, between two ranges of the mountain. It was profusely covered with willow, and through the middle of it, ran a rapid and turbulent mountain torrent, called Mallade river.[59] It contains a great abundance of beaver, their recent dams being seen in great numbers, and in the night, when all was quiet, we could hear the playful animals at their gambols, diving from the shore into the water, and striking the surface with their broad tails. The sound, altogether, was not unlike that of children at play, and the animated description of a somewhat similar scene, in the "Mohicans," recurred to my recollection, where the single-minded Gamut is contemplating with feelings of strong reprobation, the wayward freaks of what he supposes to be a bevy of young savages.

14*th.*— We travelled down the Mallade river,[60] and followed the Indian trail through the valley. The path frequently passed along near the base of the mountain, and then wound its way a considerable distance up it, to avoid rocky impediments and thick tangled bushes below, so that we had some climbing to do; but the difficulties and perils of the route of yesterday are still so fresh in our memory, that all minor things are disregarded, at least by *us.* Our poor horses, however, no doubt feel differently, as they are very tired and foot sore.

The next day we came to a close and almost impenetrable thicket of tangled willows, through which we had

---

[59] According to Wyeth's account, the expedition retraced their steps to the forks of the river, then followed the south branch, passing over the mountains which form the boundary between Custer and Blaine counties, Idaho, and emerging on Trail Creek, the affluent of the Malade, which joins the main stream at Ketchum, the present terminus of the Wood River branch of the Oregon Short Line railway.— ED.

[60] Malade (or Wood) River is a northern tributary of Lewis in Blaine County, Idaho. The mining town of Hailey is upon its banks. It was named Rivière des Malades (Sick Men's River) by Alexander Ross, who trapped upon it in 1824, and whose men fell ill from eating beaver that had fed upon a poisonous root. See Ross, *Fur Hunters* (London, 1855), ii, pp. 114-116.— ED.

great difficulty in urging our horses. The breadth of the thicket was [124] about one hundred yards, and a full hour was consumed in passing through it. We then entered immediately a rich and beautiful valley, covered profusely with a splendid blue Lupin. The mountains on either side are of much less height than those we have passed, and entirely bare, the pine trees which generally cover and ornament them, having disappeared. During the morning, we ascended and descended several high and stony hills, and early in the afternoon, emerged upon a large, level prairie, and struck a branch of Mallade river, where we encamped.

While we were unloading, we observed a number of Indians ahead, and not being aware of their character, stood with our horses saddled, while Captain W. and Richardson rode out to reconnoitre. In about half an hour they returned, and informed us that they were *Snakes* who were returning from the fisheries, and travelling towards the buffalo on the " big river," (Shoshoné.) We therefore unsaddled our poor jaded horses and turned them out to feed upon the luxuriant pasture around the camp, while we, almost equally jaded, threw ourselves down in our blankets to seek a little repose and quiet after the toils and fatigues of a long day's march.

Soon after we encamped, the Snake chief and two of his young men visited us. We formed a circle around our lodge and smoked the pipe of peace with them, after which we made them each a present of a yard of scarlet cloth for leggings, some balls and powder, a knife, and a looking glass. Captain W. then asked them a number of questions, through an interpreter, relative to the route, the fishery, &c. &c.,— and finally bought of them a small quantity of dried salmon, and a little fermented kamas or *quamash* root. The Indians remained with us until dark, and then left us quietly for their own camp. There are two lodges of them, in all about twenty persons, but none of them presumed to come near us, with the exception of the three men, two [125] squaws, and a few children. The chief is a man about fifty years of age, tall, and dignified looking, with large, strong aqualine features. His manners were cordial and agreeable, perhaps remarkably so, and he exhibited very little of that stoical indifference to surrounding objects which is so characteristic of an Indian. His dress consisted of plain leggings of deer skin, fringed at the sides, unembroidered moccasins, and a *marro* or waist-covering of antelope skin dressed without removing the hair. The upper part of his person was simply covered with a small blanket, and his ears were profusely ornamented with brass rings and beads. The men and squaws who accompanied him, were entirely naked, except that the latter had marro's of deer skin covering the loins.

The next morning we steered west across the wide prairie, crossing within every mile or two, a branch of the tortuous Mallade, near each of which good pasture was seen; but on the main prairie scarcely a blade of grass could be found, it having lately been fired by the Indians to improve the crops of next year. We have seen to-day some lava and basalt again on the sides of the hills, and on the mounds in the plain, but the level land was entirely free from it.

At noon on the 17th, we passed a deserted Indian camp, probably of the same people whose trail we have been following. There were many evident signs of the Indians having but recently left it, among which was that of several white wolves lurking around in the hope of finding remnants of meat, but, as a Scotchman would say, " I doubt they were mistaken," for meat is scarce here, and the frugal Indians rarely leave enough behind them to excite even the famished stomach of the lank and hungry wolf. The encampment here has been but a temporary one, occupying a little valley densely overgrown with willows, the tops of which have been bent over, and tied so as to form a sort of lodge; over these, they have probably stretched deer [126] skins or blankets, to exclude the rays of the sun. Of these lodges there are about forty in the valley, so that the party must have been a large one.

In the afternoon we arrived at "*Kamas prairie*," so called from a vast abundance of this esculent root which it produces, (the *Kamassa esculenta*, of Nuttall.)[61] The plain is a beautiful level one of about a mile over, hemmed in by low, rocky hills, and in spring, the pretty blue flowers of the Kamas are said to give it a peculiar, and very pleasing appearance. At this season, the flowers do not appear, the vegetable being indicated only by little dry stems which protrude all over the ground among the grass.

We encamped here, near a small branch of Mallade river; and soon after, all hands took their kettles and scattered over the prairie to dig a mess of kamas. We were, of course, eminently successful, and were furnished thereby with an excellent and wholesome meal. When boiled, this little root is palatable, and somewhat resembles the taste of the common potato; the Indian mode of preparing it, is, however, the best — that of fermenting it in pits under ground, into which hot stones have been placed. It is suffered to remain in these pits for several days; and when removed, is of a dark brown color, about the consistence of softened glue, and sweet, like molasses. It is then often made into large cakes, by being mashed, and pressed

---

[61] After crossing the Malade, the expedition moved along one of its several western branches until reaching Camas Prairie, in Elmore County.

Camas (quamash) is a bulbous root much used for food by the Indians of the Columbia. Its Shoshoni name is passheco. For further description consult Thwaites, *Original Journals of the Lewis and Clark Expedition*, iii, p.78.— ED.

together, and slightly baked in the sun. There are several other kinds of bulbous and tuberous roots, growing in these plains, which are eaten by the Indians, after undergoing a certain process of fermentation or baking. Among these, that which is most esteemed, is the white or biscuit root, the *Racine blanc* of the Canadians,— (*Eulophus ambiguus*, of Nuttall.) This is dried, pulverized with stones, and after being moistened with water, is made into cakes and baked in the sun. The taste is not unlike that of a stale [127] biscuit, and to a hungry man, or one who has long subsisted without vegetables of any kind, is rather palatable.[62]

On the morning of the 18th, we commenced ascending the hills again, and had a laborious and toilsome day's march. One of our poor wearied horses gave up, and stopped; kicking, and cuffing, and beating had no effect to make him move; the poor animal laid himself down with his load, and after this was detached and shifted to the back of another, we left him where he fell, to recruit, and fall into the hands of the Indians, or die among the arid hills. This is the first horse we have lost in this manner; but we have great fears that many others will soon fail, as their riders and drivers are compelled to use the whip constantly, to make them walk at the slowest gait. We comfort ourselves, however, by supposing that we have now nearly passed the most rugged country on the route, and hope, before many days, to reach the valley of the Shoshoné, where the country will be level, and the pasture good. We are anxious, also, to fall in with the Snake Indians, in order to get a supply of salmon, as we have been living for several days on a short allowance of wretched,

---

[62] This root is probably the one usually spoken of by the French-Canadian trappers as "white-apple" (*pomme blanche*), or "swan-apple," and well known to scientists as *Psoralea esculenta.*— ED.

dry meat, and this poor pittance is now almost exhausted.

19th.— This morning was cold, the thermometer stood at 28°, and a thick skim of ice was in the camp kettles at sunrise. Another hard day's travel over the hills, during which we lost two of our largest and stoutest horses. Towards evening, we descended to a fine large plain, and struck *Boisée*, or Big Wood river, on the borders of which we encamped.[63] This is a beautiful stream, about one hundred yards in width, clear as crystal, and, in some parts, probably twenty feet deep. It is literally *crowded* with salmon, which are springing from the water almost constantly. Our mouths are watering most abundantly for some of them, but we are not provided with suitable implements for [128] taking any, and must therefore depend for a supply on the Indians, whom we hope soon to meet.

We found, in the mountain passes, to-day, a considerable quantity of a small fruit called the choke-cherry, a species of prunus, growing on low bushes. When ripe, they are tolerable eating, somewhat astringent, however, producing upon the mouth the same effect, though in a less degree, as the unripe persimmon. They are now generally green, or we should feast luxuriantly upon them, and render more tolerable our miserable provision. We have seen, also, large patches of service bushes, but no fruit. It seems to have failed this year, although ordinarily so abundant that it constitutes a large portion of the vegetable food of both Indians and white trappers who visit these regions.

---

[63] Boise River is an important eastern affluent of Lewis, rising in the mountains of Blaine County, through which Townsend had just passed; it flows nearly west for about a hundred miles. Boise, the capital of Idaho, is upon its banks. Of the two forks which unite to form the main stream, Wyeth's expedition encountered the southern.— ED.

[129] CHAPTER VIII

August 20th.— At about daylight this morning, having charge of the last guard of the night, I observed a beautiful, sleek little *colt*, of about four months old, trot into the camp, whinnying with great apparent pleasure, and dancing and curvetting gaily amongst our sober and sedate band. I had no doubt that he had strayed from Indians, who were probably in the neighborhood; but as here, every animal that comes near us is fair game, and as we were hungry, not having eaten any thing of consequence since yesterday morning, I thought the little stranger would make a good breakfast for us. Concluding, however, that it would be best to act advisedly in the matter, I put my head into Captain W.'s tent, and telling him the news, made the proposition which had occurred to me. The captain's reply was encouraging enough,—" Down with him, if you please, Mr. T., it is the Lord's doing; let us have him for breakfast." In five minutes afterwards, a bullet sealed the fate of the unfortunate visitor, and my men were set to work making fires, and rummaging [130] out the long-neglected stew-pans, while I engaged myself in flaying the little animal, and cutting up his body in readiness for the pots.

When the camp was aroused, about an hour after, the savory steam of the cookery was rising and saluting the nostrils of our hungry people with its fragrance, who, rubbing their hands with delight, sat themselves down upon the ground, waiting with what patience they might, for the unexpected repast which was preparing for them.

It was to me almost equal to a good breakfast, to witness the pleasure and satisfaction which I had been the means of diffusing through the camp.

The repast was ready at length, and we did full justice to it; every man ate until he was filled, and all pronounced it one of the most delicious meals they had ever assisted in demolishing. When our breakfast was concluded, but little of the colt remained; that little was, however, carefully packed up, and deposited on one of the horses, to furnish, at least, a portion of another meal.

The route, this morning, lay along Boisée. For an hour, the travelling was toilsome and difficult, the Indian trail, leading along the high bank of the river, steep and rocky, making our progress very slow and laborious. We then came to a wide plain, interrupted only by occasional high banks of earth, some of them of considerable extent, across which ran the path. Towards mid-day, we lost sight of these banks, the whole country appearing level, with the exception of some distant hills in the south-west, which we suppose indicate the vicinity of some part of Snake river.

We have all been disappointed in the distance to this river, and the length of time required to reach it. Not a man in our camp has ever travelled this route before, and all we have known about it has been the general course.

[131] In the afternoon, we observed a number of Indians on the opposite side of the river, engaged in fishing for salmon. Captain W. and two men immediately crossed

over to them, carrying with them a few small articles to
exchange for fish. We congratulated ourselves upon our
good fortune in seeing these Indians, and were antici-
pating a plentiful meal, when Captain W. and his companions returned, bringing only *three* small salmon. The
Indians had been unsuccessful in fishing, not having caught
enough for themselves, and even the offer of exorbitant
sums was not sufficient to induce them to part with more.

In the afternoon, a grouse and a beaver were killed,
which, added to the remains of the colt, and our three little
salmon, made us a tolerable supper. While we were eating, we were visited by a Snake chief, a large and powerful man, of a peculiarly dignified aspect and manner.
He was naked, with the exception of a small blanket which
covered his shoulders, and descended to the middle of
the back, being fastened around the neck with a silver
skewer. As it was pudding time with us, our visitor was
of course invited to sit and eat; and he, nothing loath,
deposited himself at once upon the ground, and made a
remarkably vigorous assault upon the mixed contents of
the dish. He had not eaten long, however, before we
perceived a sudden and inexplicable change in his countenance, which was instantly followed by a violent eject-
ment of a huge mouthful of our luxurious fare. The
man rose slowly, and with great dignity, to his feet, and
pronouncing the single word " *shekum*," (horse,) in a tone
of mingled anger and disgust, stalked rapidly out of the
camp, not even wishing us a good evening. It struck me as
a singular instance of accuracy and discrimination in the
organs of taste. We had been eating of the multifarious
compound without being able to recognize, by the taste,
a single ingredient which it contained; a stranger came
amongst us, who did not know, when he [132] commenced
eating, that the dish was formed of more than one item,

and yet in less than five minutes he discovered one of the very least of its component parts.

It would seem from this circumstance that the Indians, or it may be the particular tribe to which this man belongs, are opposed to the eating of horse flesh, and yet, the natural supposition would be, that in the gameless country inhabited by them they would often be reduced to such shifts, and thus readily conquer any natural reluctance which they might feel to partake of such food. I did not think until after he left us, that if the chief knew how the horse meat he so much detested was procured, and where, he might probably have expressed even more indignation, for it is not at all unlikely that the colt had strayed from his own band.

21st.— The timber along the river banks is plentiful, and often attains a large size. It is chiefly of the species called balsam poplar, (*Populus balsamifera.*)

Towards noon to-day, we observed ahead several groups of Indians, perhaps twenty in each, and on the appearance of our cavalcade, they manifested their joy at seeing us, by the most extravagant and grotesque gestures, dancing and capering most ludicrously. Every individual of them was perfectly naked, with the exception of a small thong around the waist, to which was attached a square piece of flannel, skin, or canvass, depending half way to the knees. Their stature was rather below the middle height, but they were strongly built and very muscular. Each man carried his salmon spear, and these, with the knives stuck in their girdles, appeared to be their only weapons, not one of them having a gun. As we neared them, the first group ran towards us, crying "Shoshoné, Shoshoné," and caused some delay by their eagerness to grasp our hands and examine our garments. After one group had become satisfied with fingering [133] us, we rode on and suffered the same process by the next, and so on until we had passed the whole, every Indian crying with a loud voice, " *Tabiboo sant, tabiboo sant!* " (white man is good, white man is good.)

In a short time the chief joined us, and our party stopped for an hour, and had a " talk " with him. He told us, in answer to our questions, that his people had fish, and would give them for our goods if we would sleep one night near their camp, and smoke with them. No trade, of consequence, can ever be effected with Indians, unless the pipe be first smoked, and the matter calmly and seriously deliberated upon. An Indian chief would think his dignity seriously compromised if he were expected to do *any thing* in a hurry, much less so serious a matter as a salmon or beaver trade; and if we had refused his offered terms, he would probably have allowed us to pass on, and denied himself the darling rings, bells, and paint, rather than infringe a custom so long religiously practised by his people. We were therefore inclined to humor our Snake friend, and accordingly came to a halt, on the bank of the river.

The chief and several of his favored young braves sat with us on the bank, and we smoked with them, the other Indians forming a large circle around.

The chief is a man rather above the ordinary height, with a fine, noble countenance, and remarkably large, prominent eyes. His person, instead of being naked, as is usual, is clothed in a robe made of the skin of the mountain sheep; a broad band made of large blue beads, is fastened to the top of his head, and hangs over on his cheeks, and around his neck is suspended the foot of a huge grizzly bear. The possession of this uncouth ornament is considered among them, a great honor, since none but those whose prowess has enabled them to kill the animal, are allowed to wear it, and with their weak and inefficient weapons, [134] the destruction of so fierce and terrible a brute, is a feat that may well entitle them to some distinction.

We remained two hours at the spot where we halted, and then passed on about four miles, accompanied by the chief and his people, to their camp, where we pitched our tents for the night. In a short time the Indians came to us in great numbers, with bundles of dried salmon in their arms, and a few recent ones. We commenced our trading immediately, giving them in exchange, fish-hooks, beads, knives, paint, &c., and before evening, had procured sufficient provision for the consumption of our party until we arrive at the falls of Snake river, where we are told we shall meet the Bannecks, from whom we can doubtless trade a supply, which will serve us until we reach Walla-walla.

While we were pursuing our trade, Richardson and Mr. Ashworth rode into the camp, and I observed by the countenance of the latter, that something unusual had occurred. I felt very certain that no ordinary matter would be capable of ruffling this calm, intrepid, and almost fool-hardy young man; so it was with no little interest that I drew near, to listen to the tale which he told Captain W. with a face flushed with unusual anger, while his whole person seemed to swell with pride and disdain.

He said that while riding about five miles behind the party, (not being able to keep up with it on account of his having a worn out horse,) he was attacked by about fifty of the Indians whom we passed earlier in the day, dragged forcibly from his horse and thrown upon the ground. Here, some held their knives to his throat to prevent his rising, and others robbed him of his saddle bags, and all that they contained. While he was yet in this unpleasant situation, Richardson came suddenly upon them, and the cowardly Indians released their captive instantly, throwing the saddle bags and every thing else upon the ground and flying like frightened antelopes over the plain. The only real damage that Mr. Ashworth sustained, was the total loss of his [135] saddle bags, which were cut to pieces by the knives of the Indians, in order to abstract the contents. These, however, we think he deserves to lose, inasmuch, as with all our persuasion, we have never been able to induce him to carry a gun since we left the country infested by the Blackfeet; and to-day, the very show of such a weapon would undoubtedly have prevented the attack of which he complains.

Richardson gives an amusing account of the deportment of our young English friend while he was lying under the knives of his captors. The heavy whip of buffalo hide, which was his only weapon, was applied with great energy to the naked backs and shoulders of the Indians, who winced and stamped under the infliction, but still feared to use their knives, except to prevent his rising. Richardson, says, that until he approached closely, the blows were descending in rapid succession, and our hunter was in some danger of losing his characteristic dignity in his efforts to repress a loud and hearty laugh at the extreme ludicrousness of the whole scene.

Captain W., when the circumstances of the assault were stated to him, gave an immediate order for the suspension of business, and calling the chief to him, told him seriously, that if an attempt were again made to interrupt any of his party on their march, the offenders should be tied to a tree and whipped severely. He enforced his language by gestures so expressive that none could misunderstand him, and he was answered by a low groan from the Indians present, and a submissive bowing of their heads. The chief appeared very much troubled, and harangued his people for considerable time on the subject, repeating what the captain had said, with some additional remarks of his own, implying that even a worse fate than whipping would be the lot of future delinquents.

22d.— Last night during the second guard, while on my walk [136] around the camp, I observed one of my men squatted on the ground, intently surveying some object which appeared to be moving among the horses. At his request, I stooped also, and could distinctly perceive something near us which was certainly not a horse, and yet was as certainly a living object. I supposed it to be either a bear or a wolf, and at the earnest solicitation of the man, I gave the word " fire." The trigger was instantly pulled, the sparks flew from the flint, but the rifle was not exploded. At the sound, an Indian sprang from the grass where he had been crouching, and darted away towards the Snake camp. His object certainly was to appropriate one of our horses, and very fortunate for him was it that the gun missed fire, for the man was an unerring marksman. This little warning will probably check other similar attempts by these people.

Early in the morning I strolled into the Snake camp. It consists of about thirty lodges or wigwams, formed generally of branches of trees tied together in a conic summit, and covered with buffalo, deer, or elk skins. Men and little children were lolling about the ground all around the wigwams, together with a heterogeneous assemblance of dogs, cats, some tamed prairie wolves, and other " *varmints.*" The dogs growled and snapped when I approached, the wolves cowered and looked cross, and the cats ran away and hid themselves in dark corners. They had not been accustomed to the face of a white man, and all the quadrupeds seemed to regard me as some monstrous production, more to be feared than loved or courted. This dislike, however, did not appear to extend to the bipeds, for many of every age and sex gathered around me, and seemed to be examining me critically in all directions. The men looked complacently at me, the women, the dear creatures, smiled upon me, and the little naked, pot-bellied children crawled around my feet, examining the fashion of my hard shoes, and playing with the [137] long fringes of my leathern inexpressibles. But I scarcely know how to commence a description of the *tout en semble* of the camp, or to frame a sentence which will give an adequate idea of the extreme filth, and most horrific nastiness of the whole vicinity. I shall therefore but transiently glance at it, omitting many of the most disgusting and abominable features.

Immediately as I entered the village, my olfactories were assailed by the most vile and mephitic odors, which I found to proceed chiefly from great piles of salmon entrails and garbage which were lying festering and rotting in the sun, around the very doors of the habitations. Fish, recent and half dried, were scattered all over the ground, under the feet of the dogs, wolves and Indian children; and others which had been split, were hanging on rude platforms erected within the precincts of the camp. Some of the women were making their breakfast of the great red salmon eggs as large as peas, and using a wooden spoon to convey them to their mouths. Occasionally, also, by way of varying the repast, they would take a huge pinch of a drying fish which was lying on the ground near them. Many of the children were similarly employed, and the little imps would also have hard contests with the dogs for a favorite morsel, the former roaring and blubbering, the latter yelping and snarling, and both rolling over and over together upon the savory soil. The whole economy of the lodges, and the inside and outside appearance, was

Spearing the Salmon

of a piece with every thing else about them — filthy beyond description — the very skins which covered the wigwams were black and stiff with rancid salmon fat, and the dresses (if dresses they may be called) of the women, were of the same color and consistence, from the same cause. These *dresses* are little square pieces of deer skin, fastened with a thong around the loins, and reaching about half way to the knees; the rest of the person is entirely naked. Some of the women had little children clinging like bullfrogs to their backs, without being fastened, and in that situation [138] extracting their lactiferous sustenance from the breast, which was thrown over the shoulders.

It is almost needless to say, that I did not remain long in the Snake camp; for although I had been a considerable time estranged from the abodes of luxury, and had become somewhat accustomed to, at least, a partial assimilation to a state of nature, yet I was not prepared for what I saw here. I never had fancied any thing so utterly abominable, and was glad to escape to a purer and more wholesome atmosphere.

When I returned to our camp, the trading was going on as briskly as yesterday. A large number of Indians were assembled around, all of whom had bundles of fish, which they were anxious to dispose of. The price of a dried salmon is a straight awl, and a small fish hook, value about one cent; ten fish are given for a common butcher knife that costs eight cents. Some, however, will prefer beads, paint, &c., and of these articles, about an equal amount in value is given. A beaver skin can be had for a variety of little matters, which cost about twelve and a half cents; value, in Boston, from eight to ten dollars!

Early in the afternoon, we repacked our bales of goods and rode out of the encampment, the Indians yelling an adieu to us as we passed them. We observed that one had wrapped a buffalo robe around him, taken a bow and arrows in his hand, and joined us as we went off. Although we travelled rapidly during the afternoon, the man kept with us without apparent over-exertion or fatigue, trotting along constantly for miles together. He is probably on a visit to a village of his people who are encamped on the " Big river."

23d.— Towards noon, to-day, we fell in with a village, consisting of thirty willow lodges of Bannecks. The Indians flocked out to us by hundreds, leaving their fishing, and every other employment, to visit the strangers. The chief soon made himself known to us, and gave us a pressing invitation to stop a [139] short time with them, for the purpose of trade. Although we had a good supply of fish on hand, and did not expect soon to suffer from want, yet we knew not but we might be disappointed in procuring provision lower in the country, and concluded, therefore, to halt for half an hour, and make a small increase to our stock. We were in some haste, and anxious to travel on as quickly as possible, to Snake river. Captain W., therefore, urged the chief to have the fish brought immediately, as he intended soon to leave them. The only reply he could obtain to this request, was " *te sant*," (it is good,) accompanied by signs, that he wished to smoke. A pipe was provided, and he, with about a dozen of his young men, formed a circle near, and continued smoking, with great tranquillity, for half an hour.

Our patience became almost exhausted, and they were told that if their fish were not soon produced, we should leave them empty as we came; to this, the only answer of the chief was a sign to us to remain still, while he deliberated yet farther upon the subject.

We sat a short time longer in silent expectation, and were then preparing to mount our horses and be off, when several squaws were despatched to one of the lodges. They returned in a few minutes, bringing about a dozen dried fish. These were laid in small piles on the ground, and when the usual price was offered for them, they refused it scornfully, making the most exorbitant demands. As our articles of trade were running low, and we were not in immediate want, we purchased only a sufficiency for one day, and prepared for our departure, leaving the ground strewn with the neglected salmon. The Indians were evidently very much irritated, as we could perceive by their angry countenances, and loud words of menace. Some loosed the bows from their shoulders, and shook them at us with violent gestures of rage, and a boy, of seventeen or eighteen years of age, who stood near me, struck my horse on the head with a [140] stick, which he held in his hand. This provoked me not a little; and spurring the animal a few steps forward, I brought my heavy whip several times over his naked shoulders, and sent him screeching into the midst of his people. Several bows were drawn at me for this act, and glad would the savages have been to have had me for a short time at their mercy, but as it was, they feared to let slip their arrows, and soon dropped their points, contenting themselves with vaporing away in all the impotence of childish rage. As we rode off, they greeted us, not with the usual gay yell, but with a scornful, taunting laugh, that sounded like the rejoicings of an infernal jubilee. Had these people been provided with efficient arms, and the requisite amount of courage to use them, they might have given us some inconvenience.

Towards evening, we arrived on Snake river, crossed it at a ford, and encamped near a number of lodges along the shore. Shortly afterwards, Captain W., with three men, visited the Indians, carrying with them some small articles, to trade for fish. In about half an hour they returned, bringing only about ten salmon. They observed, among the Indians, the same disinclination to traffic that the others had manifested; or rather, like the first, they placed a higher value than usual upon the commodity, and wanted, in exchange, articles which we were not willing to spare them. They treated Captain W. with the same insolence and contempt which was so irritating from those of the other village.

This kind of conduct is said to be unusual among this tribe, but it is probably now occasioned by their having recently purchased a supply of small articles from Captain Bonneville, who, they inform us, has visited them within a few days.

Being desirous to escape from the immediate vicinity of the village, we moved our camp about four miles further, and stopped for the night.

[141] 24th.— The sudden and entire change from flesh exclusively, to fish, ditto, has affected us all more or less, with diarrhœa and pain in the abdomen; several of the men have been so extremely sick, as scarcely to be able to travel; we shall, however, no doubt, become accustomed to it in a few days.

We passed, this morning, over a flat country, very similar to that along the Platte, abounding in wormwood bushes, the pulpy-leaved thorn, and others, and deep with sand, and at noon stopped on a small stream called *Malheur's creek*.[64]

Here a party of nine men was equipped, and despatched up the river, and across the country, on a trapping expedition, with orders to join us early in the ensuing winter, at the fort on the Columbia. Richardson was the chief

[64] Malheur River rises in a lake of that name in Harney County, Oregon, and flows east and northeast into the Lewis, being one of the latter's important western tributaries.— ED.

of this party, and when I grasped the hand of our worthy hunter, and bade him farewell, I felt as though I were taking leave of a friend. I had become particularly attached to him, from the great simplicity and kindness of his heart, and his universally correct and proper deportment. I had been accustomed to depend upon his knowledge and sagacity in every thing connected with the wild and roving life which I had led for some months past, and I felt that his absence would be a real loss, as well to myself, as to the whole camp, which had profited so much by his dexterity and skill.

Our party will now consist of only seventeen men, but the number is amply sufficient, as we have passed over the country where danger is to be apprehended from Indians. We followed the course of the creek during the afternoon, and in the evening encamped on Snake river, into which Malheur empties. The river is here nearly a mile wide, but deep and clear, and for a considerable distance, perfectly navigable for steamboats, or even larger craft, and it would seem not improbable, that at some distant day, these facilities, added to the excellence of the alluvial soil, should induce the stout and hardy adventurers of our country to make permanent settlements here.

[142] I have not observed that the Indians often attempt fishing in the " big river," where it is wide and deep; they generally prefer the slues, creeks, &c. Across these, a net of closely woven willows is stretched, placed vertically, and extending from the bottom to several feet above the surface. A number of Indians enter the water about a hundred yards above the net, and, walking closely, drive the fish in a body against the wicker work. Here they frequently become entangled, and are always checked; the spear is then used dexterously, and they are thrown out, one by one, upon the shore. With industry, a vast

number of salmon might be taken in this manner; but the Indians are generally so indolent and careless of the future, that it is rare to find an individual with provision enough to supply his lodge for a week.

25th.— Early in the day the country assumed a more hilly aspect. The rich plains were gone. Instead of a dense growth of willow and the balsam poplar, low bushes of wormwood, &c., predominated, intermixed with the tall, rank prairie grass.

Towards noon, we fell in with about ten lodges of Indians, (Snakes and Bannecks,) from whom we purchased eighty salmon. This has put us in excellent spirits. We feared that we had lost sight of the natives, and as we had not reserved half the requisite quantity of provisions for our support to the Columbia, (most of our stock having been given to Richardson's trapping party,) the prospect of several days abstinence seemed very clear before us.

In the afternoon, we deviated a little from our general course, to cut off a bend in the river, and crossed a short, high hill, a part of an extensive range which we have seen for two days ahead, and which we suppose to be in the vicinity of Powder river, and [143] in the evening encamped in a narrow valley, on the borders of the Shoshoné.[65]

26th.— Last night I had the misfortune to lose my favorite, and latterly my only riding horse, the other having been left at Fort Hall, in consequence of a sudden lameness, with which he became afflicted only the night before our departure.[66] The animal was turned out as

---

[65] Lewis River here makes a considerable bend to the east, hence the short cut across country. The mountains are apparently the Burnt River Range, with Powder River beyond. Wyeth identifies this as the same place at which he encamped two years previous — near the point where the Oregon Short Line railway crosses Lewis River.— ED.

[66] I afterwards ascertained that this lameness of my "buffalo horse," was intentionally caused by one of the hopeful gentry left in charge of the fort, for the

usual, with the others, in the evening, and as I have never known him to stray in a single instance, I conclude that some lurking Indian has stolen him. It was the fattest and handsomest horse in the band, and was no doubt carefully selected, as there was probably but a single Indian, who was unable to take more, for fear of alarming the guard. This is the most serious loss I have met with. The animal was particularly valuable to me, and no consideration would have induced me to part with it here. It is, however, a kind of accident that we are always more or less liable to in this country, and as a search would certainly be fruitless, must be submitted to with as good a grace as possible. Captain W. has kindly offered me the use of horses until we arrive at Columbia.

We commenced our march early, travelling up a broad, rich valley, in which we encamped last night, and at the head of it, on a creek called Brulé, we found one family, consisting of five Snake Indians, one man, two women, and two children.[67] They had evidently but very recently arrived, probably only last night, and as they must certainly have passed our camp, we feel little hesitation in believing that my lost horse is in their possession. It is, however, impossible to prove the theft upon them in [144] any way, and time is not allowed us to search the premises. We cannot even question them concerning it, as our interpreter, McCarey, left us with the trapping party.

We bought, of this family, a considerable quantity of

purpose of rendering the animal unable to travel, and as a consequence, confining him to the fort at the time of our departure. The good qualities of the horse as a buffalo racer, were universally known and appreciated, and I had repeatedly refused large sums for him, from those who desired him for this purpose.— TOWNSEND.

[67] Burnt (Brulé) River rises in Strawberry Mountains of eastern Oregon, and flows northeast, then southeast, through Baker County into Lewis River. The Oregon Trail left the latter river at the mouth of Burnt River, and advanced up that valley to its northern bend.— ED.

dried choke-cherries, these being the only article of commerce which they possessed. This fruit they prepare by pounding it with stones, and drying it in masses in the sun. It is then good tasted, and somewhat nutritive, and it loses, by the process, the whole of the astringency which is so disagreeable in the recent fruit.

Leaving the valley, we proceeded over some high and stony hills, keeping pretty nearly the course of the creek. The travelling was, as usual in such places, difficult and laborious, and our progress necessarily slow and tedious. Throughout the day, there was no change in the character of the country, and the consequence was, that three of our poor horses gave up and stopped.

27th.— This morning, two men were left at the camp, for the purpose of collecting and bringing on, moderately, the horses left yesterday, and others that may hereafter fail. We were obliged to leave with them a stock of provision greater in proportion than our own rather limited allowance, and have thus somewhat diminished our chance of performing the remainder of the journey with satisfied appetites, but there is some small game to be found on the route, grouse, ducks, &c., and occasionally a beaver may be taken, if our necessities are pressing. We made a noon camp on Brulé, and stopped at night in a narrow valley, between the hills.

28th.— Towards noon to-day, we lost the trail among the hills, and although considerable search was made, we were not able to find it again. We then directed our course due north, and at 2 o'clock struck Powder river, a narrow and shallow stream, plentifully fringed with willows. We passed down this [145] river for about five miles and encamped.[68] Captain W. immediately left us to

---

[68] Powder River rises in the Blue Mountains and flows first east, then north, then abruptly southeast into the Lewis; the trail followed its north-bearing course.

look for the lost trail, and returned in about two hours, with the information that no trace of it could be found. He therefore concludes that it is up stream, and to-morrow we travel back to search for it in that direction. Our men killed, in the afternoon, an antelope and a deer fawn, which were particularly acceptable to us; we had been on an allowance of one dried salmon per day, and we had begun to fear that even this poor pittance would fail before we could obtain other provision. Game has been exceedingly scarce, with the exception of a few grouse, pigeons, &c. We have not seen a deer, antelope, or any other quadruped larger than a hare, since we left the confines of the buffalo country. Early this morning, one of our men, named Hubbard, left us to hunt, and as he has not joined us this evening, we fear he is lost, and feel some anxiety about him, as he has not been accustomed to finding his way through the pathless wilds. He is a good marksman, however, and will not suffer much for food; and as he knows the general course, he will probably join us at Wallawalla, if we should not see him earlier.

29th.— We commenced our march early this morning, following the river to a point about six miles above where we struck it yesterday. We then took to the hills, steering N. N. W.,— it being impossible, from the broken state of the country, to keep the river bank.

Soon after we commenced the ascent, we met with difficulties in the shape of high, steep, banks, and deep ravines, the ground being thickly strewed with sharp, angular masses of lava and basalt. As we proceeded, these difficulties increased to such a degree, as to occasion a fear that our horses could never proceed. The hills at length became like a consolidated mass of irregular rock, and

These western affluents of the Lewis (or Snake) were explored (1819) and probably named by Donald McKenzie, then of the North West Company.— Ed.

the small strips of earthy matter that occasionally appeared, were burst into wide fissures by the desiccation to which [146] the country at this season is subject. Sometimes, as we approached the verges of the cliffs, we could see the river winding its devious course many hundred feet below, rushing and foaming in eddies and whirlpools, and fretting against the steep sides of the rocks, which hemmed it in. These are what are called the cut-rocks, the sides of which are in many places as smooth and regular as though they had been worked with the chisel, and the opening between them, through which the river flows, is frequently so narrow that a biscuit might be thrown across it.

We travelled over these rocks until 1 o'clock in the day, when we stopped to rest in a small ravine, where we found a little water, and pasture for our horses. At 3, we were again on the move, making across the hills towards the river, and after a long, circuitous march, we arrived on its banks, considerably wearied, and every horse in our band lamed and completely exhausted. We have not yet found any clue to the trail for which we have been searching so anxiously; indeed it would be impossible for a distinguishable trace to be left over these rugged, stony hills, and the difficulty of finding it, or determining its direction is not a little increased by a dense fog which constantly envelopes these regions, obscuring the sun, and rendering it impossible to see an object many hundred yards in advance.

The next day we were still travelling over the high and steep hills, which, fortunately for our poor horses, were far less stony than hitherto. At about noon we descended to the plain, and struck the river in the midst of a large level prairie. We proceeded up stream for an hour, and to our great joy suddenly came in sight of a broad, open trail stretching away to the S. W. We felt, in some degree, the pleasure of a sailor who has found the port of which

he has been long and anxiously in search. We made a
noon camp here, at which we remained two hours, and
then travelled on in fine spirits over a beautiful, level, and
unobstructed country. Our horses seemed to participate
in our [147] feelings, and trotted on briskly, as though
they too rejoiced in the opportunity of escaping the dreaded
hills and rocks. Towards evening we crossed a single
range of low hills and came to a small round prairie, with
good water and excellent pasture. Here we found a family
of *Kayouse* Indians, and encamped within sight of them.
Two squaws from this family, visited us soon after, bringing
some large kamas cakes and fermented roots, which we
purchased of them.

31st.— Our route this morning, was over a country
generally level and free from rocks; we crossed, however,
one short, and very steep mountain range, thickly covered
with tall and heavy pine trees, and came to a large and
beautiful prairie, called the *Grand ronde*.[69] Here we found
Captain Bonneville's company, which has been lying here
several days, waiting the arrival of its trapping parties.
We made a noon camp near it, and were visited by Captain
Bonneville. This was the first time I had seen this gentleman. His manners were affable and pleasing, and he
seemed possessed of a large share of bold, adventurous, and
to a certain extent, romantic spirit, without which no man
can expect to thrive as a mountain leader. He stated that
he preferred the " free and easy " life of a mountain hunter
and trapper, to the comfortable and luxurious indolence
of a dweller in civilized lands, and would not exchange his
homely, but wholesome mountain fare, and his buffalo

---

[69] Grande Ronde, a noted halting place on the Oregon Trail, was so called
from its apparently circular shape, as the traveller wound down the precipitous
road into its level basin; it really is an oval twenty miles long, containing three
hundred thousand acres of rich land. It is in the present Union County, and
Grande Ronde River flows northeasterly through it.— ED.

lodge, for the most piquant dishes of the French *artiste*, and the finest palace in the land.[70] This came well from him, and I was pleased with it, although I could not altogether agree with him in sentiment, for I confess I had become somewhat weary of rough travelling and rough fare, and looked forward with no little pleasure to a long rest under a Christian roof, and a general participation in Christian living.

With the captain, came a whole troop of Indians, Kayouse, [148] Nez Percés, &c. They were very friendly towards us, each of the chiefs taking us by the hand with great cordiality, appearing pleased to see us, and anxious to point out to us the easiest and most expeditious route to the lower country. These Indians are, almost universally, fine looking, robust men, with strong aqualine features, and a much more cheerful cast of countenance than is usual amongst the race. Some of the women might almost be called beautiful, and none that I have seen are homely. Their dresses are generally of thin deer or antelope skin, with occasionally a bodice of some linen stuffs, purchased from the whites, and their whole appearance is neat and cleanly, forming a very striking contrast to the greasy, filthy, and disgusting Snake females. I observed one young and very pretty looking woman, dressed in a great superabundance of finery, glittering with rings and beads, and flaunting in broad bands of scarlet cloth. She was mounted astride,— Indian fashion,— upon a fine bay horse, whose head and tail were decorated with scarlet and blue ribbons, and the saddle, upon which the fair one sat, was ornamented all over with beads and little hawk's bells. This damsel did not do us the honor to dismount, but seemed to keep warily aloof, as though she

---

[70] For a brief sketch of Bonneville, consult Gregg's *Commerce of the Prairies* in our volume xx, p. 267, note 167.— ED.

feared that some of us might be inordinately fascinated by her fine person and splendid equipments, and her whole deportment proved to us, pretty satisfactorily, that she was no common beauty, but the favored companion of one high in office, who was jealous of her slightest movement.

After making a hasty meal, and bidding adieu to the captain, and our friendly Indian visitors, we mounted our horses, and rode off. About half an hour's brisk trotting brought us to the foot of a steep and high mountain, called the *Blue*. This is said to be the most extensive chain west of the dividing ridge, and, with one exception perhaps the most difficult of passage.[71] The whole mountain is densely covered with tall pine trees, with [149] an undergrowth of service bushes and other shrubs, and the path is strewed, to a very inconvenient degree, with volcanic rocks. In some of the ravines we find small springs of water; they are, however, rather rare, and the grass has been lately consumed, and many of the trees blasted by the ravaging fires of the Indians. These fires are yet smouldering, and the smoke from them effectually prevents our viewing the surrounding country, and completely obscures the beams of the sun. We travelled this evening until after dark, and encamped on a small stream in a gorge, where we found a plot of grass that had escaped the burning.

September 1st.— Last evening, as we were about retiring to our beds, we heard, distinctly, as we thought, a loud halloo, several times repeated, and in a tone like that of

---

[71] Blue Mountains are a continuation of the chains of western Idaho, trending southwest, then west, toward the centre of the state of Oregon, forming a watershed between the Lewis and Columbia systems. Frémont suggests that their name arises from the dark-blue appearance given to them by the pines with which they are covered. The trail led northwest from Union into Umatilla County, following the present railway route, only less circuitous.— ED.

a man in great distress. Supposing it to be a person who had lost his way in the darkness, and was searching for us, we fired several guns at regular intervals, but as they elicited no reply, after waiting a considerable time, we built a large fire, as a guide, and lay down to sleep.

Early this morning, a large panther was seen prowling around our camp, and the hallooing of last night was explained. It was the dismal, distressing yell by which this animal entices its prey, until pity or curiosity induces it to approach to its destruction. The panther is said to inhabit these forests in considerable numbers, and has not unfrequently been known to kill the horses of a camp. He has seldom the temerity to attack a man, unless sorely pressed by hunger, or infuriated by wounds.

[150] CHAPTER IX

September 1st.— The path through the valley, in which we encamped last night, was level and smooth for about a mile; we then mounted a short, steep hill, and began immediately to descend. The road down the mountain wound constantly, and we travelled in short, zig-zag lines, in order to avoid the extremely abrupt declivities; but occasionally, we were compelled to descend in places that made us pause before making the attempt: they were, some of them, almost perpendicular, and our horses would frequently slide several yards, before they could recover. To this must be added enormous jagged masses of rock, obstructing the road in many places, and pine trees projecting their horizontal branches across the path.

The road continued, as I have described it, to the valley in the plain, and a full hour was consumed before we reached it. [151] The country then became comparatively level again to the next range, where a mountain was to be ascended of the same height as the last. Here we dismounted and led our horses, it being impracticable,

in their present state, to ride them. It was the most toilsome march I ever made, and we were all so much fatigued,
when we arrived at the summit, that rest was as indispensable
to us as to our poor jaded horses. Here we made a noon
camp, with a handful of grass and no water. This last
article appears very scarce, the ravines affording none,
and our dried salmon and kamas bread were eaten un-
moistened. The route, in the afternoon, was over the
top of the mountain, the road tolerably level, but crowded
with stones. Towards evening, we commenced descending again, and in every ravine and gulley we cast our anxious
eyes in search of water; we even explored several of them,
where there appeared to exist any probability of success,
but not one drop did we find. Night at length came on,
dark and pitchy, without a moon or a single star to give
us a ray of light; but still we proceeded, depending solely
upon the vision and sagacity of our horses to keep the
track. We travelled steadily until 9 o'clock, when we
saw ahead the dark outline of a high mountain, and soon
after heard the men who rode in front, cry out, joyously,
at the top of their voices, "*water! water!*" It was truly
a cheering sound, and the words were echoed loudly by
every man in the company. We had not tasted water
since morning, and both horses and men have been suffering considerably for the want of it.

2d.— Captain W. and two men, left us early this morning for Walla-walla, where they expect to arrive this evening, and send us some provision, of which we shall be in
need, to-morrow.

Our camp moved soon after, under the direction of Captain Thing, and in about four miles reached *Utalla river*,
where it stopped, and remained until 12 o'clock.[72]

---

[72] Umatilla River, whose earlier name appears to have been Utalla. Consult Franchère's *Narrative* in our volume vi, p. 338.— Ed.

As we were approaching so near the abode of those in whose [152] eyes we wished to appear like fellow Christians, we concluded that there would be a propriety in attempting to remove at least one of the heathenish badges which we had worn throughout the journey; so Mr. N.'s razor was fished out from its hiding place in the bottom of his trunk, and in a few minutes our encumbered chins lost their long-cherished ornaments; we performed our ablutions in the river, arrayed ourselves in clean linen, trimmed our long hair, and then arranged our toilet before a mirror, with great self-complacence and satisfaction. I admired my own appearance considerably, (and this is, probably, an acknowledgement that few would make,) but I could not refrain from laughing at the strange, party-colored appearance of my physiognomy, the lower portion being fair, like a woman's, and the upper, brown and swarthy as an Indian.

Having nothing prepared for dinner to-day, I strolled along the stream above the camp, and made a meal on rose buds, of which I collected an abundance; and on returning, I was surprised to find Mr. N. and Captain T. picking the last bones of a bird which they had cooked. Upon inquiry, I ascertained that the subject was an unfortunate owl which I had killed in the morning, and had intended to preserve, as a specimen. The temptation was too great to be resisted by the hungry Captain and naturalist, and the bird of wisdom lost the immortality which he might otherwise have acquired.

In the afternoon, soon after leaving the Utalla, we ascended a high and very steep hill, and came immediately in view of a beautiful, and regularly undulating country of great extent. We have now probably done with high, rugged mountains; the sun shines clear, the air is bracing and elastic, and we are all in fine spirits.

The next day, the road being generally level, and tolerably free from stones, we were enabled to keep our horses at the swiftest gait to which we dare urge them. We have been somewhat [153] disappointed in not receiving the expected supplies from Walla-walla, but have not suffered for provision, as the grouse and hares are very abundant here, and we have shot as many as we wished.

At about noon we struck the Walla-walla river, a very pretty stream of fifty or sixty yards in width, fringed with tall willows, and containing a number of salmon, which we can see frequently leaping from the water. The pasture here, being good, we allowed our horses an hour's rest to feed, and then travelled on over the plain, until near dark, when, on rising a sandy hill, the noble Columbia burst at once upon our view. I could scarcely repress a loud exclamation of delight and pleasure, as I gazed upon the magnificent river, flowing silently and majestically on, and reflected that I had actually crossed the vast American continent, and now stood upon a stream that poured its waters directly into the Pacific. This, then, was the great Oregon, the first appearance of which gave Lewis and Clark so many emotions of joy and pleasure, and on this stream our indefatigable countrymen wintered, after the toils and privations of a long, and protracted journey through the wilderness. My reverie was suddenly interrupted by one of the men exclaiming from his position in advance, "there is the fort." We had, in truth approached very near, without being conscious of it.[73] There

---

[73] Fort Walla Walla (or Nez Percés) was built by Alexander Ross of the North West Company in July, 1818 — see Ross, *Fur Hunters*, i, p. 171, for description and representation. It passed into the possession of the Hudson's Bay Company upon the consolidation of the corporations, and being rebuilt of adobé after its destruction by fire, was maintained until 1855–56, when it was abandoned during an Indian war. It was near the sight of the present Wallula, Washington, on the left bank of the Columbia, about half a mile above Walla Walla River.— ED.

stood the fort on the bank of the river; horses and horned cattle were roaming about the vicinity, and on the borders of the little Walla-walla, we recognized the white tent of our long lost missionaries. These we soon joined, and were met and received by them like brethren. Mr. N. and myself were invited to sup with them upon a dish of stewed hares which they had just prepared, and it is almost needless to say that we did full justice to the good men's cookery. They told us that they had travelled comfortably from Fort Hall, without any unusual fatigue, and like ourselves, had no particularly stirring adventures. Their [154] route, although somewhat longer, was a much less toilsome and difficult one, and they suffered but little for food, being well provided with dried buffalo meat, which had been prepared near Fort Hall.

Mr. Walker, (a young gentleman attached to the band,) related an anecdote of Mr. Lee, the principal, which I thought eminently characteristic. The missionaries were, on one occasion, at a considerable distance behind the main body, and had stopped for a few moments to regale themselves on a cup of milk from a cow which they were driving. Mr. L. had unstrapped the tin pan from his saddle, and was about applying himself to the task, when a band of a dozen Indians was descried at a distance, approaching the little party at full gallop. There was but little time for consideration. The rifles were looked to, the horses were mounted in eager haste, and all were ready for a long run, except Mr. Lee himself, who declared that nothing should deprive him of his cup of milk, and that he meant to "lighten the old cow before he moved." He accordingly proceeded coolly to fill his tin pan, and, after a hearty drink, grasped his rifle, and mounted his horse, at the very moment that the Indians had arrived to within speaking distance. To the great relief of most of the party, these proved to be of the friendly Nez Percé tribe, and after a cordial greeting, they travelled on together.

The missionaries informed us that they had engaged a large barge to convey themselves and baggage to Fort Vancouver, and that Captain Stewart and Mr. Ashworth were to be of the party. Mr. N. and myself were very anxious to take a seat with them, but to our disappointment, were told that the boat would scarcely accommodate those already engaged. We had therefore to relinquish it, and prepare for a journey on horseback to the *Dalles*, about eighty miles below, to which place Captain W. would [155] precede us in the barge, and engage canoes to convey us to the lower fort.

This evening, we purchased a large bag of Indian meal, of which we made a kettle of mush, and mixed with it a considerable quantity of horse tallow and salt. This was, I think, one of the best meals I ever made. We all ate heartily of it, and pronounced it princely food. We had been long without bread stuff of any kind, and the coarsest farinaceous substance, with a proper allowance of grease, would have been highly prized.

The next morning, we visited Walla-walla Fort, and were introduced, by Captain W., to Lieutenant Pierre S. Pambrun, the superintendent.[74] Wyeth and Mr. Pambrun had met before, and were well acquainted; they had, therefore, many reminiscences of by-gone days to recount, and

---

[74] Lieutenant Pierre Chrysologue Pambrun was born near Quebec in 1792. In the War of 1812–15, he was an officer in the Canadian light troops, and soon after peace was declared entered the employ of the Hudson's Bay Company. At the Red River disturbances (1816) he was taken prisoner, but soon released. Later he served at several far Western fur-trade posts, and coming to the Columbia was placed in charge at Fort Walla Walla (1832). He showed many courtesies to the overland emigrants, but refused supplies to Captain Bonneville as being a rival trader; he appears, however, to have had no such feeling with regard to Captain Wyeth. Pambrun was severely hurt by a fall from his horse (1840), and died of the injury at Walla Walla.— ED.

long conversations, relative to the variety of incidents which had occurred to each, since last they parted.

The fort is built of drift logs, and surrounded by a stoccade of the same, with two bastions, and a gallery around the inside. It stands about a hundred yards from the river, on the south bank, in a bleak and unprotected situation, surrounded on every side by a great, sandy plain, which supports little vegetation, except the wormwood and thorn-bushes. On the banks of the little river, however, there are narrow strips of rich soil, and here Mr. Pambrun raises the few garden vegetables necessary for the support of his family. Potatoes, turnips, carrots, &c., thrive well, and Indian corn produces eighty bushels to the acre.

At about 10 o'clock, the barge got under way, and soon after, our company with its baggage, crossed the river in canoes, and encamped on the opposite shore.

There is a considerable number of Indians resident here, Kayouse's and a collateral band of the same tribe, called Walla-wallas.[75] [156] They live along the bank of the river, in shantys or wigwams of drift wood, covered with buffalo or deer skins. They are a miserable, squalid looking people, are constantly lolling around and in the fort, and annoy visitors by the importunate manner in which they endeavor to force them into some petty trade for a pipe, a hare, or a grouse. All the industrious and enterprising men of this tribe are away trading salmon, kamas root, &c. to the mountain companies.

Notwithstanding the truly wretched plight in which these poor people live, and the privations which they must necessarily have to suffer, they are said to be remarkably honest and upright in their dealings, and generally correct

[75] For the Walla Walla Indians, see Ross's *Oregon Settlers*, in our volume vii, p. 137, note 37.— ED.

in their moral deportment. Although they doubtless have
the acquisitive qualities so characteristic of the race, they
are rarely known to violate the principles of common honesty. A man may leave his tent unguarded, and richly
stored with every thing which ordinarily excites the cu-
pidity of the Indian, yet, on returning after a long absence,
he may find all safe. What a commentary is this on the
habits and conduct of our *Christian* communities!

The river is here about three-fourths of a mile in width,—
a clear, deep, and rapid stream, the current being generally from three to four miles an hour. It is the noblest
looking river I have seen since leaving our Delaware. The
banks are in many places high and rocky, occasionally
interrupted by broad, level sandy beaches. The only
vegetation along the margin, is the wormwood, and other
low, arid plants, but some of the bottoms are covered with
heavy, rank grass, affording excellent pasture for horses.

5th.—This morning we commenced our march down
the Columbia. We have no provision with us except
flour and horse tallow, but we have little doubt of meeting Indians daily, with whom we can trade for fish. Our
road will now be a rather monotonous one [157] along
the bank of the river, tolerably level, but often rocky, so
that very rapid travelling is inadmissible. The mallard
duck, the widgeon, and the green-winged teal are tolerably
abundant in the little estuaries of the river. Our men
have killed several, but they are poor, and not good.

6th.— We have observed to-day several high, conical
stacks of drift-wood near the river. These are the graves
of the Indians. Some of these cemeteries are of considerable
extent, and probably contain a great number of bodies.
I had the curiosity to peep into several of them, and even
to remove some of the coverings, but found nothing to
compensate for the trouble.

We bought some salmon from Indians whom we met
to-day, which, with our flour and tallow, enable us to live
very comfortably.

7th.— We frequently fall in with large bands of Indian
horses. There are among them some very beautiful animals, but they are generally almost as wild as deer, seldom
permitting an approach to within a hundred yards or more.
They generally have owners, as we observe upon many
of them strange hieroglyphic looking characters, but there
are no doubt some that have never known the bit, and
will probably always roam the prairie uncontrolled. When
the Indians wish to catch a horse from one of these bands,
they adopt the same plan pursued by the South Americans
for taking the wild animal.

8th.— Our road to-day has been less monotonous, and
much more hilly than hitherto. Along the bank of the
river, are high mountains, composed of basaltic rock and
sand, and along their bases enormous drifts of the latter
material. Large, rocky promontories connected with these
mountains extend into the river to considerable distances,
and numerous islands of the same dot its surface.

We are visited frequently as we travel along, by Indians
of [158] the Walla-walla and other tribes, whose wigwams
we see on the opposite side of the river. As we approach
these rude huts, the inhabitants are seen to come forth
in a body; a canoe is immediately launched, the light bark
skims the water like a bird, and in an incredibly short
time its inmates are with us. Sometimes a few salmon
are brought to barter for our tobacco, paint, &c., but more
frequently they seem impelled to the visit by mere curiosity.
To-day a considerable number have visited us, and among
them some very handsome young girls. I could not but
admire the gaiety and cheerfulness which seemed to ani-
mate them. They were in high spirits, and evidently

very much pleased with the unusual privilege which they were enjoying.

At our camp in the evening, eight Walla-walla's came to see us. The chief was a remarkably fine looking man, but he, as well as several of his party, was suffering from a severe purulent ophthalmia which had almost deprived him of sight. He pointed to his eyes, and contorting his features to indicate the pain he suffered, asked me by signs to give him medicine to cure him. I was very sorry that my small stock of simples did not contain anything suited to his complaint, and I endeavored to tell him so. I have observed that this disease is rather prevalent among the Indians residing on the river, and I understood from the chief's signs that most of the Indians towards the lower country were similarly affected.

9th.— The character of the country has changed considerably since we left Walla-walla. The river has become gradually more narrow, until it is now but about two hundred yards in width, and completely hemmed in by enormous rocks on both sides. Many of these extend for considerable distances into the stream in perpendicular columns, and the water dashes and breaks against them until all around is foam. The current is here very swift, probably six or seven miles to the hour; and the [159] Indian canoes in passing down, seem literally to *fly* along its surface. The road to-day has been rugged to the very last degree. We have passed over continuous masses of sharp rock for hours together, sometimes picking our way along the very edge of the river, several hundred feet above it; again, gaining the back land, by passing through any casual chasm or opening in the rocks, where we were compelled to dismount, and lead our horses.

This evening, we are surrounded by a large company of Chinook Indians, of both sexes, whose temporary wig-

wams are on the bank of the river. Many of the squaws
have young children sewed up in the usual Indian fashion,
wrapped in a skin, and tied firmly to a board, so that
nothing but the head of the little individual is seen.[76]

These Indians are very peaceable and friendly. They
have no weapons except bows, and these are used more
for amusement and exercise, than as a means of procuring
them sustenance, their sole dependence being fish and
beaver, with perhaps a few hares and grouse, which are
taken in traps. We traded with these people for a few
fish and beaver skins, and some roots, and before we retired for the night, arranged the men in a circle, and gave
them a smoke in token of our friendship.

10th.— This afternoon we reached the *Dalles.*[77] The
entire water of the river here flows through channels of
about fifteen feet in width, and between high, perpendicular rocks; there are several of these channels at distances of from half a mile to a mile apart, and the water
foams and boils through them like an enormous cauldron.

On the opposite side of the river there is a large Indian
village, belonging to a chief named Tilki, and containing
probably five hundred wigwams. As we approached, the
natives swarmed like bees to the shore, launched their
canoes, and joined us in a few [160] minutes. We were
disappointed in not seeing Captain W. here, as this was
the spot where we expected to meet him; the chief, however, told us that we should find him about twelve miles
below, at the next village. We were accordingly soon

---

[76] This must have been a roving party, far from their base, for the Chinook
were rarely found so high up the Columbia.— ED.

[77] The first obstruction in the Columbia on descending from Walla Walla
consists of the Falls and Long and Short Narrows frequently called the Dalles.
See descriptions in *Original Journals of the Lewis and Clark Expedition*, iii, pp.
146–173; Franchère's *Narrative*, in our volume vi, p. 337; and Ross's *Oregon
Settlers*, our volume vii, pp. 128–133.— ED.

on the move again, and urging our horses to their fastest gait, we arrived about sunset. The captain, the chief of the village, and several other Indians, came out to meet us and make us welcome. Captain W. has been here two days, and we were pleased to learn that he had completed all the necessary arrangements for transporting ourselves and baggage to Vancouver in canoes. The route by land is said to be a very tedious and difficult one, and, in some places, almost impassable, but even were it otherwise, I believe we should all much prefer the water conveyance, as we have become very tired of riding.

Since leaving the upper village this afternoon, we have been followed by scores of Indians on foot and on horseback; some of the animals carrying three at a time; and although we travelled rapidly, the pedestrians were seldom far behind us.

We have concluded to leave our horses here, in charge of the chief of the village, who has promised to attend to them during the winter, and deliver them to our order in the spring. Captain W. having been acquainted with this man before, is willing to trust him.

11*th.*— Early this morning, we launched our three canoes, and each being provided with an Indian, as helmsman, we applied ourselves to our paddles, and were soon moving briskly down the river. In about an hour after, the wind came out dead ahead, and although the current was in favor, our progress was sensibly checked. As we proceeded, the wind rose to a heavy gale, and the waves ran to a prodigious height. At one moment our frail bark danced upon the crest of a wave, and at the next, fell with a surge into the trough of the sea, and as we looked at the swell before us, it seemed that in an instant we [161] must inevitably be engulphed. At such times, the canoe ahead of us was entirely hidden from view, but she was observed to rise again like a seagull, and hurry on into the same danger. The Indian in my canoe soon became completely frightened; he frequently hid his face with his hands, and sang, in a low melancholy voice, a prayer which we had often heard from his people, while at their evening devotions. As our dangers were every moment increasing, the man became at length absolutely childish, and with all our persuasion and threats, we could not induce him to lay his paddle into the water. We were all soon compelled to put in shore, which we did without sustaining any damage; the boats were hauled up high and dry, and we concluded to remain in our quarters until to-morrow, or until there was a cessation of wind. In about an hour it lulled a little, and Captain W. ordered the boats to be again launched, in the hope of being able to weather a point about five miles below, before the gale again commenced, where we could lie by until it should be safe to proceed. The calm proved, as some of us had suspected, a treacherous one; in a very few minutes after we got under way, we were contending with the same difficulties as before, and again our cowardly helmsman laid by his paddle and began mumbling his prayer. It was too irritating to be borne. Our canoe had swung round broad side to the surge, and was shipping gallons of water at every dash.

At this time it was absolutely necessary that every man on board should exert himself to the utmost to head up the canoe and make the shore as soon as possible. Our Indian, however, still sat with his eyes covered, the most abject and contemptible looking thing I ever saw. We took him by the shoulders and threatened to throw him overboard, if he did not immediately lend his assistance: we might as well have spoken to a stone. He was finally aroused, however, by our presenting a loaded gun at his breast; he dashed the muzzle away, seized his paddle [162] again, and worked with a kind of desperate and wild energy, until he sank back in the canoe completely exhausted. In the mean time the boat had become half full of water, shipping a part of every surf that struck her, and as we gained the shallows every man sprang overboard, breast deep, and began hauling the canoe to shore. This was even a more difficult task than that of propelling her with the oars; the water still broke over her, and the bottom was a deep kind of quicksand, in which we sank almost to the knees at every step, the surf at the same time dashing against us with such violence as to throw us repeatedly upon our faces. We at length reached the shore, and hauled the canoe up out of reach of the breakers. She was then unloaded as soon as possible, and turned bottom upwards. The goods had suffered considerably by the wetting; they were all unbaled and dried by a large fire, which we built on the shore.

We were soon visited by several men from the other boats, which were ahead, and learned that their situation had been almost precisely similar to our own, except that their Indians had not evinced, to so great a degree, the same unmanly terror which had rendered ours so inefficient and useless. They were, however, considerably frightened, much more so than the white men. It would seem strange that Indians, who have been born, and have lived during their whole lives, upon the edge of the water, who have been accustomed, from infancy, to the management of a canoe, and in whose childish sports and manly pastimes these frail barks have always been employed, should exhibit, on occasions like this, such craven and womanly fears; but the probability is, as their business is seldom of a very urgent nature, that they refrain from making excursions of any considerable extent in situations known to be dangerous, except during calm weather; it is possible, also, that such gales may be rare, and they have not been accustomed to them. Immediately after we landed, our redoubtable helmsman broke away from us, [163] and ran at full speed back towards the village. We have doubtless lost him entirely, but we do not much regret his departure, as he proved himself so entirely unequal to the task he had undertaken.[78]

12th.— The gale continues with the same violence as yesterday, and we do not therefore think it expedient to leave our camp. Mr. N.'s large and beautiful collection of new and rare plants was considerably injured by the wetting it received; he has been constantly engaged since we landed yesterday, in opening and drying them. In this task he exhibits a degree of patience and perseverance which is truly astonishing; sitting on the ground, and steaming over the enormous fire, for hours together, drying the papers, and re-arranging the whole collection, specimen by specimen, while the great drops of perspiration roll unheeded from his brow. Throughout the whole of our long journey, I have had constantly to admire the ardor and perfect indefatigability with which he has devoted himself to the grand object of his tour. No difficulty, no danger, no fatigue has ever daunted him, and he finds his rich reward in the addition of nearly *a thousand* new species of American plants, which he has been enabled to make to the already teeming flora of our vast continent. My bale of birds, which was equally exposed to the action of the water, escaped without any material injury.

In the afternoon, the gale not having abated, Captain W. became impatient to proceed, as he feared his business at Vancouver would suffer by delay; he accordingly

---

[78] On this matter consult *Original Journals of the Lewis and Clark Expedition,* iii, pp. 166–210, 217, 221, 256, where the Indians are represented as venturing forth into rough water that no white man dared breast.— ED.

proposed taking one canoe, and braving the fury of the elements, saying that he wished five men, who were not afraid of water, to accompany him. A dozen of our fearless fellows volunteered in a moment, and the captain selecting such as he thought would best suit his purpose, lost no time in launching his canoe, and away she went over the foaming waters, dashing the spray from her bows, and laboring through the heavy swells until she was lost to our view. [164] The more sedate amongst us did not much approve of this somewhat hasty measure of our principal; it appeared like a useless and daring exposure of human life, not warranted by the exigencies of the case. Mr. N. remarked that he would rather lose all his plants than venture his life in that canoe.

On the 13th the wind shifted to due north, and was blowing somewhat less furiously than on the previous day. At about noon we loaded our canoes, and embarked; our progress, however, during the afternoon, was slow; the current was not rapid, and the wind was setting up stream so strongly that we could not make much headway against it; we had, also, as before, to contend with turbulent waves, but we found we could weather them with much less difficulty, since the change of the wind.

14*th*.— Before sunrise, a light rain commenced, which increased towards mid-day to a heavy shower, and continued steadily during the afternoon and night. There was, in the morning, a dead calm, the water was perfectly smooth, and disturbed only by the light rain pattering upon its surface. We made an early start, and proceeded on very expeditiously until about noon, when we arrived at the "cascades," and came to a halt above them, near a small Indian village. These cascades, or cataracts are formed by a collection of large rocks, in the bed of the river, which extend, for perhaps half a mile. The current for a short distance above them, is exceedingly rapid, and there is said to be a gradual fall, or declivity of the river, of about twenty feet in the mile. Over these rocks, and across the whole river, the water dashes and foams most furiously, and with a roar which we heard distinctly at the distance of several miles.[79]

It is wholly impossible for any craft to make its way through these difficulties, and our light canoes would not live an instant in them. It is, therefore, necessary to make a portage, either by carrying the canoes over land to the opposite side of the cataracts, or by wading in the water near the shore, where the surges are [165] lightest, and dragging the unloaded boat through them by a cable. Our people chose the latter method, as the canoes felt very heavy and cumbersome, being saturated with the rain which was still falling rapidly. They were accordingly immediately unloaded, the baggage placed on the shore, and the men entered the water to their necks, headed by Captain Thing, and addressed themselves to the troublesome and laborious task. In the meantime, Mr. N., and myself were sent ahead to take the best care of ourselves that our situation and the surrounding circumstances permitted. We found a small Indian trail on the river bank, which we followed in all its devious windings, up and down hills, over enormous piles of rough flinty rocks, through brier bushes, and pools of water, &c. &c., for about a mile, and descending near the edge of the river, we observed a number of white men who had just succeeded in forcing a large barge through the torrent, and were then warping her into still water near the shore.

---

[79] The cascades are the last obstructions on the Lower Columbia. Consult *Original Journals of the Lewis and Clark Expedition*, iii, pp. 179–185; Franchère's *Narrative* in our volume vi, p. 336; and Ross's *Oregon Settlers* in our volume vii, pp. 121–125.— ED.

Upon approaching them more closely, we recognised, to our astonishment, our old friend Captain Stewart, with the good missionaries, and all the rest who left us at Walla-walla on the 4th. Poor fellows! Every man of them had been over breast deep in water, and the rain, which was still falling in torrents, was more than sufficient to drench what the waves did not cover, so that they were most abundantly soaked and bedraggled. I felt sadly inclined to laugh heartily at them, but a single glance at the sorry appearance of myself and my companion was sufficient to check the feeling. We joined them, and aided in kindling a fire to warm and dry ourselves a little, as there was not a dry rag on us, and we were all in an ague with cold. After a very considerable time, we succeeded in igniting the wet timber, and had a tolerably large fire. We all seated ourselves on the ground around it, and related our adventures. They had, like ourselves, suffered somewhat from the head-wind and heavy swells, but unlike us they had a craft that would weather it easily; even they, however, [166] shipped some water, and made very little progress for the last two days. They informed us that Captain W.'s canoe had been dashed to pieces on the rocks above, and that he and all his crew were thrown into the water, and forced to swim for their lives. They all escaped, and proceeded down the river, this morning, in a canoe, hired of the Indians here, one of whom accompanied them, as pilot.

After a hasty meal of fish, purchased on the spot, our friends reloaded their boat and got under way, hoping to reach Vancouver by next morning. Mr. N. and myself remained some time longer here, expecting intelligence from our people behind; we had begun to feel a little uneasy about them, and thought of returning to look into their situation, when Captain T. came in haste towards us, with the mortifying intelligence that one canoe had been stove upon the rocks, and the other so badly split, that he feared she would not float; the latter was, however, brought on by the men, and moored where we had stopped. A man was then despatched to an Indian village, about five miles below, to endeavor to procure one or two canoes and a pilot. In the mean time, we had all to walk back along the circuitous and almost impassable Indian trail, and carry our wet and heavy baggage from the spot where the boats had been unloaded. The distance, as I have stated, was a full mile, and the road so rough and encumbered as to be scarcely passable. In walking over many of the large and steep rocks, it was often necessary that the hands should be used to raise and support the body; this, with a load, was inconvenient. Again, in ascending and descending the steep and slippery hills, a single mis-step was certain to throw us in the mud, and bruise us upon the sharp rocks which were planted all around. This accident occurred several times with us all.

Over this most miserable of all roads, with the cold rain dashing and pelting upon us during the whole time, until we felt as [167] though we were frozen to the very marrow, did we all have to travel and return four separate times, before our baggage was properly deposited. It was by far the most fatiguing, cheerless, and uncomfortable business in which I was ever engaged, and truly glad was I to lie down at night on the cold, wet ground, wrapped in my blankets, out of which I had just wrung the water, and I think I never slept more soundly or comfortably than that night.[80]

I arose the next morning rested and refreshed, though somewhat sore from sundry bruises received on the hills to which I have alluded.

---

[80] I could not but recollect at that time, the last injunction of my dear old grandmother, not to sleep in damp beds! ! — TOWNSEND.

15th.— The rain still continued falling, but lightly, the weather calm and cool. The water immediately below the cascades foams and boils in a thousand eddies, forming little whirlpools, which, however insignificant they may appear, are exceedingly dangerous for light canoes, whirling their bows around to the current, and capsising them in an instant. Near the shore, at the foot of the cataract, there is a strong backward tow, through which it is necessary to drag the canoe, by a line, for the distance of a hundred yards; here it feels the force of the opposite current, and is carried on at the rate of seven or eight miles to the hour.

The man whom we sent yesterday to the village, returned this morning; he stated that one canoe only could be had, but that three Indians, accustomed to the navigation, would accompany us; that they would soon be with us, and endeavor to repair our damaged boat. In an hour they came, and after the necessary clamping and caulking of our leaky vessel, we loaded, and were soon moving rapidly down the river. The rain ceased about noon, but the sun did not appear during the day.

[168] *16th.*— The day was a delightful one; the sky was robed in a large flaky cumulus, the glorious sun occasionally bursting through among the clouds, with dazzling splendor. We rose in the morning in fine spirits, our Indians assuring us that " King George," as they called the fort, was but a short distance from us. At about 11 o'clock, we arrived, and stepped on shore at the *end of our journey.*

It is now three days over six months since I left my beloved home. I, as well as the rest, have been in some situations of danger, of trial, and of difficulty, but I have passed through them all unharmed, with a constitution strengthened, and invigorated by healthful exercise, and a heart which I trust can feel deeply, sincerely thankful to that kind and overruling Providence who has watched over and protected me.

We have passed for months through a country swarming with Indians who thirsted for our blood, and whose greatest pride and glory consisted in securing the scalp of a white man. Enemies, sworn, determined enemies to all, both white and red, who intrude upon his hunting grounds, the Blackfoot roams the prairie like a wolf seeking his prey, and springing upon it when unprepared, and at the moment when it supposes itself most secure. To those who have always enjoyed the comforts and security of civilized life, it may seem strange that persons who know themselves to be constantly exposed to such dangers — who never lie down at night without the weapons of death firmly grasped in their hands, and who are in hourly expectation of hearing the terrific war whoop of the savage, should yet sleep soundly and refreshingly, and feel themselves at ease; such however is the fact. I never in my life enjoyed rest more than when travelling through the country of which I speak. I had become accustomed to it: I felt constant apprehension certainly, but not to such an extent as to deprive me of any of the few comforts which I could command in such an uncomfortable country. The [169] guard might pass our tent, and cry "all's well," in his loudest key, without disturbing my slumbers: but if the slightest *unusual* noise occurred, I was awake in an instant, and listening painfully for a repetition of it.

On the beach in front of the fort, we were met by Mr. Lee, the missionary, and Dr. John McLoughlin, the chief factor, and Governor of the Hudson's Bay posts in this vicinity. The Dr. is a large, dignified and very noble looking man, with a fine expressive countenance, and remarkably bland and pleasing manners. The missionary introduced Mr. N. and myself in due form, and we were greeted and received with a frank and unassuming politeness which was most peculiarly grateful to our feelings. He requested us to consider his house our home, provided a separate room for our use, a servant to wait upon us, and furnished us with every convenience which we could possibly wish for. I shall never cease to feel grateful to him for his disinterested kindness to the poor houseless and travel-worn strangers.[81]

---

[81] Dr. John McLoughlin, born near Quebec, October 19, 1784, was educated as a physician, and for a time studied in Paris. Early in the nineteenth century he entered the North West Company's employ, and was stationed at Fort William, on Lake Superior, where he knew Sir Alexander Mackenzie and other frontier celebrities. In 1818 he married Margaret, widow of Alexander McKay, who perished in the "Tonquin" (1811). In 1824 McLoughlin was transferred to the Columbia, as chief factor for the Hudson's Bay Company in all the transmontane region. Making his headquarters at Fort Vancouver, he for upwards of twenty years ruled with a firm but mild justice this vast forest empire. On the great American emigration to Oregon, McLoughlin's humanity and kindness of heart led him to succor the weary homeseekers, for which cause he was reprimanded by the company and thereupon resigned (1846). The remainder of his life was passed at Oregon City, and was somewhat embittered by land controversies. He became a naturalized American citizen, and after his death (September 7, 1857) the Oregon legislature made to his heirs restitution of his lands, in recognition of the great service of the "Father of Oregon." Brief sketches from his life are included in E. E. Dye, *McLoughlin and Old Oregon, a Chronicle* (Chicago, 1900).— ED.

[170] CHAPTER X

Fort Vancouver — Agricultural and other improvements — Vancouver "camp" — Approach of the rainy season — Expedition to the Wallammet — The falls — A village of Klikatat Indians — Manner of flattening the head — A Flathead infant — Brig "May Dacre" — Preparations for a settlement — Success of the naturalists — Chinook Indians — their appearance and costume — Ague and fever — Superstitious dread of the Indians — Desertion of the Sandwich Islanders from Captain Wyeth's party — Embarkation for a trip to the Islands — George, the Indian pilot — Mount Coffin — A visit to the tombs — Superstition — Visit to an Indian house — Fort George — Site of Astoria — A blind Indian boy — Cruel and unfeeling conduct of the savages — their moral character — Baker's Bay — Cape Disappointment — Dangerous bar at the entrance of the river — The sea beach — Visit of Mr. Ogden — Passage across the bar. . . .

FORT VANCOUVER is situated on the north bank of the Columbia on a large level plain, about a quarter of a mile from the shore.[82] The space comprised within the stoccade is an oblong square, of about one hundred, by two hundred and fifty feet. The houses built of logs and frame-work, to the number of ten or twelve, are ranged around in a quadrangular form, the one occupied by the doctor being in the middle. In front, and enclosed on three sides by the buildings, is a large open space, where all the in-door work of the establishment is done. Here the Indians assemble with their multifarious articles of trade, beaver,

[82] Fort Vancouver was the centre of the Hudson's Bay Company's operations in Oregon, and the most important post in that country. Built in 1824–25 under the supervision of Dr. John McLoughlin, who decided to transfer thither his headquarters from Fort George (Astoria), its site was on the north bank of the Columbia, a hundred and fourteen miles from the mouth of the river, and six miles above that of the Willamette. It was not a formidable enclosure, for the Indians thereabout were in general peaceful, and a large farm and an agricultural settlement were attached to the post. After McLoughlin resigned (1846), James Douglas was chief factor until the American possession. In 1849 General Harney took charge, and by orders from Washington destroyed part of the trading post, and established a United States military post now known as Vancouver Barracks.— ED.

otter, venison, and various other game, and here, once a week, several scores of Canadians are employed, beating the furs which have been collected, in order to free them from dust and vermin.

[171] Mr. N. and myself walked over the farm with the doctor, to inspect the various improvements which he has made. He has already several hundred acres fenced in, and under cultivation, and like our own western prairie land, it produces abundant crops, particularly of grain, without requiring any manure. Wheat thrives astonishingly; I never saw better in any country, and the various culinary vegetables, potatoes, carrots, parsnips, &c., are in great profusion, and of the first quality. Indian corn does not flourish so well as at Walla-walla, the soil not not being so well adapted to it; melons are well flavored, but small; the greatest curiosity, however, is the apples, which grow on small trees, the branches of which would be broken without the support of props. So profuse is the quantity of fruit that the limbs are covered with it, and it is actually *packed* together precisely in the same manner that onions are attached to ropes when they are exposed for sale in our markets.

On the farm is a grist mill, a threshing mill, and a saw mill, the two first, by horse, and the last, by water power; besides many minor improvements in agricultural and other matters, which cannot but astonish the stranger from a civilized land, and which reflect great credit upon the liberal and enlightened chief factor.

In the propagation of domestic cattle, the doctor has been particularly successful. Ten years ago a few head of neat cattle were brought to the fort by some fur traders from California; these have now increased to near seven hundred. They are a large framed, long horned breed, inferior in their milch qualities to those of the United States, but the beef is excellent, and in consequence of the mildness of the climate, it is never necessary to provide them with fodder during the winter, an abundant supply of excellent pasture being always found.

On the farm, in the vicinity of the fort, are thirty or forty log huts, which are occupied by the Canadians, and others attached [172] to the establishment. These huts are placed in rows, with broad lanes or streets between them, and the whole looks like a very neat and beautiful village. The most fastidious cleanliness appears to be observed; the women may be seen sweeping the streets and scrubbing the door-sills as regularly as in our own proverbially cleanly city.[83]

Sunday, September 25th.— Divine service was performed in the fort this morning by Mr. Jason Lee. This gentleman and his nephew had been absent some days in search of a suitable place to establish themselves, in order to fulfil the object of their mission. They returned yesterday, and intend leaving us to-morrow with their suite for the station selected, which is upon the Wallammet river, about sixty miles south of the fort.[84]

In the evening we were gratified by the arrival of Captain Wyeth from below, who informed us that the brig from Boston, which was sent out by the company to which Wyeth

---

[83] I have given this notice of the suburbs of the fort, as I find it in my journal written at the time; I had reason, subsequently, to change my opinion with regard to the scrupulous cleanliness of the Canadians' Indian wives, and particularly after inspecting the internal economy of the dwellings. What at first struck me as neat and clean, by an involuntary comparison of it with the extreme filthiness to which I had been accustomed amongst the Indians, soon revealed itself in its proper light, and I can freely confess that my first estimate was too high.— TOWNSEND.

[84] Jason Lee had intended to settle among the Flatheads; but upon the advice of McLoughlin, reinforced by his own observations, the missionary decided to establish his first station in the fertile Willamette valley. He proceeded to the small settlement of French Canadian ex-servants of the company and built his house on the east side of the river, at Chemyway, in Marion County.— ED.

is attached, had entered the river, and was anchored about twenty miles below, at a spot called Warrior's point, near the western entrance of the Wallammet.[85]

Captain W. mentioned his intention to visit the Wallammet country, and seek out a convenient location for a fort which he wishes to establish without delay, and Mr. N. and myself accepted an invitation to accompany him in the morning. He has brought with him one of the brig's boats, and eight oarsmen, five of whom are Sandwich Islanders.

We have experienced for several days past, gloomy, lowering, and showery weather; indeed the sun has scarcely been seen for [173] a week past. This is said to indicate the near approach of the rainy season, which usually sets in about the middle of October, or even earlier. After this time, until December, there is very little clear weather, showers or heavy clouds almost constantly prevailing.

On the 29th, Captain Wyeth, Mr. N., and myself, embarked in the ship's boat for our exploring excursion. We had a good crew of fine robust sailors, and the copper-colored islanders,— or *Kanakas*, as they are called,— did their duty with great alacrity and good will.

At about five miles below the fort, we entered the upper mouth of the Wallammet. This river is here about half the width of the Columbia, a clear and beautiful stream, and navigable for large vessels to the distance of twenty-five miles. It is covered with numerous islands, the largest of which is that called *Wappatoo Island*, about twenty miles in length.[86] The vegetation on the main land is

---

[85] Warriors' Point is at the lower end of Wappato (or Sauvie) Island, the eastern boundary of the lower Willamette mouth. Probably it received its name from a party of Indians who in 1816 fired upon a trading party from Fort George and drove them back from the Willamette; see Alexander Ross, *Fur Hunters*, i, pp. 100, 101.— ED.

[86] This large island across the mouth of the Willamette valley was by Lewis and Clark named Image-Canoe, later Wappato Island. It is now known as Sauvie

good, the timber generally pine and post oak, and the river is margined in many places with a beautiful species of willow with large ob-lanceolate leaves like those of the peach, and white on their under surface. The timber on the islands is chiefly oak, no pine growing there. At about 10 o'clock we overtook three men whom Captain W. had sent ahead in a canoe and we all landed soon after on the beach and dined on a mess of salmon and peas which we had provided. We were under way again in the afternoon, and encamped at about sunset. We have as yet seen no suitable place for an establishment, and to-morrow we proceed to the falls of the river, about fifteen miles further. Almost all the land in the vicinity is excellent and well calculated for cultivation, and several spots which we have visited, would be admirably adapted to the captain's views, but that there is not a sufficient extent unincumbered, or which could be fitted for the purposes of tillage in a space of time short enough [174] to be serviceable; others are at some seasons inundated, which is an insurmountable objection.

We embarked early the next morning, and at 11 o'clock arrived at the falls, after encountering some difficulties from rapids, through which we had to warp our boat.[87] There are here three falls on a line of rocks extending across the river, which forms the bed of the upper channel. The water is precipitated through deep abrazed gorges,

for Jean Baptiste Sauvé, who was for many years a faithful servant of the Hudson's Bay Company, and maintained the dairy farm on this island.— ED.

[87] The falls of Willamette were not discovered by Lewis and Clark, who explored that river only to the site of Portland. Probably the first white men to visit them were a party led by Franchère and William Henry in 1814; see Franchère's *Narrative* in our volume vi, p. 313. McLoughlin staked out a claim around these falls in 1829, and made some improvements. Later (1840) his claims were contested, but in 1842 the land was laid off in lots and entitled Oregon City. The falls are now passed by locks, in order to facilitate navigation on the upper Willamette.— ED.

and falls perhaps forty feet at an angle of about twenty degrees. It was a beautiful sight when viewed from a distance, but it became grand and almost sublime as we approached it nearer. I mounted the rocks and stood over the highest fall, and although the roar of the cataract was almost deafening, and the rays of the bright sun reflected from the white and glittering foam threatened to deprive me of sight, yet I became so absorbed in the contemplation of the scene, and the reflections which were involuntarily excited, as to forget every thing else for the time, and was only aroused by Captain W. tapping me on the shoulder, and telling me that every thing was arranged for our return. While I visited the falls, the captain and his men had found what they sought for; and the object of our voyage being accomplished, we got on board immediately and shaped our course down the river with a fair wind, and the current in favor.

About two miles below the cataract is a small village of Klikatat Indians.[88] Their situation does not appear different from what we have been accustomed to see in the neighborhood of the fort. They live in the same sort of miserable loose hovels, and are the same wretched, squalid looking people. Although enjoying far more advantages, and having in a much greater degree the means of rendering themselves comfortable, yet their mode of living, their garments, their wigwams, and every thing connected with them, is not much better than the Snakes and [175] Bannecks, and very far inferior to that fine, noble-looking race, the Kayouse, whom we met on the *Grand ronde*.

---

[88] The Klikitat were a Shahaptian tribe, near kin to the Yakima. Their habitat was on both sides of the Cascade Range, north of the Columbia. Early in the nineteenth century they made a futile attempt to settle in the Willamette valley. They were probably the Wahhowpums of Lewis and Clark.— Ed.

A custom prevalent, and almost universal amongst these Indians, is that of flattening, or mashing in the whole front of the skull, from the superciliary ridge to the crown. The appearance produced by this unnatural operation is almost hideous, and one would suppose that the intellect would be materially affected by it. This, however, does not appear to be the case, as I have never seen, (with a single exception, the Kayouse,) a race of people who appeared more shrewd and intelligent. I had a conversation on this subject, a few days since, with a chief who speaks the English language. He said that he had exerted himself to abolish the practice in his own tribe, but although his people would listen patiently to his talk on most subjects, their ears were firmly closed when this was mentioned; " they would leave the council fire, one by one, until none but a few squaws and children were left to drink in the words of the chief." It is even considered among them a degradation to possess a round head, and one whose *caput* has happened to be neglected in his infancy, can never become even a subordinate chief in his tribe, and is treated with indifference and disdain, as one who is unworthy a place amongst them.

The flattening of the head is practiced by at least ten or twelve distinct tribes of the lower country, the Klikatats, Kalapooyahs, and Multnomahs, of the Wallammet, and its vicinity;[89] the Chinooks, Klatsaps, Klatstonis, Kowalitsks, Katlammets, Killemooks, and Chekalis of the lower Columbia and its tributaries, and probably by others both north and south.[90] The tribe called Flatheads, or *Salish*,

---

[89] For the Kalapuya and Multnomah tribes of the Willamette valley, consult Ross's *Oregon Settlers*, in our volume vii, p. 230, note 80, and Franchère's *Narrative* in our volume vi, p. 247, note 53, respectively.— ED.

[90] Consult Franchère's *Narrative*, notes 39, 40, 49, 65, 67, and Ross's *Oregon Settlers*, pp. 102, 103, note 13.— ED.

who reside near the sources of the Oregon, have long since abolished this custom.[91]

The mode by which the flattening is effected, varies considerably with the different tribes. The Wallammet Indians place the infant, soon after birth, upon a board, to the edges of which [176] are attached little loops of hempen cord or leather, and other similar cords are passed across and back, in a zig-zag manner, through these loops, enclosing the child, and binding it firmly down. To the upper edge of this board, in which is a depression to receive the back part of the head, another smaller one is attached by hinges of leather, and made to lie obliquely upon the forehead, the force of the pressure being regulated by several strings attached to its edge, which are passed through holes in the board upon which the infant is lying, and secured there.

The mode of the Chinooks, and others near the sea, differs widely from that of the upper Indians, and appears somewhat less barbarous and cruel. A sort of cradle is formed by excavating a pine log to the depth of eight or ten inches. The child is placed in it on a bed of little grass mats, and bound down in the manner above described. A little boss of tightly plaited and woven grass is then applied to the forehead, and secured by a cord to the loops at the side. The infant is thus suffered to remain from four to eight months, or until the sutures of the skull have in some measure united, and the bone become solid and firm. It is seldom or never taken from the cradle, ex-

---

[91] For the use of Flathead as a generic term, consult Franchère's *Narrative*, p. 340, note 145. Lewis and Clark noted that instances of the custom of flattening the forehead by pressure diminished in frequency from the coast east: among the tribes of eastern Oregon and Washington, only an occasional female appeared with flattened head, while among the coast tribes the custom was universal for both sexes.— ED.

cept in case of severe illness, until the flattening process is completed.[92]

I saw, to-day, a young child from whose head the board had just been removed. It was, without exception, the most frightful and disgusting looking object that I ever beheld. The whole front of the head was completely flattened, and the mass of brain being forced back, caused an enormous projection there. The poor little creature's eyes protruded to the distance of half an inch, and looked inflamed and discolored, as did all the surrounding parts. Although I felt a kind of chill creep over me from the contemplation of such dire deformity, yet there was something so stark-staring, and absolutely queer in the physiognomy, that I could not repress a smile; and when the mother amused the little object and made it laugh, it looked so irresistibly, [177] so *terribly* ludicrous, that I and those who were with me, burst into a simultaneous roar, which frightened it and made it cry, in which predicament it looked much less horrible than before.

On the 1st of November we arrived at the brig. She was moored, head and stern, to a large rock near the lower mouth of the Wallammet. Captain Lambert with his ship's company, and our own mountain men, were all actively engaged at various employments; carpenters, smiths, coopers, and other artisans were busy in their several vocations; domestic animals, pigs, sheep, goats, poultry, &c., were roaming about as if perfectly at home, and the whole scene looked so like the entrance to a country village, that it was difficult to fancy oneself in a howling wilderness inhabited only by the wild and improvident Indian, and his scarcely more free and fearless neighbors, the bear

---

[92] See illustration in *Original Journals of the Lewis and Clark Expedition*, iv, p. 10.— ED.

and the wolf.[93] An excellent temporary storehouse of twigs, thatched with grass, has been erected, in which has been deposited the extensive assortment of goods necessary for the settlement, as well as a number of smaller ones, in which the men reside. It is intended as soon as practicable, to build a large and permanent dwelling of logs, which will also include the store and trading establishment, and form the groundwork for an *American fort* on the river Columbia.

5th.— Mr. N. and myself are now residing on board the brig, and pursuing with considerable success our scientific researches through the neighborhood. I have shot and prepared here several new species of birds, and two or three undescribed quadrupeds, besides procuring a considerable number, which, though known to naturalists, are rare, and therefore valuable. My companion is of course in his element; the forest, the plain, the rocky hill, and the mossy bank yield him a rich and most abundant supply.

[178] We are visited daily by considerable numbers of Chinook and Klikatat Indians, many of whom bring us provisions of various kinds, salmon, deer, ducks, &c., and receive in return, powder and shot, knives, paint, and *Indian rum*, i. e. rum and water in the proportion of one part of the former to two of the latter. Some of these Indians would be handsome were it not for the abominable practice, which, as I have said, is almost universal amongst them, of destroying the form of the head. The features of many are regular, though often devoid of expression, and

---

[93] The brig was the "May Dacre;" Captain Lambert had been in command of Wyeth's earlier vessel, the "Sultana," which was wrecked on a South Pacific reef. He later made many voyages in command of various vessels, the last of which sailed from Hawaii to New Bedford, Massachusetts. He died at "Sailor's Snug Harbor" on Staten Island. See F. H. Victor, "Flotsom and Jetsom of the Pacific," in *Oregon Historical Society Quarterly*, ii, pp. 36–54.— ED.

the persons of the men generally are rather symmetrical; their stature is low, with light sinewy limbs, and remarkably small delicate hands. The women are usually more rotund, and, in some instances, even approach obesity. The principal clothing worn by them is a sort of short petticoat made of strands of pine bark or twisted hempen strings, tied around the loins like a marro. This article they call a *kalaquarté*; and is often their only dress; some, however, cover the shoulders with a blanket, or robe made of muskrat or hare skins sewed together.[94]

A disease of a very fatal character is prevalent among these Indians; many of them have died of it; even some of those in the neighborhood of the fort, where medical assistance was always at hand. The symptoms are a general coldness, soreness and stiffness of the limbs and body, with violent tertian ague. Its fatal termination is attributable to its tendency to attack the liver, which is generally affected in a few days after the first symptoms are developed. Several of the white people attached to the fort have been ill with it, but no deaths have occurred amongst them, the disease in their case having yielded to the simple tonic remedies usually employed at home. This I have no doubt would be equally the case with the Indians, were they [179] willing to submit to proper restrictions during the time of administering medicine.

Captain Lambert informs me that on his first landing here the Indians studiously avoided his vessel, and all kind of intercourse with his crew, from the supposition, (which they have since acknowledged) that the malady which they dread so much was thus conveyed. As in a short time it became desirable, on account of procuring supplies of provision, to remove this impression, some

---

[94] See *Original Journals of the Lewis and Clark Expedition*, iii, pp. 239–242.— ED.

pains were taken to convince the Indians of their error, and they soon visited the ship without fear.

Mr. N. and myself have been anxious to escape the wet and disagreeable winter of this region, and visit some other portion of the country, where the inclemency of the season will not interfere with the prosecution of our respective pursuits. After some reflection and consultation, we concluded to take passage in the brig, which will sail in a few weeks for the Sandwich Islands. We shall remain there about three months, and return to the river in time to commence our peregrinations in the spring.

23d.— At Fort Vancouver. A letter was received yesterday by Dr. McLoughlin, from Captain Wyeth, dated Walla-walla, stating that the twelve Sandwich Islanders whom he took with him a week since for a journey to Fort Hall, had deserted, each taking a horse. They had no doubt heard from some of their countrymen, whom they met at the fort, of the difficulties of the route before them, which were probably very much exaggerated. Captain W. is on the alert to find them, and is sending men on their trail in every direction, but it is more than probable that they will not be overtaken, and the consequence will then be, that the expedition must be abandoned, and the captain return to the fort to spend the winter.

December 3d.— Yesterday Mr. N. and myself went down the river to the brig, and this morning early the vessel left her [180] moorings, and with her sails unloosed stood out into the channel way. The weather was overcast, and we had but little wind, so that our progress during the morning was necessarily slow. In the afternoon we ran aground in one and a half fathoms water, but as the tide was low, we were enabled to get her clear in the evening. The navigation of this river is particularly difficult in consequence of numerous shoals and sand bars, and good

pilots are scarce, the Indians alone officiating in that capacity. Towards noon the next day, a Kowalitsk Indian
with but one eye, who said his name was *George*, boarded
us, and showed a letter which he carried, written by Captain McNeall, in the Hudson's Bay service, recommending
said George as a capable and experienced pilot. We
accepted his services gladly, and made a bargain with him
to take us into Baker's bay near the cape, for four bottles
of rum; with the understanding, however, that every time
the brig ran aground, one bottle of the precious liquor
was to be forfeited.[95] George agreed to the terms, and
taking his station at the bow, gave his orders to the man
at the wheel like one having authority, pointing with his
finger when he wished a deviation from the common course,
and pronouncing in a loud voice the single word *ookook*,
(here.)

On the afternoon of the 4th, we passed along a bold
precipitous shore, near which we observed a large isolated
rock, and on it a great number of canoes, deposited above
the reach of the tides. This spot is called *Mount Coffin*,
and the canoes contain the dead bodies of Indians. They
are carefully wrapped in blankets, and all the personal
property of the deceased, bows and arrows, guns, salmon
spears, ornaments, &c., are placed within, and around
his canoe. The vicinity of this, and all other cemeteries,
is held so sacred by the Indians, that they never approach
it, except to make similar deposits; they will often even
travel a considerable distance out of their course, in order
to avoid intruding upon the sanctuary of their dead.[96]

[181] We came to anchor near this rock in the evening,
and Captain Lambert, Mr. N., and myself visited the tombs.

[95] For Baker's Bay, and the origin of its name, see Franchère's *Narrative*, our
volume vi, p. 234, note 38.— ED.

[96] For Mount Coffin see both Franchère and Ross, volume vi, p. 244, and
volume vii, pp. 117, 118, respectively.— ED.

We were especially careful not to touch or disarrange any of the fabrics, and it was well we were so, for as we turned to leave the place, we found that we had been narrowly watched by about twenty Indians, whom we had not seen when we landed from our boat. After we embarked, we observed an old withered crone with a long stick or wand in her hand, who approached, and walked over the ground which we had defiled with our sacrilegious tread, waving her enchanted rod over the mouldering bones, as if to purify the atmosphere around, and exorcise the evil spirits which we had called up.

I have been very anxious to procure the skulls of some of these Indians, and should have been willing, so far as I alone was concerned, to encounter some risk to effect my object, but I have refrained on account of the difficulty in which the ship and crew would be involved, if the sacrilege should be discovered; a prejudice might thus be excited against our little colony which would not soon be overcome, and might prove a serious injury.

6th.— The weather is almost constantly rainy and squally, making it unpleasant to be on deck; we are therefore confined closely to the cabin, and are anxious to get out to sea as soon as possible, if only to escape this.

In the afternoon, the captain and myself went ashore in the long-boat, and visited several Indian houses upon the beach. These are built of roughly hewn boards and logs, usually covered with pine bark, or matting of their own manufacture, and open at the top, to allow the smoke to escape. In one of these houses we found men, women, and children, to the number of fifty-two, seated as usual, upon the ground, around numerous fires, the smoke from which filled every cranny of the building, and to us was almost stifling, although the Indians did not appear to suffer [182] any inconvenience from it. Although living in a state of the most abject poverty, deprived of most of the absolute necessaries of life, and frequently enduring the pangs of protracted starvation, yet these poor people appear happy and contented. They are scarcely qualified to enjoy the common comforts of life, even if their indolence did not prevent the attempt to procure them.

On the afternoon of the 8th, we anchored off *Fort George*, as it is called, although perhaps it scarcely deserves the name of a fort, being composed of but one principal house of hewn boards, and a number of small Indian huts surrounding it, presenting the appearance, from a distance, of an ordinary small farm house with its appropriate outbuildings. There is but one white man residing here, the superintendent of the fort; but there is probably no necessity for more, as the business done is not very considerable, most of the furs being taken by the Indians to Vancouver. The establishment is, however, of importance, independent of its utility as a trading post, as it is situated within view of the dangerous cape, and intelligence of the arrival of vessels can be communicated to the authorities at Vancouver in time for them to render adequate assistance to such vessels by supplying them with pilots, &c. This is the spot where once stood the fort established by the direction of our honored countryman, John Jacob Astor. One of the chimneys of old Fort Astoria is still standing, a melancholy monument of American enterprise and domestic misrule. The spot where once the fine parterre overlooked the river, and the bold stoccade enclosed the neat and substantial fort, is now overgrown with weeds and bushes, and can scarce be distinguished from the primeval forest which surrounds it on every side.[97]

---

[97] Compare Franchère's *Narrative*, in our volume vi, p. 241, note 42, and Ross's *Oregon Settlers*, our volume vii, pp. 243–247, 250. The fort had been abandoned in 1824, but later was restored as a post of observation.— ED.

Captain Lambert, Mr. N. and myself visited the Indian houses in the neighborhood. In one of them we saw a poor little boy about three years of age who had been blind from his birth. He [183] was sitting on the ground near the fire, surrounded by a quantity of fish bones which he had been picking. Our sympathy was very much excited for the poor little unfortunate, particularly as he was made a subject for the taunting jibes and laughter of a number of men and women, squatting around, and his mother sat by with the most cruel apathy and unconcern, and only smiled at the commiseration which we expressed for her innocent and peculiarly unhappy offspring. It seems difficult to believe that those who possess the form and countenance of human creatures, should so debase the natural good feelings which God has implanted in them: but these ignorant and gross wretches seemed to take credit to themselves in rendering this afflicted being unhappy, and smiled and looked at each other when we endeavored to infuse a little pity into them. The child had evidently been very much neglected, and almost starved, and the little articles which we presented it, (in the hope, that the Indians on seeing us manifest an interest in it, would treat it more tenderly,) it put to its mouth eagerly, but finding them not eatable, threw them aside in disgust. Oh! how I wished at that moment for a morsel of bread to give this little famished and neglected creature. We soon left the place, and returned to the brig, but I could think of nothing during the remainder of the evening but the little blind child, and at night I dreamed I saw it, and it raised its dim and sightless orbs, and stretched out its little emaciated arms towards me, as if begging for a crumb to prevent its starving.

These people, as I have already said, do not appear to possess a particle of natural good feeling, and in their moral character, they are little better than brutes. In the case of the blind boy, they seemed to take pride in tormenting it, and rendering it miserable, and vied with each other in the skill and dexterity with which they applied to it the most degrading and insulting epithets. These circumstances, with others, in regard to their [184] moral character, which I shall not even mention, have tended very considerably to lower the estimation in which I have always held the red man of the forest, and serve to strengthen the opinion which I had long since formed, that nothing but the introduction of civilization, with its good and wholesome laws, can ever render the Indian of service to himself, or raise him from the state of wretchedness which has so long characterized his expiring race.

The next morning, we ran down into Baker's bay, and anchored within gunshot of the cape, when Captain Lambert and myself went on shore in the boat, to examine the channel, and decide upon the prospect of getting out to sea. This passage is a very dangerous one, and is with reason dreaded by mariners. A wide bar of sand extends from Cape Disappointment to the opposite shore,— called Point Adams,— and with the exception of a space, comprehending about half a mile, the sea at all times breaks furiously, the surges dashing to the height of the mast head of a ship, and with the most terrific roaring.[98] Sometimes the water in the channel is agitated equally with that which covers the whole length of the bar, and it is then a matter of imminent risk to attempt a passage. Vessels have occasionally been compelled to lie in under the cape for several weeks, in momentary expectation of the subsidence of the dangerous breakers, and they have not unfrequently been required to stand off shore, from without,

---

[98] For Cape Disappointment, and Point Adams, consult Franchère's *Narrative*, in our volume vi, p. 233, notes 36, 37.— ED.

until the crews have suffered extremely for food and water. This circumstance must ever form a barrier to a permanent settlement here; the sands, which compose the bar, are constantly shifting, and changing the course and depth of the channel, so that none but the small coasting vessels in the service of the company can, with much safety, pass back and forth.

Mr. N. and myself visited the sea beach, outside the cape, in the hope of finding peculiar marine shells, but although we [185] searched assiduously during the morning, we had but little success. We saw several deer in the thick forest on the side of the cape, and a great number of black shags, or cormorants, flying over the breakers, and resting upon the surf-washed rocks.

On the morning of the 11th, Mr. Hanson, the mate, returned from the shore, and reported that the channel was smooth; it was therefore deemed safe to attempt the passage immediately. While we were weighing our anchor, we descried a brig steering towards us, which soon crossed the bar, and ran up to within speaking distance. It was one of the Hudson's Bay Company's coasters, and, as we were getting under way, a boat put off from her, and we were boarded by Mr. Ogden, a chief factor from one of the Company's forts on the coast.[99] He informed us that the brig left Naas about the first of October, but had been delayed by contrary winds, and rough, boisterous

---

[99] Peter Skeen Ogden was the son of Isaac, chief justice of the Province of Quebec — originally a loyalist from New York. Early entering the fur-trade, young Ogden was sent out to Astoria, arriving after its transference to the British. He thereupon entered the North West Company, and spent his life in the Oregon country. A successful trapper and trader, he led for many years parties into the interior, where he explored the Yellowstone and Lewis River countries, and Utah, giving his name to Ogden's Hole and the Utah city therein. In 1825 he had a disastrous encounter with Ashley, and from that time onward competition with American traders was keen. He followed Jedidiah S. Smith west to California, trapping on the upper Sacramento and discovering Ogden River — which Fré-

weather.[100]   Thus the voyage which usually requires but
about eight days for its performance, occupied upwards
of *two months*.   They had been on an allowance of a pint
of water per day, and had suffered considerably for fresh
provision.   Mr. Ogden remained with us but a short time,
and we stood out past the cape.

When we entered the channel, the water which had
before been so smooth, became suddenly very much agitated, swelling, and roaring, and foaming around us, as
if the surges were upheaved from the very bottom, and
as [if] our vessel would fall in the trough of the sea, pitching
down like a huge leviathan seeking its native depths, I
could not but feel positive, that the enormous wave, which
hung like a judgment over our heads, would inevitably
engulph us; but the good ship, like a creature instinct
with life, as though she knew her danger, gallantly rose
upon it, and but dipped her bows into its crest, as if in scorn
of its mighty and irresistible power.   This is my first sea
voyage, and every thing upon the great deep is of course
novel and interesting to me.   During the scene which I
have just described, although I was [186] aware of our
imminent peril, and the tales that I had frequently heard
of vessels perishing in this very spot, and in precisely such
a sea, recurred to my mind with some force, yet I could
not but feel a kind of secret and wild joy at finding myself
in a situation of such awful and magnificent grandeur.
I thought of the lines of Shelley, and repeated them to
myself in a kind of ecstasy.

---

mont renamed Humboldt.   In 1835 Ogden was appointed chief factor of New Caledonia, and made his headquarters at Fort St. James, on Stuart Lake.   Ogden
married Julia, daughter of a Flathead chief, and her intrepidity and understanding of Indian nature aided her husband's undertakings.   He died at Oregon City
in 1854, aged about sixty years.— ED.

[100] Nass Bay and Harbor, in upper British Columbia, near the Alaska boundary.— ED.

" And see'st thou, and hear'st thou,
And fear'st thou, and fear'st thou,
And ride we not free
O'er the terrible sea,
    I and thou ? "

In about twenty minutes we had escaped all the danger, and found ourselves riding easily in a beautiful placid sea. We set the sails, which had been shortened on the bar, and the gallant vessel feeling the impulse of the wind, rushed ahead as if exulting in the victory she had achieved.

.   .   .   .

CHAPTER XII

. . . Arrival at the Columbia.

[217] On the 15th,[101] the wind, which had for several days been light, began steadily to increase, until we were running ten knots by the log. In the afternoon, the atmosphere became thick and hazy, indicating our approach to the shores of the continent. In a short time, a number of the small Auks,— of which we saw a few immediately after leaving the Columbia,— were observed sporting in the waves, close under our bows; then several gulls of the species common on the river, and soon after large flocks of geese and canvass-back ducks.

The sea gradually lost its legitimate deep blue color, and assumed a dirty, green appearance, indicating soundings. Upon heaving the lead here, we got only eleven fathoms, and found that we had approached nearer than was prudent, having been misled by the haze. Wore ship immediately, and soon saw land, bearing east, which we ascertained to be south of Cape Disappointment. Stood off during the night, and the next morning at 4 o'clock, the wind favoring us, we bore up for the cape, and at 7 crossed the dangerous bar safely, and ran direct for the river.

---

[101] This date is April 15, 1835. The interval between this and December 11, 1834 (the part omitted) was spent in a visit to the Hawaiian Islands. Townsend returned on Wyeth's vessel, the "May Dacre."— ED.

[218] CHAPTER XIII

Passage up the Columbia — Birds — A trip to the Wallammet — Methodist missionaries — their prospects — Fort William — Band-tail pigeons — Wretched condition of the Indians at the falls — A Kallapooyah village — Indian cemetery — Superstitions — Treatment of diseases — Method of steaming — "Making medicine" — Indian sorcerers — An interruption of festivities — Death of Thornburg — An inquest — Verdict of the jury — Inordinate appetite for ardent spirits — Misfortunes of the American Company — Eight men drowned — Murder of two trappers by the Banneck Indians — Arrival of Captain Thing — His meeting and skirmish with the Blackfeet Indians — Massacre — A narrow escape.

On the 16th, we anchored abreast of Oak point.[102] Our decks were almost immediately crowded with Indians to welcome us, and among them we recognised many faces with which we were familiar. *Chinamus*, the Chinook chief, was the principal of these, who, with his wife, *Aillapust*, or *Sally*, as she is called at the fort, paid us an early visit, and brought us red deer and sturgeon to regale upon after our voyage.

On the afternoon of the next day, we ran up to Warrior's point, the brig's old mooring ground. The people here had been anxious to see us; extensive preparations had been made to prosecute the salmon fishery, and the coopers have been engaged the whole winter in making barrels to accommodate them. Mr. Walker, the missionaries' quondam associate, was in charge of the post, and he informed us that Captain Wyeth had returned only a few weeks since from the upper country, where he had been spending the winter, engaged in the arduous business of [219] trap-

---

[102] For a brief account of Oak Point, see Franchère's *Narrative* in our volume vi, p. 261, note 74.— Ed.

ping, in the prosecution of which he had endured great and various hardships.[103]

May 12th.— The rainy season is not yet over; we have had almost constant showers since we arrived, but now the weather appears settled. Birds are numerous, particularly the warblers, (*Sylvia*.) Many of these are migratory, remaining but a few weeks: others breed here, and reside during the greater part of the summer. I have already procured several new species.

20th.— Mr. Wyeth, came down from Walla-walla yesterday, and this morning I embarked with him in a large canoe, manned by Kanakas, for a trip to the Wallammet falls in order to procure salmon. We visited fort William, (Wyeth's new settlement upon Wappatoo island,) which is about fifteen miles from the lower mouth of the Wallammet.[104] We found here the missionaries, Messrs. Lee and Edwards, who arrived to-day from their station, sixty miles above. They give flattering accounts of their prospects here; they are surrounded by a considerable number of Indians who are friendly to the introduction of civilization and religious light, and who treat them with the greatest hospitality and kindness. They have built several comfortable log houses, and the soil in their vicinity they represent as unusually rich and productive. They have, I think, a good prospect of being serviceable to this miserable and degraded people; and if they commence their operations judiciously, and pursue a steady, unwavering

[103] Captain Wyeth returned to Fort Vancouver February 12, 1835. The journal of his hardships during this trapping expedition is in his *Oregon Expeditions*, pp. 234–250.— ED.

[104] According to Wyeth's statements, Fort William was eight miles from Vancouver, on the southwest side of the island. Built in the spring of 1835, it was upon Wyeth's return to the United States (1836) left in charge of C. M. Walker, who came out with Jason Lee. Walker was given instructions to lease the place, but no tenant offering, it was soon abandoned, and the Hudson's Bay Company established a dairy farm near the site.— ED.

course, the Indians in this section of country may yet be redeemed from the thraldom of vice, superstition, and indolence, to which they have so long submitted, and above which their energies have not enabled them to rise.

The spot chosen by Captain W. for his fort is on a high piece of land, which will probably not be overflown by the periodical freshets, and the soil is the rich black loam so plentifully distributed through this section of country. The men now live in tents and temporary huts, but several log houses are constructing [220] which, when finished, will vie in durability and comfort with Vancouver itself.

21st.— The large band-tail pigeon (*Colomba fasciata*) is very abundant near the river, found in flocks of from fifty to sixty, and perching upon the dead trees along the margin of the stream. They are feeding upon the buds of the balsam poplar; are very fat, and excellent eating. In the course of the morning, and without leaving the canoe, I killed enough to supply our people with provision for two days.

24th.— We visited the falls to-day, and while Captain W. was inspecting the vicinity to decide upon the practicability of drawing his seine here, I strolled into the Indian lodges on the bank of the river. The poor creatures were all living miserably, and some appeared to be suffering absolute want. Those who were the best supplied, had nothing more than the fragments of a few sturgeons and lamprey eels, kamas bread, &c. To the roofs of the lodges were hung a number of crooked bladders, filled with rancid seal oil, used as a sort of condiment with the dry and unsavory sturgeon.

On the Klakamas river,[105] about a mile below, we found

---

[105] Clackamas River rises in the Cascade Range, between Mounts Hood and Jefferson, and flows northwest through a county of the same name into the Willamette, at the present Oregon City.— ED.

a few lodges belonging to Indians of the Kalapooyah tribe. We addressed them in Chinook, (the language spoken by all those inhabiting the Columbia below the cascades,)[106] but they evidently did not comprehend a word, answering in a peculiarly harsh and gutteral language, with which we were entirely unacquainted. However, we easily made them understand by signs that we wanted salmon, and being assured in the same significant manner that they had none to sell, we decamped as soon as possible, to escape the fleas and other vermin with which the interior of their wretched habitations were plentifully supplied. We saw here a large Indian cemetery. The bodies had been buried under the ground, and each tomb had a board at its head, upon which was rudely painted some strange, uncouth figure. The [221] pans, kettles, clothing, &c., of the deceased, were all suspended upon sticks, driven into the ground near the head board.

June 6th.— The Indians frequently bring us salmon, and we observe that, invariably, before they part with them, they are careful to remove the hearts. This superstition, is religiously adhered to by all the Chinook tribe. Before the fish is split and prepared for eating, a small hole is made in the breast, the heart taken out, roasted, and eate in silence, and with great gravity. This practice is continued only during the first month in which the salmon make their appearance, and is intended as a kind of propitiation to the particular deity or spirit who presides over the finny tribes. Superstition in all its absurd and most revolting aspects is rife among this people. They believe in " black spirits, and white, blue spirits, and grey," and to each grizzly monster some peculiar virtue or ghastly

---

[106] On the Chinook jargon — the medium of communication between the whites and Indians of the Northwest coast — see Franchère's *Narrative* in our volume vi, p. 240, note 40.— ED.

terror is attributed. When a chief goes on a hunting or fishing excursion, he puts himself under the care of one of these good spirits, and if his expedition is unsuccessful, he affirms that the antagonist evil principle has gained the victory; but this belief does not prevent his making another, and another attempt, in the hope, each time, that his guardian genius will have the ascendency.

In their treatment of diseases, they employ but few remedies, and these are generally simple and inefficacious. Wounds are treated with an application of green leaves, and bound with strips of pine bark, and in some febrile cases, a sweat is administered. This is effected by digging a hole two or three feet deep in the ground, and placing within it some hemlock or spruce boughs moistened with water; hot stones are then thrown in, and a frame work of twigs is erected over the opening, and covered closely with blankets to prevent the escape of the steam. Under this contrivance, the patient is placed; and after remaining [222] fifteen or twenty minutes, he is removed, and plunged into cold water.

Their mode of " *making medicine,*" to use their own term, is, however, very different from this. The sick man is laid upon a bed of mats and blankets, elevated from the ground, and surrounded by a raised frame work of hewn boards. Upon this frame two " medicine men " (sorcerers) place themselves, and commence chaunting, in a low voice, a kind of long drawn, sighing song. Each holds a stout stick, of about four feet long, in his hand, with which he beats upon the frame work, and keeps accurate time with the music. After a few minutes, the song begins to increase in loudness and quickness, (a corresponding force and celerity being given to the stick,) until in a short time the noise becomes almost deafening, and may well serve, in many instances, to accelerate the exit of him whom it is their intention to benefit.

During the administration of the medicine, the relations and friends of the patient are often employed in their usual avocations in the same house with him, and by his bedside; the women making mats, moccasins, baskets, &c., and the men lolling around, smoking or conversing upon general subjects. No appearance of sorrow or concern is manifested for the brother, husband, or father, expiring beside them, and but for the presence and ear-astounding din of the medicine men, you would not know that anything unusual had occurred to disturb the tranquillity of the family circle.

These medicine men are, of course, all impostors, their object being simply the acquisition of property; and in case of the recovery of the patient, they make the most exorbitant demands of his relations; but when the sick man dies, they are often compelled to fly, in order to escape the vengeance of the survivors, who generally attribute the fatal termination to the evil influence of the practitioner.

[223] *July 4th.*— This morning was ushered in by the firing of cannon on board our brig, and we had made preparations for spending the day in festivity, when, at about 9 o'clock, a letter was received from Mr. Walker, who has charge of the fort on Wappatoo island, stating that the tailor, Thornburg, had been killed this morning by Hubbard, the gunsmith, and requesting our presence immediately, to investigate the case, and direct him how to act.

Our boat was manned without loss of time, and Captain L. and myself repaired to the fort, where we found every thing in confusion. Poor Thornburg, whom I had seen but two days previously, full of health and vigor, was now a lifeless corpse; and Hubbard, who was more to be pitied, was walking up and down the beach, with a countenance pale and haggard, from the feelings at war within.

We held an inquest over the body, and examined all
the men of the fort severally, for the purpose of eliciting
the facts of the case, and, if warranted by the evidence,
to exculpate Hubbard from blame in the commission of
the act. It appeared that, several weeks since, a dispute
arose between Hubbard and Thornburg, and the latter
menaced the life of the former, and had since been frequently heard to declare that he would carry the threat
into effect on the first favorable opportunity. This morning, before daylight, he entered the apartment of Hubbard,
armed with a loaded gun, and a large knife, and after
making the most deliberate preparations for an instant departure from the room, as soon as the deed should be committed, cocked his gun, and prepared to shoot at his
victim. Hubbard, who was awakened by the noise of
Thornburg's entrance, and was therefore on the alert,
waited quietly until this crisis, when cocking his pistol,
without noise, he took deliberate aim at the assassin, and
fired. Thornburg staggered back, his gun fell from his
grasp, and the two combatants struggled hand to hand.
The tailor, being wounded, [224] was easily overcome,
and was thrown violently out of the house, when he fell
to the ground, and died in a few minutes. Upon examining the body, we found that the two balls from the pistol
had entered the arm below the shoulder, and escaping
the bone, had passed into the cavity of the chest. The
verdict of the jury was " justifiable homicide," and a properly attested certificate, containing a full account of the
proceedings, was given to Hubbard, as well for his satisfaction, as to prevent future difficulty, if the subject should
ever be investigated by a judicial tribunal.

This Thornburg was an unusually bold and determined
man, fruitful in inventing mischief, as he was reckless and
daring in its prosecution. His appetite for ardent spirits

was of the most inordinate kind. During the journey across the country, I constantly carried a large two-gallon bottle of whiskey, in which I deposited various kinds of lizards and serpents and when we arrived at the Columbia the vessel was almost full of these crawling creatures. I left the bottle on board the brig when I paid my first visit to the Wallammet falls, and on my return found that Thornburg had decanted the liquor from the precious reptiles which I had destined for immortality, and he and one of his pot companions had been "happy" upon it for a whole day. This appeared to me almost as bad as the "tapping of the Admiral," practised with such success by the British seamen; but unlike their commander, I did not discover the theft until too late to save my specimens, which were in consequence all destroyed.

11*th.*— Mr. Nuttall, who has just returned from the dalles, where he has been spending some weeks, brings distressing intelligence from above. It really seems that the "Columbia River Fishing and Trading Company" is devoted to destruction; disasters meet them at every turn, and as yet none of their schemes have prospered. This has not been for want of energy or exertion. Captain W. has pursued the plans which seemed [225] to him best adapted for insuring success, with the most indefatigable perseverance and industry, and has endured hardships without murmuring, which would have prostrated many a more robust man; nevertheless, he has not succeeded in making the business of fishing and trapping productive, and as we cannot divine the cause, we must attribute it to the Providence that rules the destinies of men and controls all human enterprises.

Two evenings since, eight Sandwich Islanders, a white man and an Indian woman, left the cascades in a large canoe laden with salmon, for the brig. The river was as usual rough and tempestuous, the wind blew a heavy gale, the canoe was capsized, and eight out of the ten sank to rise no more. The two who escaped, islanders, have taken refuge among the Indians at the village below, and will probably join us in a few days.

Intelligence has also been received of the murder of one of Wyeth's principal trappers, named Abbot, and another white man who accompanied him, by the Banneck Indians. The two men were on their way to the Columbia with a large load of beaver, and had stopped at the lodge of the Banneck chief, by whom they had been hospitably entertained. After they left, the chief, with several of his young men, concealed themselves in a thicket, near which the unsuspicious trappers passed, and shot and scalped them both.

These Indians have been heretofore harmless, and have always appeared to wish to cultivate the friendship of the white people. The only reason that can be conceived for this change in their sentiments, is that some of their number may lately have received injury from the white traders, and, with true Indian animosity, they determined to wreak their vengeance upon the whole race. Thus it is always unsafe to travel among Indians, as no one [226] knows at what moment a tribe which has always been friendly, may receive ill treatment from thoughtless, or evil-designing men, and the innocent suffer for the deeds of the guilty.

August 19th.— This morning, Captain Thing (Wyeth's partner) arrived from the interior. Poor man! he looks very much worn by fatigue and hardships, and seven years older than when I last saw him. He passed through the Snake country from Fort Hall, without knowing of the hostile disposition of the Bannecks, but, luckily for him, only met small parties of them, who feared to attack his camp. He remarked symptoms of distrust and coolness in their manner, for which he was, at the time, unable to account. As I have yet been only an hour in his company, and as a large portion of this time was consumed in his business affairs, I have not been able to obtain a very particular account of his meeting and skirmish with the Blackfeet last spring, a rumor of which we heard several weeks since. From what I have been enabled to gather, amid the hurry and bustle consequent upon his arrival, the circumstances appear to be briefly these. He had made a camp on Salmon river, and, as usual, piled up his goods in front of it, and put his horses in a pen erected temporarily for the purpose, when, at about daybreak, one of his sentries heard a gun discharged near. He went immediately to Captain T.'s tent to inform him of it, and at that instant a yell sounded from an adjacent thicket, and about five hundred Indians,— three hundred horse and two hundred foot,— rushed out into the open space in front. The mounted savages were dashing to and fro across the line of the camp, discharging their pieces with frightful rapidity, while those who had not horses, crawled around to take them in the rear.

Nothwithstanding the galling fire which the Indians were constantly pouring into them, Captain T. succeeded in driving his horses into the thicket behind, and securing them there, placing over them a guard of three men as a check to the savages who [227] were approaching from that quarter. He then threw himself with the remainder of his little band, behind the bales of goods, and returned the fire of the enemy. He states that occasionally he was gratified by the sight of an Indian tumbling from his horse, and at such times a dismal, savage yell was uttered by the rest, who then always fell back a little, but returned immediately to the charge with more than their former fury.

At length the Indians, apparently wearied by their unsuccessful attempts to dislodge the white men, changed their mode of attack, and rode upon the slight fortification, rapidly and steadily. Although they lost a man or two by this (for them) unusually bold proceeding, yet they succeeded in driving the brave little band of whites to the cover of the bushes. They then took possession of the goods, &c., which had been used as a defence, and retired to a considerable distance, where they were soon joined by their comrades on foot, who had utterly failed in their attempt to obtain the horses. In a short time, a man was seen advancing from the main body of Indians towards the scene of combat, holding up his hand as a sign of amity, and an intimation of the suspension of hostilities, and requested a " talk " with the white people. Captain T., with difficulty repressing his inclination to shoot the savage herald down, was induced, in consideration of the safety of his party, to dispatch an interpreter towards him. The only information that the Blackfeet wished to communicate was, that having obtained all the goods of the white people, they were now willing that they should continue their journey in peace, and that they should not again be molested. The Indians then departed, and the white men struck back on their trail, towards Fort Hall. Captain Thing lost every thing he had with him, all his clothing, papers, journals, &c. But he should probably be thankful that he escaped with his life, for [228] it is known to be very unusual for these hostile Indians to spare the lives of white men, when in their power, the acquisition of property being generally with them only a secondary consideration.

Captain T. had two men severely, but not mortally, wounded. The Indians had seven killed, and a considerable number wounded.

20th.— Several days since a poor man came here in a most deplorable condition, having been gashed, stabbed, and bruised in a manner truly frightful. He had been travelling on foot constantly for fifteen days, exposed to the broiling sun, with nothing to eat during the whole of this time, except the very few roots which he had been able to find. He was immediately put in the hospital here, and furnished with every thing necessary for his comfort, as well as surgical attendance. He states that he left Monterey, in California, in the spring, in company with seven men, for the purpose of coming to the Wallammet to join Mr. Young, an American, who is now settled in that country.[107] They met with no accident until they arrived at a village of *Potámeos* Indians,[108] about ten days journey south of this. Not knowing the character of these Indians, they were not on their guard, allowing them to enter their camp, and finally to obtain possession of their weapons.[109] The Indians then fell upon the defenceless little band with their tomahawks and knives, (having no fire arms themselves, and not knowing the use of those they had taken,) and, ere the white men had recovered from the panic which the sudden and unexpected attack occasioned, killed four

[107] This was a party arranged by John Turner, who had previously visited Oregon with Jedidiah S. Smith. For Ewing Young, see our volume xx, p.23, note 2. The wounded man was Dr. William J. Bailey, an Englishman who, after being educated for a physician, enlisted as a sailor, and after much roving had been a year or two in California. On recovering from his wounds, he settled in Willamette valley, married Margaret Smith, a mission teacher, and had a large farm and an important practice. Bailey became a man of note in early Oregon history, was a member of the executive committee of the provisional government in 1844, and died at Champoeg in 1876.— ED.

[108] Called by the inhabitants of this country, the "*rascally Indians*," from their uniformly evil disposition, and hostility to white people.— TOWNSEND.

[109] The Loloten or Tototen tribe of Klamath Indians. From their hostile and thievish disposition, their habitat was styled Rogue River, and they are usually spoken of as Rogue River Indians. The river is in southwestern Oregon, and the tribe related to those of northern California. Trouble arose between this tribe and the miners, lasting from 1850 to 1854, in which several battles were fought. There were in 1903 but fifty-two survivors, on Grande Ronde Reservation, in western Oregon.— ED.

of them. The remaining four fought with their knives as
long as they were able, but were finally overpowered, and
this poor fellow left upon the ground, covered with wounds,
and in a state [229] of insensibility. How long he remained
in this situation, he has no means of ascertaining; but
upon recovering, the place was vacated by all the actors
in the bloody scene, except his three dead companions,
who were lying stark and stiff where they fell. By considerable exertion, he was enabled to drag himself into
a thicket near, for the purpose of concealment, as he rightly
conjectured that their captors would soon return to secure
the trophies of their treacherous victory, and bury the
corpses. This happened almost immediately after; the
scalps were torn from the heads of the slain, and the mangled bodies removed for interment. After the most dread-
ful and excruciating sufferings, as we can well believe,
the poor man arrived here, and is doing well under the
excellent and skilful care of Doctor Gairdner.[110] I examined most of his wounds yesterday. He is literally
covered with them, but one upon the lower part of his
face is the most frightful. It was made by a single blow
of a tomahawk, the point of which entered the upper lip,
just below the nose, cutting entirely through both the upper
and lower jaws and chin, and passing deep into the side
of the neck, narrowly missing the large jugular vein. He
says he perfectly recollects receiving this wound. It was
inflicted by a powerful savage, who at the same time
tripped him with his foot, accelerating his fall. He also
remembers distinctly feeling the Indian's long knife pass

---

[110] Dr. Gairdner was a young English physician and scientist who had studied
with Ehrenberg, in Germany, and Sir William Hooker, in Scotland. Under the
patronage of the latter he had come as physician to Fort Vancouver. He died
in Hawaii, whither he had gone for his health. His name is perpetuated in that
of one of the Columbia salmon.— ED.

five separate times into his body; of what occurred after this he knows nothing. This is certainly by far the most horrible looking wound I ever saw, rendered so, however, by injudicious treatment and entire want of care in the proper apposition of the sundered parts; he simply bound it up as well as he could with his handkerchief, and his extreme anguish caused him to forget the necessity of accuracy in this respect. The consequence is, that the lower part of his face is dreadfully contorted, one side being considerably lower than the other. A union by the [230] first intention has been formed, and the ill-arranged parts are uniting.

This case has produced considerable excitement in our little circle. The Potámeos have more than once been guilty of acts of this kind, and some of the gentlemen of the fort have proposed fitting out an expedition to destroy the whole nation, but this scheme will probably not be carried into effect.

[231] CHAPTER XIV

THE Indians of the Columbia were once a numerous and powerful people; the shore of the river, for scores of miles, was lined with their villages; the council fire was frequently lighted, the pipe passed round, and the destinies of the nation deliberated upon. War was declared against neighboring tribes; the deadly tomahawk was lifted, and not buried until it was red with the blood of the savage; the bounding deer was hunted, killed, and his antlers ornamented the wigwam of the red man; the scalps of his enemies hung drying in the smoke of his lodge, and the Indian was happy. Now, alas! where is he? — gone; — gathered to his fathers and to his happy hunting grounds; his place knows him no more. The spot where once stood the thickly peopled village, the smoke curling and wreathing above the closely packed lodges, the lively children playing in the front, and their indolent [232] parents lounging on their mats, is now only indicated by a heap of undistinguishable ruins. The depopulation here has been truly fearful. A gentleman told me, that only four years ago, as he wandered near what had formerly been a thickly peopled village, he counted no less than sixteen dead, men and women, lying unburied and festering in the sun in front of their habitations. Within the houses all were sick; not one had escaped the contagion; upwards of a hundred individuals, men, women, and children, were writhing in agony on the floors of the houses, with no one to render them any assistance. Some were in the dying struggle, and clenching with the convulsive grasp of death their disease-worn companions, shrieked and howled in the last sharp agony.

Probably there does not now exist one, where, five years ago, there were a hundred Indians; and in sailing up the river, from the cape to the cascades, the only evidence of the existence of the Indian, is an occasional miserable wigwam, with a few wretched, half-starved occupants. In some other places they are rather more numerous; but the thoughtful observer cannot avoid perceiving that in a very few years the race must, in the nature of things, become extinct; and the time is probably not far distant, when the little trinkets and toys of this people will be picked up by the curious, and valued as mementoes of a nation passed away for ever from the face of the earth. The aspect of things is very melancholy. It seems as if the fiat of the Creator had gone forth, that these poor denizens of the forest and the stream should go hence, and be seen of men no more.[111]

In former years, when the Indians were numerous, long after the establishment of this fort, it was not safe for the

---

[111] When Lewis and Clark visited the Columbia (1805–06), they noted signs of a declining population, and thought it due to an epidemic of small-pox that a few years before had decimated the native population. In 1829, shortly after the ground had been broken for a farm at Fort Vancouver, a form of intermittent fever broke out among both white men and Indians. To the latter it proved deadly, and for three years raged without abatement. This epidemic had occasioned the desolation noted by Townsend.— ED.

white men attached to it to venture beyond the protection of its guns without being fully armed. Such was the jealousy of the natives towards them, that various deep laid schemes were practised to obtain possession of the post, and massacre all whom it had harbored; [233] now, however, they are as submissive as children. Some have even entered into the services of the whites, and when once the natural and persevering indolence of the man is worn off, he will work well and make himself useful.

About two hundred miles southward, the Indians are said to be in a much more flourishing condition, and their hostility to the white people to be most deadly. They believe that we brought with us the fatal fever which has ravaged this portion of the country, and the consequence is, that they kill without mercy every white man who trusts himself amongst them.

October 1st. — Doctor Gairdner, the surgeon of Fort Vancouver, took passage a few days ago to the Sandwich Islands, in one of the Company's vessels. He has been suffering for several months, with a pulmonary affection, and is anxious to escape to a milder and more salubrious climate. In his absence, the charge of the hospital will devolve on me, and my time will thus be employed through the coming winter. There are at present but few cases of sickness, mostly ague and fever, so prevalent at this season. My companion, Mr. Nuttall, was also a passenger in the same vessel. From the islands, he will probably visit California, and either return to the Columbia by the next ship, and take the route across the mountains, or double Cape Horn to reach his home.

16th.— Several days since, the Rev. Samuel Parker, of Ithaca, N. York, arrived at the fort. He left his home last May, travelled to the rendezvous on the Colorado, with the fur company of Mr. Fontinelle, and performed

the remainder of the journey with the Nez Percé or Cheap-
tin Indians. His object is to examine the country in respect to its agricultural and other facilities, with a view
to the establishment of missions among the Indians.[112]
He will probably return to the States next spring, and report the [234] result of his observations to the board of
commissioners, by whose advice his pioneer journey has
been undertaken.[113]

On the 17th, I embarked with this gentleman in a canoe,
for a visit to the lower part of the river. We arrived at
the American brig in the afternoon, on board of which
we quartered for the night, and the next morning early,
the vessel cast off from the shore. She has her cargo of
furs and salmon on board, and is bound to Boston, via
the Sandwich and Society Islands. Mr. Parker took passage in her to Fort George, and in the afternoon I returned
in my canoe to Vancouver.[114]

December 1st.— The weather is now unusually fine. Instead of the drenching rains which generally prevail during
the winter months, it has been for some weeks clear and
cool, the thermometer ranging from 35° to 45°.

[112] Reverend Samuel Parker was born in New Hampshire (1779); educated
at Williams and Andover, he settled at Ithaca, where he died in 1866. At the meeting of the American Board of Commissioners for Foreign Missions (1834), the
subject of an Oregon mission was discussed and Parker appointed to make inves-
tigations. Arriving at St. Louis too late for the annual brigade, he returned home,
only to come out the succeeding year in company with Marcus Whitman. At the
Green River rendezvous, Whitman went back for reinforcements, but Parker
pushed on, with Nez Percés as his sole companions, as far as Fort Walla Walla,
where he arrived October 6, 1835. He remained in Oregon until June, 1836,
then embarked for Hawaii, reaching home in May, 1837.— ED.

[113] Mr. Parker has since published an account of this tour, to which the reader
is referred, for much valuable information, relative to the condition of the Indians
on our western frontier.— TOWNSEND.

*Comment by Ed. The Journal of an Exploring Tour beyond the Rocky Moun-
tains* (Ithaca, 1838). Five American editions and one English appeared. The
popularity of the work was considerable, and it spread information concerning the
Oregon country.

[114] This was Wyeth's vessel, the "May Dacre."— ED.

The ducks and geese, which have swarmed throughout the country during the latter part of the autumn, are leaving us, and the swans are arriving in great numbers. These are here, as in all other places, very shy; it is difficult to approach them without cover; but the Indians have adopted a mode of killing them which is very successful; that of drifting upon the flocks at night, in a canoe, in the bow of which a large fire of pitch pine has been kindled. The swans are dazzled, and apparently stupefied by the bright light, and fall easy victims to the craft of the sportsman.

20th.—Yesterday one of the Canadians took an enormous wolf in a beaver-trap. It is probably a distinct species from the common one, (*lupus,*) much larger and stronger, and of a yellowish cinereous color.[115] The man states that he found considerable difficulty in capturing him, even after the trap had been fastened on [235] his foot. Unlike the lupus, (which is cowardly and cringing when made prisoner,) he showed fight, and seizing the pole in his teeth, with which the man attempted to despatch him, with one backward jerk, threw his assailant to the ground, and darted at him, until checked by the trap chain. He was finally shot, and I obtained his skin, which I have preserved.

I have just had a visit from an old and intelligent Indian chief, who lives near. It is now almost midnight, but for the last hour I have heard the old man wandering about like an unquiet 'spirit, in the neighborhood of my little mansion, and singing snatches of the wild, but sweetly musical songs of his tribe. It is a bitter night, and supposing the old man might be cold, I invited him to a seat by my comfortable fire.

---

[115] Probably an individual of what Lewis and Clark call the large brown wolf of the wooded regions of the Columbia (*canis lupus occidentalis*).— Ed.

He says, " eighty snows have chilled the earth since *Maniquon* was born." Maniquon has been a great warrior; he has himself taken twenty scalps between the rising and setting of the sun. Like most old people, he is garrulous, and, like all Indians, fond of boasting of his warlike deeds. I can sit for hours and hear old Maniquon relate the particulars of his numerous campaigns, his ambushes, and his " scrimmages," as old Hawk-eye would say. When he once gets into the spirit of it, he springs upon his feet, his old, sunken eyes sparkle like diamonds set in bronze, and he whirls his shrunken and naked arm around his head, as though it still held the deadly tomahawk. But in the midst of his excitement, seeming suddenly to recollect his fallen state, he sinks into his chair.

" Maniquon is not a warrior now — he will never raise his axe again — his young men have deserted his lodge — his sons will go down to their graves, and the squaws will not sing of their great deeds."

I have several times heard him speak the substance of these words in his own language, and in one instance he concluded thus:

[236] " And who made my people what they are ? " This question was put in a low voice, almost a whisper, and was accompanied by a look so savage and malignant, that I almost quailed before the imbecile old creature. I, however, answered quickly, without giving him time to reply to his own question.

" The Great Spirit, Maniquon," pointing with my finger impressively upwards.

" Yes, yes — it *was* the Great Spirit; it was not the *white man*!" I could have been almost angry with the old Indian for the look of deadly hostility with which he uttered these last words, but that I sympathized with his wounded pride, and pitied his sorrows too much to harbor any other feeling than commiseration for his manifold wrongs.

February 3d, 1836.— During a visit to Fort William, last week, I saw, as I wandered through the forest, about three miles from the house, a canoe, deposited, as is usual, in the branches of a tree, some fourteen feet from the ground. Knowing that it contained the body of an Indian, I ascended to it for the purpose of abstracting the skull; but upon examination, what was my surprise to find a perfect, embalmed body of a young female, in a state of preservation equal to any which I had seen from the catacombs of Thebes. I determined to obtain possession of it, but as this was not the proper time to carry it away, I returned to the fort, and said nothing of the discovery which I had made.

That night, at the witching hour of twelve, I furnished myself with a rope, and launched a small canoe, which I paddled up against the current to a point opposite the mummy tree. Here I ran my canoe ashore, and removing my shoes and stockings, proceeded to the tree, which was about a hundred yards from the river. I ascended, and making the rope fast around the body, lowered it gently to the ground ; then arranging the fabric which had been displaced, as neatly as the darkness allowed, I descended, and taking the body upon my shoulders, bore it to my [237] canoe, and pushed off into the stream. On arriving at the fort, I deposited my prize in the store house, and sewed around it a large Indian mat, to give it the appearance of a bale of guns. Being on a visit to the fort, with Indians whom I had engaged to paddle my canoe, I thought it unsafe to take the mummy on board when I returned to Vancouver the next day, but left directions with Mr. Walker to stow it away under the hatches of a little schooner, which was running twice a week between the two forts.

On the arrival of this vessel, several days after, I received, instead of the body, a note from Mr. Walker, stating that an Indian had called at the fort, and demanded the corpse. He was the brother of the deceased, and had been in the habit of visiting the tomb of his sister every year. He had now come for that purpose, from his residence near the "*tum-water*," (cascades,) and his keen eye had detected the intrusion of a stranger on the spot hallowed to him by many successive pilgrimages. The canoe of his sister was tenantless, and he knew the spoiler to have been a white man, by the tracks upon the beach, which did not incline inward like those of an Indian.

The case was so clearly made out, that Mr. W. could not deny the fact of the body being in the house, and it was accordingly delivered to him, with a present of several blankets, to prevent the circumstance from operating upon his mind to the prejudice of the white people. The poor Indian took the body of his sister upon his shoulders, and as he walked away, grief got the better of his stoicism, and the sound of his weeping was heard long after he had entered the forest.

25th.— Several weeks ago the only son of Ke-ez-a-no, the principal chief of the Chinooks, died.[116] The father was almost distracted with grief, and during the first paroxysm attempted to take the life of the boy's mother, supposing that she had exerted an evil influence over him which had caused his death. She [238] was compelled to fly in consequence, and put herself under the protection of Dr. McLoughlin, who found means to send her to her people below. Disappointed in this scheme of vengeance, the chief determined to sacrifice all whom he thought had ever wronged his son, or treated him with indignity; and

[116] This appears to be the chief mentioned by Franchh, in our volume vi, p. 246, and by Ross in our volume vii, p. 118.

the first victim whom he selected was a very pretty and accomplished Chinook girl, named Waskéma, who was remarkable for the exceeding beauty of her long black hair. Waskéma had been solicited by the boy in marriage, but had refused him, and the matter had been long forgotten, until it was revived in the recollection of the father by the death of his son. Ke-ez-a-no despatched two of his slaves to Fort William, (where the girl was at that time engaged in making moccasins for Mr. W. and where I had seen her a short time previously,) who hid themselves in the neighborhood until the poor creature had embarked in her canoe alone to return to her people, when they suddenly rushed upon her from the forest which skirted the river, and shot two balls through her bosom. The body was then thrown into the water, and the canoe broken to pieces on the beach.

Tapeo the brother of Waskéma delivered to me a letter from Mr. W. detailing these circumstances, and amid an abundance of tears which he shed for the loss of his only and beloved sister, he denounced the heaviest vengeance upon her murderer. These threats, however, I did not regard, as I knew the man would never dare to raise his hand against his chief, but as expression relieves the overcharged heart, I did not check his bursts of grief and indignation.

A few days after this, Ke-ez-a-no himself stalked into my room. After sitting a short time in silence, he asked if I believed him guilty of the murder of Waskéma. I replied that I did, and that if the deed had been committed in my country, he would be hanged. He denied all agency in the matter, and placing one hand upon his bosom, and pointing upwards with the other, called [239] God to witness that he was innocent. For the moment I almost believed his asseverations; but calling to mind the strong and undeniable evidence against him, with a feeling of horror and repugnance, I opened the door and bowed him out of the house.

March 1st.— There is an amusing little Indian living in this neighborhood, who calls himself " *tanas tie,*" (little chief,) and he is so probably in every sense of the term. In person, he stands about four feet six, in his moccasins; but no exquisite in the fashionable world, no tinselled dandy in high life, can strut and stamp, and fume with more dignity and self consequence. His name, he says, is Quâlaskin; but in the fort, he is known by the cognomen of " *busy body,*" from his restless anxiety to pry into every body's business, and his curiosity to know the English name of every article he sees; *ikata ookook?— ikata ookook?* (what is this? — what is this?) *kahtah pasiooks yahhalle?* (what is its English name?) are expressions which he is dinning in your ears, whenever he enters a room in the fort. If you answer him, he attempts the pronunciation after you, and it is often not a little ludicrous. He is evidently proud of the name the white people have given him, not understanding its import, but supposing it to be a title of great honor and dignity. If he is asked his Indian name, he answers very modestly, Quâlaskin, (muddy river,) but if his *pasiooks yahhalle* is required, he puffs up his little person to its utmost dimensions, and tells you with a simper of pride and self complacency, that it is "*mizzy moddy.*"

16th.— Doctor W. F. Tolmie, one of the surgeons of the Hudson's Bay Company, has just arrived from Fort Langley, on the coast, and has relieved me of the charge of the hospital, which will afford me the opportunity of peregrinating again in pursuit of specimens.[117] The spring

---

[117] Dr. William Fraser Tolmie was born in Inverness, educated at Glasgow, and joined (1832) the Hudson's Bay Company as a physician. The following spring he arrived at Vancouver by way of Cape Horn, and was sent north to the

is just opening, the birds are arriving, the plants are starting from the ground, and in a few weeks, the wide prairies
of the Columbia will appear like the richest flower gardens.

[240] *May 13th.*— Two days ago I left the fort, and am
now encamped on a plain below Warrior's point. Near
me are several large lodges of Kowalitsk Indians;[118] in
all probably one hundred persons. As usual, they give
me some trouble by coming around and lolling about my
tent, and importuning me for the various little articles
that they see. My camp-keeper, however, (a Klikatat,)
is an excellent fellow, and has no great love for Kowalitsk
Indians, so that the moment he sees them becoming
troublesome, he clears the coast, *sans ceremonie.* There
is in one of the lodges a very pretty little girl, sick with
intermittent fever; and to-day the "medicine man" has
been exercising his functions upon the poor little patient;
pressing upon its stomach with his brawny hands until it
shrieked with the pain, singing and muttering his incanta-
tions, whispering in its ears, and exhorting the evil spirit
to pass out by the door, &c. These exhibitions would be
laughable did they not involve such serious consequences,
and for myself I always feel so much indignation against
the unfeeling impostor who operates, and pity for the de-
luded creatures who submit to it, that any emotions but
those of risibility are excited.

Puget Sound region with a party engaged in planting a new post. There he remained until the return noted by Townsend. He lived at Fort Vancouver and
vicinity until 1841. A visit to England (1841–43) was made in the interest of the
Puget Sound Agricultural Company, of which Tolmie was superintendent at Fort
Nisqually (1843–59). Upon the final cession of all the territory to the United States,
Dr. Tolmie removed to Victoria, British Columbia, where he was still living in
1878.

Fort Langley was founded in 1827 upon the left bank of the Fraser River, about
thirty miles above its mouth.— ED.

[118] For the habitat of this tribe, see Franchère's *Narrative*, in our volume vi,
p. 245, note 49.— ED.

I had a serious conversation with the father of this child, in which I attempted to prove to him, and to some twenty or thirty Indians who were squatted about the ground near, that the "medicine man" was a vile impostor, that he was a fool and a liar, and that his manipulations were calculated to increase the sufferings of the patient instead of relieving them. They all listened in silence, and with great attention to my remarks, and the wily conjurer himself had the full benefit of them: he stood by during the whole time, assuming an expression of callous indifference which not even my warmest vituperations could affect. Finally I offered to exhibit the strongest proof of the truth of what I had been saying, by pledging myself to cure the child in three days, provided the "medicine man" was dismissed without delay. This, the father told me, required some consideration [241] and consultation with his people, and I immediately left the lodge and took the way to my camp, to allow them an opportunity of discussing the matter alone.

Early next morning the Indian visited me, with the information that the "medicine man" had departed, and he was now anxious that I should make trial of my skill. I immediately administered to the child an active cathartic, followed by sulphate of quinine, which checked the disease, and in two days the patient was perfectly restored.

In consequence of my success in this case, I had an application to administer medicine to two other children similarly affected. My stock of quinine being exhausted, I determined to substitute an extract of the bark of the dogwood, (*Cornus Nuttalli*,) and taking one of the parents into the wood with his blanket, I soon chipped off a plentiful supply, returned, boiled it in his own kettle, and completed the preparation in his lodge, with most of the Indians standing by, and staring at me, to comprehend the process.

This was exactly what I wished; and as I proceeded, I took some pains to explain the whole matter to them, in order that they might at a future time be enabled to make use of a really valuable medicine, which grows abundantly every where throughout the country. I have often thought it strange that the sagacity of the Indians should not long ago have made them acquainted with this remedy; and I believe, if they had used it, they would not have had to mourn the loss of hundreds, or even thousands of their people who have been swept away by the demon of ague and fever.

I administered to each of the children about a scruple of the extract per day. The second day they escaped the paroxysm, and on the third were entirely well.

June 26th.— I left Vancouver yesterday, with the summer brigade, for a visit to Walla-walla, and its vicinity. The gentlemen [242] of the party are, Peter Ogden, Esq., chief factor, bound to New Caledonia, Archibald McDonald, Esq., for Colville, and Samuel Black, Esq., for Thompson's river, and the brigade consists of sixty men, with nine boats.[119]

---

[119] Archibald McDonald was a Hudson's Bay officer who had been in charge of forts in the Thompson River district (1822–26), when he became chief factor for Kamloops. In 1828 he was chosen to accompany Sir George Simpson in a transmontane tour, and his diary thereof was published as *Peace River: A Canoe Voyage from Hudson Bay to the Pacific* (Ottawa, 1872). On this expedition he was left in charge of the newly-built Fort Langley, where he remained about eight years, constructing Fort Nisqually on Puget Sound (1833). In 1836 he was appointed to Fort Colville, where he remained for many years. This post was on the upper Columbia, not far from Kettle Falls, in the present state of Washington; built in 1825, it was maintained by the Hudson's Bay Company until the discovery of gold in that region (1858), whereupon the stockade was removed across the border into British Columbia, to avoid United States customs duties.

Samuel Black had been a North West Company trader; but later was placed in charge of Hudson's Bay posts at Fort Dunveyan (1823) and at Walla Walla (1828). He commanded at Fort Kamloops (see our volume vii, p. 199, note 64), on Thompson's River for some years, before his murder (1841) by a neighboring native.— ED.

27th.—We arrived yesterday at the upper cascades, and made in the course of the day three portages. As is usual in this place, it rained almost constantly, and the poor men engaged in carrying the goods, were completely drenched. A considerable number of Indians are employed here in fishing, and they supply us with an abundance of salmon. Among them I recognise many of my old friends from below.

29th.—This morning the Indian wife of one of the men gave birth to a little girl. The tent in which she was lying was within a few feet of the one which I occupied, and we had no intimation of the matter being in progress until we heard the crying of the infant. It is truly astonishing with what ease the parturition of these women is performed; they generally require no assistance in delivery, being fully competent to manage the whole paraphernalia themselves. In about half an hour after this event we got under way, and the woman walked to the boat, carrying her new born infant on her back, embarked, laughed, and talked as usual, and appeared in every respect as well as if nothing had happened.

This woman is a most noble specimen of bone and muscle, and so masculine in appearance, that were she to cast the petticoat, and don the breeches, the cheat would never be discovered, and but few of the *lords of the creation* would be willing to face the Amazon. She is particularly useful to her husband. As he is becoming rather infirm, she can protect him most admirably. If he wishes to cross a stream in travelling without horses or boats, she plunges in without hesitation, takes him upon her back, and lands him safely and expeditiously upon the opposite bank. She can also kill and dress an elk, run down and shoot a buffalo, [243] or spear a salmon for her husband's breakfast in the morning, as well as any man-servant he could employ. Added to all this, she has, in several instances, saved his life in skirmishes with Indians, at the imminent risk of her own, so that he has some reason to be proud of her.

In the afternoon, we passed the bold, basaltic point, known to the *voyageurs* by the name of " Cape Horn." [120] The wind here blew a perfect hurricane, and but for the consummate skill of those who managed our boats, we must have had no little difficulty.

30th.— We were engaged almost the whole of this day in making portages, and I had, in consequence, some opportunity of prosecuting my researches on the land. We have now passed the range of vegetation; there are no trees or even shrubs; nothing but huge, jagged rocks of basalt, and interminable sand heaps. I found here a large and beautiful species of marmot, (the *Arctomys Richardsonii,*) several of which I shot. Encamped in the evening at the village of the Indian chief, *Tilki.* I had often heard of this man, but I now saw him for the first time. His person is rather below the middle size, but his features are good, with a Roman cast, and his eye is deep black, and unusually fine. He appears to be remarkably intelligent, and half a century before the generality of his people in civilization.

July 3d.— This morning we came to the open prairies, covered with wormwood bushes. The appearance, and strong odor of these, forcibly remind me of my journey across the mountains, when we frequently saw no vegetation for weeks, except this dry and barren looking shrub.

The Indians here are numerous, and are now engaged in catching salmon, lamprey eels, &c. They take thousands

---

[120] Cape Horn is a high basaltic cliff towering two thousand five hundred feet above the river bank, not far above Vancouver, in Skamania County, Washington. It was so named because boats were frequently wind-bound in passing this point.— ED.

of the latter, and they are seen hanging in great numbers in their lodges to dry in the smoke. As soon as the Indians see us approach, they leave their wigwams, and run out towards us, [244] frequently wading to their breasts in the water, to get near the boats. Their constant cry is *pi-pi*, *pi-pi*, (tobacco, tobacco,) and they bring a great variety of matters to trade for this desirable article; fish, living birds of various kinds, young wolves, foxes, minks, &c.

On the evening of the 6th, we arrived at Walla-walla or Nez Percés fort, where I was kindly received by Mr. Pambrun, the superintendent.

The next day the brigade left us for the interior, and I shouldered my gun for an excursion through the neighborhood. On the west side of the little Walla-walla river, I saw, during a walk of two miles, at least thirty rattlesnakes, and killed five that would not get out of my way. They all seemed willing to dispute the ground with me, shaking their rattles, coiling and darting at me with great fury. I returned to the fort in the afternoon with twenty-two sharp-tailed grouse, (*Tetrao phasianellus*,) the product of my day's shooting.

25th.— I mounted my horse this morning for a journey to the Blue mountains. I am accompanied by a young half breed named Baptiste Dorion,[121] who acts as guide, groom, interpreter, &c., and I have a pack horse to carry my little *nick-nackeries*. We shaped our course about N. E. over the sandy prairie, and in the evening encamped on the Morro river,[122] having made about thirty miles.

---

[121] This is the son of old Pierre Dorion, who makes such a conspicuous figure in Irving's "Astoria."— TOWNSEND.

Comment by Ed. Consult Bradbury's *Travels* in our volume v, p. 38, note 7; also Ross's *Oregon Settlers*, our volume vii, pp. 265–269, wherein the murder of the elder Dorion and the escape of his wife and children are related

[122] The direction appears to be wrong, as a northern course would be directly away from the Blue Mountains; moreover it would necessitate crossing Walla

On our way, we met two Walla-walla Indians driving down
a large band of horses.   They inform us that the Snakes
have crossed the mountain to commence their annual
thieving of horses, and they are taking them away to have
them secure.   I shall need to keep a good look out to my
own small caravan, or I shall be under the necessity of
turning pedestrian.

Walla River before reaching Umatilla.   It should therefore, obviously, be read
"S. E. over the sandy prairie."   Morro River must be an upper affluent of Walla
Walla (or Umatilla).— ED.

[245] CHAPTER XV

July 26th.— At noon, to-day, we arrived at the Utalla, or Emmitilly river, where we found a large village of Kayouse Indians, engaged in preparing kamas. Large quantities of this root were strewed about on mats and buffalo robes; some in a crude state, and a vast quantity pounded, to be made into cakes for winter store. There are of the Indians, about twelve or fifteen lodges. A very large one, about sixty feet long by fifteen broad, is occupied by the chief, and his immediate family. This man I saw when I arrived at Walla-walla, and I have accepted an invitation to make my home in his lodge while I remain here. The house is really a very comfortable one; the rays of the sun are completely excluded, and the ground is covered with buffalo robes. There are in the chief's lodge about twenty women, all busy as usual; some pounding kamas, others making [246] leathern dresses, moccasins, &c. Several of the younger of these are very good looking,— I might almost say handsome. Their heads are of the natural form,— not flattened and contorted in the horrible manner of the Chinooks; — their faces are inclining to oval, and their eyes have a peculiarly sleepy and languishing appearance. They seem as if naturally inclined to lasciviousness, but if this feeling exists, it is effectually checked by their self-enacted laws, which are very severe in this respect, and in every instance rigidly enforced. The dresses of the women, (unlike the Chinooks, they all *have* dresses,) are of deer or antelope skin, more or less ornamented with beads and *hyquâs*.[123] It consists of one piece, but the part covering the bust, projects over the lower portion of the garment, and its edges are cut into strings, to which a quantity of blue beads are generally attached.

In the evening all the Indians belonging to the village assembled in our lodge, and, with the chief for minister, performed divine service, or family worship. This, I learn, is their invariable practice twice every twenty-four hours, at sunrise in the morning, and after supper in the evening. When all the people had gathered, our large lodge was filled. On entering, every person squatted on the ground, and the *clerk* (a sort of sub-chief) gave notice that the Deity would now be addressed. Immediately the whole audience rose to their knees, and the chief supplicated for about ten minutes in a very solemn, but low tone of voice, at the conclusion of which an amen was pronounced by the whole company, in a loud, swelling sort of groan. Three hymns were then sung, several of the individuals present leading in rotation, and at the conclusion of each, another amen. The chief then pronounced a short exhortation, occupying about fifteen minutes, which was repeated by the clerk at his elbow in a voice loud enough to be heard by the whole assembly. At the [247] conclusion of this, each person rose, and walked to one of the doors of the lodge, where, making a low inclination of his body, and pro-

---

[123] A· long white shell, of the genus *Dentalium*, found on the coast.— TOWNSEND.

nouncing the words "*tots sekan*," (good night,) to the chief, he departed to his home.

I shall hear this ceremony every night and morning while I remain, and so far from being irksome, it is agreeable to me. It is pleasant to see these poor degraded creatures performing a religious service; for to say nothing of the good influence which it will exert in improving their present condition, it will probably soften and harmonize their feelings, and render them fitter subjects for the properly qualified religious instruction which it is desirable they may some day receive.

The next morning, my friend the chief furnished me with fresh horses, and I and my attendant, with two Indian guides, started for a trip to the mountain. We passed up one of the narrow valleys or gorges which here run at right angles from the alpine land, and as we ascended, the scenery became more and more wild, and the ground rough and difficult of passage, but I had under me one of the finest horses I ever rode; he seemed perfectly acquainted with the country; I had but to give him his head, and not attempt to direct him, and he carried me triumphantly through every difficulty. Immediately as we reached the upper land, and the pine trees, we saw large flocks of the dusky grouse, (*Tetrao obscurus*,) a number of which we killed. Other birds were, however, very scarce. I am at least two months too late, and I cannot too much regret the circumstance. Here is a rich field for the ornithologist at the proper season. We returned to our lodge in the evening loaded with grouse, but with very few specimens to increase my collection.

29th.— Early this morning our Indians struck their lodges, and commenced making all their numerous movables into bales for packing on the horses. I admired the facility and despatch with which this was done; the women alone worked at it, the [248] men lolling around, smoking and talking, and not even once directing their fair partners in their task. The whole camp travelled with me to Walla-walla, where we arrived the next day.

Sept. 1st.— Mr. John M'Leod, a chief trader of the Hudson's Bay Company, arrived this morning from the rendezvous, with a small trading party.[124] I had been anxiously expecting this gentleman for several weeks, as I intended to return with him to Vancouver. He is accompanied by several Presbyterian missionaries, the Rev. Mr. Spalding and Doctor Whitman,[125] with their wives,

---

[124] John McLeod had for some years been with the Hudson's Bay Company. He was in charge at Kamloops from 1822 to 1826, and in the latter year built Norway House. In 1832 he founded, in conjunction with Michel La Framboise, Fort Umpqua, the only establishment of the company south of the Columbia. At the time Townsend met him he appears to have headed the Snake country brigade.— ED.

[125] Henry H. Spalding was born in Bath County, New York, in 1803. He studied at Western Reserve, and afterwards at Lane Theological Seminary, which latter school he left to join Dr. Whitman (1836) in a mission to Oregon. Settled at Lapwai, in western Idaho, among the Nez Percés, he maintained the mission at that place until the Whitman massacre in 1847. Narrowly escaping therefrom, he accepted in 1850, at the solicitation of the missionary board, the position of United States Indian agent, and served also as commissioner of schools (1850-55). In 1862 he returned to Lapwai to re-commence mission work, and died among the Nez Percés in 1874.

Dr. Marcus Whitman was born in Rushville, New York, in 1802. Graduating as a physician he was appointed to the Oregon mission in 1834, actually reaching his station in September, 1836, as Townsend narrates — see note 112, p. 335, *ante*. He established his mission at Waiilatpu among the Cayuse, and there labored until 1842, when news from the mission board, advising abandonment of his station, caused his return to the United States. This was the journey regarding which so much controversy has arisen. According to some writers, Whitman's object was to awaken the United States authorities to the necessity of occupying Oregon, and how "Marcus Whitman saved Oregon" to the United States has been much discussed. Recently exceptions have been taken to this view, and eminent historical scholars have minimized Whitman's national services. The first stage of the controversy began about 1883. See Myron Eells, *Marcus Whitman, M. D., Proofs of his work in Saving Oregon to the United States* (Portland, 1883). Later Professor Edward G. Bourne took up the subject and presented a paper at the American Historical Association meeting of 1900 (published in *American Historical Review*, vii, pp. 276-300); this has been expanded into "The Legend of Marcus

and Mr. Gray, teacher.[126] Doctor Whitman presented me with a large pacquet of letters from my beloved friends at home. I need not speak of the emotions excited by their reception, nor of the trembling anxiety with which I tore open the envelope and devoured the contents. This is the first intelligence which I have received from them since I left the state of Missouri, and was as unexpected as it was delightful.[127]

Mr. M'Leod informed me of the murder of Antoine Goddin, the half-breed trapper, by the Blackfeet Indians, at Fort Hall.— A band of these Indians appeared on the shore of the Portneuf river, opposite the fort, headed by a white man named Bird.— This man requested Goddin, whom he saw on the opposite side of the river, to cross to him with a canoe, as he had beaver which he wished to

Whitman" in *Essays in Historical Criticism* (New York, 1901). William I. Marshall of Chicago, discussed Professor Bourne's paper (see American Historical Association *Report* for 1900, i, pp. 219-236) offering additional evidence. Marshall has since published *History vs. the Whitman Saved Oregon Story* (Chicago, 1904). Myron Eells also issued *A Reply to Professor Bourne's "The Whitman Legend"* (Walla Walla, 1902). William A. Mowry essays a defense in *Marcus Whitman and the early days of Oregon* (New York, 1901) which contains a good bibliography. See also additional evidence in articles by William E. Griffis and others, contributed to the *Sunday School Times*, Philadelphia, August 9, November 1, 8, 15, 22, 29, December 3, 1902; January 10, 29, 1903. Whitman returned to his mission, and despite threatening aspects, remained at Waiilatpu until 1847, when suddenly in October the Cayuse arose and massacred most of the members of the mission, including both Dr. Whitman and his wife.— ED.

[126] William H. Gray (born in Utica, New York, in 1810) joined Dr. Whitman as business manager and agent of the expedition. In 1837 he went East for reinforcements, and married Mary Augusta Dix, with whom he returned to Oregon in September, 1838. They labored at Lapwai and Waiilatpu until 1842, when Gray resigned and retired to the Willamette, where he was instrumental in establishing the provisional government. In 1849 Gray went to California during the gold excitement, but returned to Oregon, settling first at Clatsop Plains, and later in Astoria, where he died in 1889. His *History of Oregon* (Portland, San Francisco, and New York, 1870) is a main source for the early decades.— ED.

[127] See reference to this fact and to the meeting with Townsend, in Mrs. Whitman's "Journal," published in Oregon Pioneer Association *Transactions* (1891), pp. 57, 63.— ED.

trade. The poor man accordingly embarked alone, and landing near the Indians, joined the circle which they had made, and *smoked the pipe of peace with them*. While Goddin was smoking in his turn, Bird gave a sign to the Indians, and a volley was fired into his back. While he was yet living, Bird himself tore the scalp from the poor fellow's head, and deliberately cut Captain Wyeth's initials, N. J. W. in large letters upon his forehead. He then hallooed to the fort people, telling them to bury the carcass if they wished, and immediately went off with his party.

[249] This Bird was formerly attached to the Hudson's Bay Company, and was made prisoner by the Blackfeet, in a skirmish several years ago. He has since remained with them, and has become a great chief, and leader of their war parties. He is said to be a man of good education, and to possess the most unbounded influence over the savage people among whom he dwells. He was known to be a personal enemy of Goddin, whom he had sworn to destroy on the first opportunity.

We also hear, that three of Captain Wyeth's men who lately visited us, had been assaulted on their way to Fort Hall, by a band of Walla-walla Indians, who, after beating them severely, took from them all their horses, traps, ammunition, and clothing. They were, however, finally induced to return them each a horse and gun, in order that they might proceed to the interior, to get fresh supplies. This was a matter of policy on the part of the Indians, for if the white men had been compelled to travel on foot, they would have come immediately here to procure fresh horses, &c., and thus exposed the plunderers. Mr. Pambrun is acquainted with the ringleader of this band of marauders, and intends to take the first opportunity of inflicting upon him due punishment, as well as to compel him to make ample restitution for the stolen property, and broken heads of the unoffending trappers.

I have had this evening, some interesting conversation with our guests, the missionaries. They appear admirably qualified for the arduous duty to which they have devoted themselves, their minds being fully alive to the mortifications and trials incident to a residence among wild Indians; but they do not shrink from the task, believing it to be their religious duty to engage in this work. The ladies have borne the journey astonishingly; they look robust and healthy.[128]

3d.—Mr. M'Leod and myself embarked in a large batteau, with six men, and bidding farewell to Mr. Pambrun and the missionaries, were soon gliding down the river. We ran, to-day, [250] several rapids, and in the evening encamped about fifteen miles below the mouth of the Utalla river.

This running of rapids appears rather a dangerous business to those unaccustomed to it, and it is in reality sufficiently hazardous, except when performed by old and skilful hands. Every thing depends upon the men who manage the bow and stern of the boat. The moment she enters the rapid, the two guides lay aside their oars taking in their stead paddles, such as are used in the management of a canoe. The middle-men ply their oars; the guides brace themselves

---

[128] Mrs. Narcissa Prentice Whitman was a native of Prattsburgh, Steuben County, New York, and married Dr. Whitman just before his journey across the plains (1836). She was of much assistance to him in the mission work, and perished in the massacre of 1847. See her letters and "Journal" in Oregon Pioneer Association *Transactions* (1891). She and Mrs. Spalding were the first white women to cross the plains to Oregon.

Mrs. Spalding (*née* Eliza Hart) was born in Connecticut (1807) and reared in Ontario County, New York. She was less strong than Mrs. Whitman, and her journey at first fatigued her so greatly that it was feared she would not reach its end. Her health improved after passing the mountains, and she was an efficient aid in the mission, learning the Indian languages with great aptitude. After the Whitman massacre she never recovered from the shock, and died in 1851.— ED.

against the gunwale of the boat, placing their paddles edge-wise down her sides, and away she goes over the curling, foaming, and hissing waters, like a race horse.

We passed to-day several large lodges of Indians, from whom we wished to have purchased fish, but they had none, or were not willing to spare any, so that we were compelled to purchase a *dog* for supper. I have said *we*, but I beg leave to correct myself, as I was utterly averse to the proceeding; not, however, from any particular dislike to the quality of the food, (I have eaten it repeatedly, and relished it,) but I am always unwilling, unless when suffering absolute want, to take the life of so noble and faithful an animal. Our hungry oarsmen, however, appeared to have no such scruples. The Indian called his dog, and he came to him, *wagging his tail*! He sold his companion for ten balls and powder! One of our men approached the poor animal with an axe. I turned away my head to avoid the sight, but I heard the dull, *sodden* sound of the blow. The tried friend and faithful companion lay quivering in the agonies of death at its master's feet.

We are enjoying a most magnificent sight at our camp this evening. On the opposite side of the river, the Indians have fired the prairie, and the whole country for miles around is most brilliantly illuminated. Here am I sitting cross-legged on the [251] ground, scribbling by the light of the vast conflagration with as much ease as if I had a ton of oil burning by my side; but my eyes are every moment involuntarily wandering from the paper before me, to contemplate and admire the grandeur of the distant scene. The very heavens themselves appear ignited, and the fragments of ashes and burning grass-blades, ascending and careering about through the glowing firmament, look like brilliant and glorious birds let loose to roam and revel amid this splendid scene. It is past midnight: every one in the camp is asleep, and I am this moment visited by half a dozen Indian fishermen, who are peering over my shoulders, and soliciting a smoke, so that I shall have to stop, and fill my calamet.

5th.—The Indians are numerous along the river, and all engaged in fishing; as we pass along, we frequently see them posted upon the rocks overhanging the water, surveying the boiling and roaring flood below, for the passing salmon. In most instances, an Indian is seen entirely alone in these situations, often standing for half an hour perfectly still, his eyes rivetted upon the torrent, and his long fish spear poised above his head. The appearance of a solitary and naked savage thus perched like an eagle upon a cliff, is sometimes, — when taken in connexion with the wild and rugged river scenery, — very picturesque. The spear is a pole about twelve feet in length, at the end of which a long wooden fork is made fast, and between the tines is fixed a barbed iron point. They also, in some situations, use a hand scoop-net, and stand upon scaffolds ingeniously constructed over the rapid water. Their winter store of dried fish is stowed away in little huts of mats and branches, closely interlaced, and also in *caches* under ground. It is often amusing to see the hungry ravens tearing and tugging at the strong twigs of the houses, in a vain attempt to reach the savory food within.

In the afternoon, we passed John Day's river,[129] and encamped about sunset at the "'shoots." Here is a very large village of [252] Indians, (the same that I noticed in my journal, on the passage down,) and we are this evening surrounded by some scores of them.

---

[129] For the pioneer in whose honor this river was named, see Bradbury's *Travels* in our volume v, p. 181, note 104. The John Day River rises in the Blue Mountains and flows west and northwest, entering the Columbia a few miles above the falls. It is an important stream for central Oregon, forming the boundary, in part, of several counties.— ED.

6th.—We made the portage of the shoots this morning by carrying our boat and baggage across the land, and in half an hour, arrived at one of the upper *dalles*. Here Mr. M'Leod and myself debarked, and the men ran the dall. We walked on ahead to the most dangerous part, and stood upon the rocks about a hundred feet above to observe them. It really seemed exceedingly dangerous to see the boat dashing ahead like lightning through the foaming and roaring waters, sometimes raised high above the enormous swells, and dashed down again as if she were seeking the bottom with her bows, and at others whirled around and nearly sucked under by the whirlpools constantly forming around her. But she stemmed every thing gallantly, under the direction of our experienced guides, and we soon embarked again, and proceeded to the lower dalles. Here it is utterly impossible, in the present state of the water, to pass, so that the boat and baggage had to be carried across the whole portage. This occupied the remainder of the day, and we encamped in the evening at a short distance from the lower villages. The Indians told us with sorrowful faces of the recent death of their principal chief, Tilki. Well, thought I, the white man has lost a friend, and long will it be before we see his like again! The poor fellow was unwell when I last saw him, with a complaint of his breast, which I suspected to be pulmonary. I gave him a few simple medicines, and told him I should soon see him again. Well do I remember the look of despondency with which he bade me farewell, and begged me to return soon and give him more medicine. About two weeks since he ruptured a blood vessel, and died in a short time.

We see great numbers of seals as we pass along. Immediately [253] below the Dalles they are particularly abundant, being attracted thither by the vast shoals of salmon which seek the turbulent water of the river. We occasionally shoot one of them as he raises his dog-like head above the surface, but we make no use of them; they are only valuable for the large quantity of oil which they yield.

We observe on the breasts and bellies of many of the Indians here, a number of large red marks, mostly of an oval form, sometimes twenty or thirty grouped together. These are wounds made by their own hands, to display to their people the unwavering and stoical resolution with which they can endure pain. A large fold of the skin is taken up with the fingers, and sliced off with a knife; the surrounding fibre then retreats, and a large and ghastly looking wound remains. Many that I saw to-day are yet scarcely cicatrized. There is a chief here who obtained the dignity which he now enjoys, solely by his numerous and hardy feats of this kind. He was originally a common man, and possessed but one wife; he has now *six*, and any of the tribe would think themselves honored by his alliance. He is a most gigantic fellow, about six feet four inches in height, and remarkably stout and powerful. The whole front of his person is covered with the red marks of which I have spoken, and he displays with considerable pride the two scars of a bullet, which entered the left breast, and passed out below the shoulder blade. This wound he also made with his own hand, by placing the muzzle of his gun against his breast, and pressing the trigger with his toe; and by this last, and most daring act, he was raised to the chief command of all the Indians on the north side of the river. Now that Tilki is no more, he will probably be chosen chief of all the country from the cascades to Walla-walla. I asked him if he felt no fear of death from the wound in his chest, at the time it was inflicted. He said, no; that his heart was strong, and that a bullet could never kill him. He told me that he was entirely [254] well in a week after this occurrence, but that for two days he vomited blood constantly. He is named by the Indians "*Skookoom*," (the strong.)

About six weeks after, Mr. M'Leod, who again returned from a visit to Walla-walla, informed me that the strong chief was dead. A bullet, (or rather two of them,) killed him at last, in spite of his supposed invulnerability. He was shot by one of his people in a fit of jealousy. *Skookoom* had assisted Mr. M'Leod with his boats across the portage, and, being a chief, he of course received more for the service than a common man. This wretch, who was but a serf in the tribe, chose to be offended by it, and vented his rage by murdering his superior. He fired a ball from his own gun into his breast, which brought him to the ground, and then despatched him with a second, which he seized from another. So poor Skookoom has passed away, and such is the frail tenure upon which an Indian chief holds his authority and his life. The murderer will no doubt soon die by the hand of some friend or relative of the deceased; he in his turn will be killed by another, and as usual, the bloody business will go on indefinitely, and may even tend to produce an open war between the rival parties.

I saw an old man here, apparently eighty years of age, who had given himself three enormous longitudinal gashes in his leg, to evince his grief for the loss of Tilki. From the sluggishness of the circulation in the body of the poor old creature, combined with a morbid habit, these wounds show no disposition to heal. I dressed his limb, and gave him a strict charge to have it kept clean, but knowing the universal carelessness of Indians in this respect, I fear my directions will not be attended to, and the consequence will probably be, that the old man will die miserably. I spoke to him of the folly of such inflictions, and took this opportunity of delivering a short lecture upon the same subject to the others assembled in his lodge.

[255] At 11 o'clock next day we arrived at the cascades, where we made the long portage, and at nine in the evening encamped in an ash grove, six miles above *Prairie de Thê*.

On the 8th, reached Vancouver, where we found two vessels which had just arrived from England.

On the 24th, I embarked in a canoe with Indians for Fort George, and arrived in two days. Here I was kindly received by the superintendent, Mr. James Birnie,[130] and promised every assistance in forwarding my views.

30*th.* — I visited to-day some cemeteries in the neighborhood of the fort, and obtained the skulls of four Indians. Some of the bodies were simply deposited in canoes, raised five or six feet from the ground, either in the forks of trees, or supported on stakes driven into the earth. In these instances it was not difficult to procure the skulls without disarranging the fabric; but more frequently, they were nailed in boxes, or covered by a small canoe, which was turned bottom upwards, and placed in a larger one, and the whole covered by strips of bark, carefully arranged over them. It was then necessary to use the utmost caution in removing the covering, and also to be careful to leave every thing in the same state in which it was found. I thought several times to-day, as I have often done in similar situations before: — Now suppose an Indian were to step in here, and see me groping among the bones of his fathers, and laying unhallowed hands upon the mouldering remains of his people, what should I say? — I know well what the Indian would *do*. He would instantly shoot me, unless I

---

[130] James Birnie was a native of Aberdeen, Scotland. Coming early to America he entered the North West Company's employ and was on the Columbia before 1820, when he was in charge of the post at the Dalles. He was then retained by the Hudson's Bay Company, and given command at Fort George (Astoria) where he remained many years. Later he became a naturalized American, and resided at Cathlamet.— Ed.

took the most effectual measures to prevent it; but could I have time allowed me to temporize a little, I could easily disarm his hostility and ensure his silence, by the offer of a shirt or a blanket; but the difficulty in most cases would be, that in a paroxysm of rage he would put a bullet through your head, and then good bye to temporizing. Luckily for my pursuits in this way, there are at present but few Indians here, and I do not therefore incur [256] much risk; were it otherwise, there would be no little danger in these aggressions.

The corpses of the several different tribes which are buried here, are known by the difference in the structure of their canoes; and the *sarcophagi* of the chiefs from those of the common people, by the greater care which has been manifested in the arrangement of the tomb.

October 14th.— I walked to-day around the beach to the foot of Young's bay,[131] a distance of about ten miles, to see the remains of the house in which Lewis and Clark's party resided during the winter which they spent here. The logs of which it is composed, are still perfect, but the roof of bark has disappeared, and the whole vicinity is overgrown with thorn and wild currant bushes.[132]

One of .Mr. Birnie's children found, a few days since, a large silver medal, which had been brought here by Lewis and Clark, and had probably been presented to some chief, who lost it. On one side was a head, with the name "Th. Jefferson, President of the United States, 1801." On the other, two hands interlocked, surmounted by a pipe

---

[131] For Young's Bay, see Franchére's *Narrative*, our volume vi, p. 259, note 69.— ED.

[132] This is an interesting description of the place, seen thirty years later, where the explorers passed the dismal winter months of 1805-06. For a ground plan of the fort, known as Fort Clatsop, see Thwaites, *Original Journals of the Lewis and Clark Expedition*, iii, pp. 282, 283, 298.— ED.

and tomahawk; and above the words, "Peace and Friend-ship." [133]

15th.—This afternoon I embarked in a canoe with *China-mus*, and went with him to his residence at Chinook.[134]   The chief welcomed me to his house in a style which would do no discredit to a more civilized person.   His two wives were ordered to make a bed for me, which they did by piling up about a dozen of their soft mats, and placing my blankets upon them, and a better bed I should never wish for.   I was regaled, before I retired, with sturgeon, salmon, wappatoos, cranberries, and every thing else that the mansion afforded, and was requested to ask for any thing I wanted, and it should be furnished me.   Whatever may be said derogatory to these people, I can testify that inhospitality is not among the number of their failings.   I never went into the [257] house of an Indian in my life, in any part of the country, without being most cordially received and welcomed.

The chief's house is built in the usual way, of logs and hewn boards, with a roof of cedar bark, and lined inside with mats. The floor is boarded and matted, and there is a depression in the ground about a foot in depth and four feet in width, extending the whole length of the building in the middle, where the fires are made.

In this, as in almost every house, there is a large figure, or idol, rudely carved and painted upon a board, and oc-cupying a conspicuous place.   To this figure many of the Indians ascribe supernatural powers.   Chinamus says that if he is in any kind of danger, and particularly, if he is under the influence of an evil spell, he has only to place himself

---

[133] A close description of the medals carried by the expedition.   See engraving in O. D. Wheeler, *On the Trail of Lewis and Clark* (New York, 1904), ii, pp. 123, 124.— ED.

[134] The site of this Chinook village opposite Astoria, was probably that of the present Fort Columbia, built to protect the entrance to the river.— ED.

against the image, and the difficulty, of whatever kind, vanishes at once. This certainly savors of idolatry, although I believe they never address the uncouth figure as a deity. Like all other Indians, they acknowledge a great and invisible spirit, who governs and controls, and to whom all adoration is due.

Attached to this establishment, are three other houses, similarly constructed, inhabited by about thirty Indians, and at least that number of dogs. These, although very useful animals in their place, are here a great nuisance. They are of no possible service to the Indians, except to eat their provisions, and fill their houses with fleas, and a stranger approaching the lodges, is in constant danger of being throttled by a legion of fierce brutes, who are not half as hospitable as their masters.

I remained here several days, making excursions through the neighborhood, and each time when I returned to the lodge, the dogs growled and darted at me. I had no notion of being bitten, so I gave the Indians warning, that unless the snarling beasts were tied up when I came near, I would shoot every one of them. The threat had the effect desired, and after this, whenever [258] I approached the lodges, there was a universal stir among the people, and the words, "*iskam kahmooks, iskam kahmooks, kalak'alah tie chahko,*" (take up your dogs, take up your dogs, the *bird chief* is coming,) echoed through the little village, and was followed by the yelping and snarling of dozens of wolf-dogs, and "curs of low degree," all of which were gathered in haste to the cover and protection of one of the houses.

[259] CHAPTER XVI

Northern excursion — Large shoals of salmon — Indian mode of catching them — House near the beach — Flathead children — A storm on the bay — Loss of provision — Pintail ducks — Simple mode of killing salmon — Return to Chinook — Indian garrulity — Return to Fort George — Preparations for a second trip to the Sandwich Islands — Detention within the cape. . . .

October 17th.— I left Chinook this morning in a canoe with Chinamus, his two wives, and a slave, to procure shell-fish, which are said to be found in great abundance towards the north. We passed through a number of narrow *slues* which connect the numerous bays in this part of the country, and at noon debarked, left our canoe, took our blankets on our shoulders, and struck through the midst of a deep pine forest. After walking about two miles, we came to another branch, where we found a canoe which had been left there for us yesterday, and embarking in this, we arrived in the evening at an Indian house, near the seaside, where we spent the night.

In our passage through some of the narrow channels today, we saw vast shoals of salmon, which were leaping and curvetting [260] about in every direction, and not unfrequently dashing their noses against our canoe, in their headlong course. We met here a number of Indians engaged in fishing. Their mode of taking the salmon is a very simple one. The whole of the tackle consists of a pole about twelve feet long, with a large iron hook attached to the end. This machine they keep constantly trailing in the water, and when the fish approaches the surface, by a quick and dexterous jerk, they fasten the iron into his side, and shake him off into the canoe. They say they take so many fish that it is necessary for them to land about three times a day to deposit them.

The house in which we sleep to-night is not near so comfortable as the one we have left. It stinks intolerably of salmon, which are hanging by scores to the roof, to dry in the smoke, and our bed being on the dead level, we shall probably suffer somewhat from fleas, not to mention another unmentionable insect which is apt to inhabit these dormitories in considerable profusion. There are here several young children; beautiful, flat-headed, broad-faced, little individuals. One of the little dears has taken something of a fancy to me, and is now hanging over me, and staring at my book with its great goggle eyes. It is somewhat strange, perhaps, but I have become so accustomed to this universal deformity, that I now scarcely notice it. I have often been evilly disposed enough to wish, that if in the course of events one of these little beings should die, I could get possession of it. I should like to plump the small carcass into a keg of spirits, and send it home for the observation of the curious.

18th.—Last night the wind rose to a gale, and this morning it is blowing most furiously, making the usually calm water of these bays so turbulent as to be dangerous for our light craft. Notwithstanding this disadvantage, the Indians were in favor of starting for the sea, which we accordingly did at an early hour. Soon after we left, in crossing one of the bays, about three-quarters [261] of a mile in width, the water suddenly became so agitated as at first nearly to upset our canoe. A perfect hurricane was blowing right ahead, cold as ice, and the water was dashing over us, and into our little bark, in a manner to frighten even the experienced chief who was acting as helmsman. In a few minutes we were sitting nearly up to our waistbands in water, although one of the women and myself were constantly bailing it out, employing for the purpose the only two hats belonging to the party, my own and that of the chief. We arrived at the shore at length in safety, although there was scarcely a dry thread on us, and built a tremendous fire with the drift-wood which we found on the beach. We then dried our clothes and blankets as well as we could, cooked some ducks that we killed yesterday, and made a hearty breakfast. My stock of bread, sugar, and tea, is completely spoiled by the salt water, so that until I return to Fort George, I must live simply; but I think this no hardship: what has been done once can be done again.

In the afternoon the women collected for me a considerable number of shells, several species of *Cardium*, *Citherea*, *Ostrea*, &c., all edible, and the last very good, though small.

The common pintail duck, (*Anas acuta*,) is found here in vast flocks. The chief and myself killed *twenty-six* to-day, by a simultaneous discharge of our guns. They are exceedingly fat and most excellent eating; indeed all the game of this lower country is far superior to that found in the neighborhood of Vancouver. The ducks feed upon a small submerged vegetable which grows in great abundance upon the reedy islands in this vicinity.

The next day we embarked early, to return to Chinook. The wind was still blowing a gale, but by running along close to the shore of the stormy bay, we were enabled, by adding greatly to our distance, to escape the difficulties against which we contended [262] yesterday, and regained the slues with tolerably dry garments.

At about 10 o'clock, we arrived at the portage, and struck into the wood, shouldering our baggage as before. We soon came to a beautiful little stream of fresh water, where we halted, and prepared our breakfast. In this stream, (not exceeding nine feet at the widest part,) I was surprised to observe a great number of large salmon. Beautiful fellows, of from fifteen to twenty-five pounds weight, darting and playing about in the crystal water, and often exposing three-fourths of their bodies in making their way through the shallows. I had before no idea that these noble fish were ever found in such insignificant streams, but the Indians say that they always come into the rivulets at this season, and return to the sea on the approach of winter. Our slave killed seven of these beautiful fish, while we made our hasty breakfast, his only weapon being a light cedar paddle.

We reached Chinook in the evening, and as we sat around the fires in the lodge, I was amused by the vivid description given to the attentive inhabitants by Chinamus and his wives, of the perils of our passage across the stormy bay. They all spoke at once, and described most minutely every circumstance that occurred, the auditors continually evincing their attention to the relation by a pithy and sympathizing *hugh*. They often appealed to me for the truth of what they were saying, and, as in duty bound, I gave an assenting nod, although at times I fancied they were yielding to a propensity, not uncommon among those of Christian lands, and which is known by the phrase, " drawing a long bow."

21st.—The wind yesterday was so high, that I did not consider it safe to attempt the passage to Fort George. This morning it was more calm, and we put off in a large canoe at sunrise. When we had reached the middle of Young's bay, the wind again rose, and the water was dashing over us in fine style, so that we [263] were compelled to make for the shore and wait until it subsided. We lay by about an hour, when, the water becoming more smooth, we again got under way, and arrived at Fort George about noon.

On the 5th of November, I returned to Vancouver, and immediately commenced packing my baggage, collection, &c., for a passage to the Sandwich Islands, in the barque Columbia, which is now preparing to sail for England. This is a fine vessel, of three hundred tons, commanded by Captain Royal; we shall have eight passengers in the cabin; Captain

Darby, formerly of this vessel, R. Cowie, chief trader, and others.

On the 21st, we dropped down the river, and in two days anchored off the cape. We have but little prospect of being able to cross the bar; the sea breaks over the channel with a roar like thunder, and the surf dashes and frets against the rocky cape and drives its foam far up into the bay.

I long to see blue water again. I am fond of the sea; it suits both my disposition and constitution; and then the reflection, that now every foot I advance will carry me nearer to my beloved home, is in itself a most powerful inducement to urge me on. But much as I desire again to see home, much as I long to embrace those to whom I am attached by the strongest ties, I have nevertheless felt something very like regret at leaving Vancouver and its kind and agreeable residents. I took leave of Doctor McLoughlin with feelings akin to those with which I should bid adieu to an affectionate parent; and to his fervent, "God bless you, sir, and may you have a happy meeting with your friends," I could only reply by a look of the sincerest gratitude. Words are inadequate to express my deep sense of the obligations which I feel under to this truly generous and excellent man, and I fear I can only repay them by the sincerity with which I shall always cherish the recollection of his kindness, and the ardent prayers I shall breathe for his prosperity and happiness.

[264] 30*th.*—At daylight this morning, the wind being fair, and the bar more smooth, we weighed anchor and stood out. At about 9 o'clock we crossed the bar, and in a few minutes were hurrying along on the open sea before a six-knot breeze. We are now out, and so good bye to Cape Disappointment and the Columbia, and now for *home*, dear home again!